William Makepeace Thayer

From Tannery to the White House

The Life of Ulysses S. Grant

William Makepeace Thayer

From Tannery to the White House
The Life of Ulysses S. Grant

ISBN/EAN: 9783337372019

Printed in Europe, USA, Canada, Australia, Japan

Cover: Foto ©Thomas Meinert / pixelio.de

More available books at **www.hansebooks.com**

*
****
*

FROM THE TANNERY

TO THE WHITE HOUSE

*
*

Story of the life
of Ulysses S. Grant,
his boyhood, youth, **
manhood, public and ****
private life and services

by

William M. Thayer

*   *   *
** *** *** **
*
*
*
xxx*xxxx

Hurst & Company
Publishers
New York
1885

TO ALL WHO

HONOR NOBLE MANHOOD,

THIS LIFE OF

Ulysses S. Grant,

FROM

BOYHOOD TO MANHOOD,

"THE MAN OF DEEDS, NOT WORDS,"

STEADFAST, BRAVE, LOYAL, FAITHFUL, AND TRUE,

THE

GREAT GENERAL AND TRUSTED PRESIDENT,

IS RESPECTFULLY DEDICATED.

PREFACE.

This Life of General Grant is designed to be a companion volume, in the author's Series of Presidents who have occupied the White House, to the Life of Garfield — "FROM LOG CABIN TO WHITE HOUSE" — of which more than two hundred and fifty thousand copies have been sold. The other volumes in the Series, are the Life of Abraham Lincoln — "FROM PIONEER HOME TO WHITE HOUSE" — and the Life of Washington — "FROM FARM HOUSE TO WHITE HOUSE."

The aim of this volume is, like that of its predecessors, which was to show the elements of character that made the subjects great. That a man almost unknown to fame at thirty years of age, struggling to support his family, and scarcely succeeding in filling a clerkship at eight hundred dollars a year in a country village, unassuming, shy, and of supposed moderate abilities, should prove himself to be the greatest general of modern times, and, later, the wise statesman and foremost man of his age, is stranger than fiction. For this reason, man have pronounced his life an "accident." Others have claimed that he was born under a "lucky star." Not a few have regarded him as a "child of destiny." But these pages will prove conclusively to the reader, that the boy Grant and the man Grant were as nearly related as bud and fruit — that the latter cannot be accounted for without the former is studied, and that the former would have remained inexplicable without the latter. Hence, incidents crowd these pages to tell their story — facts from the life of one of the most *real* boys who ever lived, and from one of the most *real* men the world has known. There is no fiction here, no creation of the fancy, no attempt at concealment, no extravagant eulogy; but facts speak for themselves; and they tell the story of one of the most marvellous lives on record, from earliest boyhood to ripe manhood — a fit companion for Washington, Lincoln, and Garfield!

The author, while availing himself of the information furnished by the numerous works on General Grant's life and public services, has, in addition, had access to fresh sources of knowledge, including the assistance of an army officer, who accompanied General Grant through his remarkable campaigns in the West, for two and a half years, to the fall of Vicksburg.

The life of General Grant, as a whole, presents one of the most unique and beautiful characters for young and old to study. The hero was not perfect. "Great men have great faults"; Grant had his. "Great men make great mistakes"; Grant was no exception. And yet, his CHARACTER challenges universal admiration. Parents may study it with profit, and hold it up for a model to their children. Children may accept it, not as the example of one too far above them for imitation, but of one who cultivated the commonplace virtues of truthfulness, obedience, industry, perseverance, self-reliance, honesty, loyalty, and fidelity. The masses of people, men and women, may find material in his life for their instruction. He was born of common people, lived with them, fought for them, presided over them, and never rose above them in his heart. He was the same in renown and power that he was in poverty and obscurity, as modest and unassuming, as quiet, amiable, self-forgetful, and simple in his habits.

We have adopted the title which this volume bears, not only because it is appropriate, but, also, that it may harmonize with the names of its companions. W. M. T.

FRANKLIN, MASS., 1885.

CONTENTS.

I.
BALLOTING FOR A NAME.

Point Pleasant — Jesse Grant's Son — General Joy — Ten Pounds and Three-quarters — The Young Couple Popular — Naming the Baby — A Difficult Problem — Visit to Grandpa Simpson's — A Scene — Discussing a Name — Proposition to Ballot for It — Hannah's Perplexity — Ulysses the Name Chosen — The Other Ballots, and Who Cast Them — Mrs. Simpson's Remark — The Grandfather's Disappointment — How Baptized — Only Child Named by Ballot — Reason of the Singular Demonstration — A New Country — Pioneers — James A. Garfield Eight Years after Ulysses — Grant's Small Opportunities 21

II.
"CHIP OF THE OLD BLOCK."

Genealogy by Richard A. Wheeler — A Dialogue about His Ancestry — Seventeen Ship-loads in 1630 — "Honest Matthew Grant" — Religious People — Settled Near Boston — Short of Food — Matthew's Wife Dies — He Goes to Connecticut Valley — Influential Man — Fights Schism in Church — Marries Again and Has Eight Children — Matthew's Son Samuel — Samuel's Son Samuel — Second Samuel's Son Noah — Noah's Son Noah — Heroic Officers in Wars — The Military Noah removes to Pennsylvania — Two Years Later Removes to Ohio — Jesse Grant Married — Ulysses Born — Indian Troubles — Jesse at Five Years of Age — Loyalty Hereditary — Carrying Grist to Mill — In Trouble — Family Broken Up

— Home at Judge Tod's — Silver Spoons — Learning Tanning Business — Setting Up for Himself — Marrying at Twenty-five — Courting in a Business Way — Married — Speaker and Poet — Educated by Business — CHIP LARGER THAN THE BLOCK 33

III.
HOME AND MOTHER.

A Scholar's Remark — John Adams' Letter — Jesse Grant's Estimate of His Wife — A Neighbor's Opinion — Key to His Home Life — His Home More Attractive Than Beer-shop — Fired a Pistol at Two Years of Age — Difference between Mr. and Mrs. Grant — Her Modesty and Humility — Force of This Quality in the Family — An Amusing Incident — What Ulysses' Father Said of His Modesty — Riding a Pony when Two Years Old — Later a Furious Pony Ride — No Element of Fear — His Mother's View 4f

IV.
THE LOG SCHOOL-HOUSE.

Beginning of School Days — Poor Schools and Teachers — Slow Not Brilliant — The Difficult Lesson — His Nicknames — The Teacher's Rebuke and Advice — Talent and Energy — "Ulysses Grant" — Excelled in Arithmetic — The Declamation — His Canadian Cousin — Military Ancestors — A Contest over Washington — The Reproof of His Mother — His Father's Interference — The Phrenologist and His Remark — Love of Games — Nice Sense of Honor and Justice — The Broken Pane — Expert in Drawing Horses — Love of Horses Interferes with Studies — Going to School in Kentucky — At School in Ripley — Too Large to be Educated by Schools — Washington Greater than Schools — Abraham Lincoln Too Large for Any School Curriculum — True also of James A. Garfield — True of U. S. Grant 5f

V.
THE TANNER BOY.

The Tanning Business — The Bark Mill — Process of Grinding Described — Does Not Like the Tannery — Hauling Brush with

the Colt—Propriety of the Beast—The Pile of Brush—His
Father's Wonder—The Result—The Drunken Journeyman
and His Expulsion—Teaming at Eight Years of Age—Taking Care of the Span—Driving a Pair of Horses to Cincinnati—Meeting William Dennison, a Future Governor—Laying Up Twenty Dollars—Buying a Horse for Himself—His
Father's Opinion—Standing on His Colt to Ride—Best
Rider and Trainer of Horses at Ten—Truthful, Obedient,
Never Profane—Buying a Horse for His Father—The
Cheater Outwitted—Made a Good Tanner—Tact, Push, and
Principle 67

VI.

A NOTABLE TRIP.

Death of Mr. Marshall—Ulysses Goes to the Funeral—The Trip
and Steamer—Remains Three Weeks at Deerfield—Return
to Georgetown—Difficulties Encountered—Steamer *Lady Byron*—Mischief Planned at Wheeling—Sorry for the Deed—
Six Days on the Return—A Good School—Building a New
House—Ulysses Drawing Materials—No Play—Teaching
a Horse to Pace—The Trick Exposed—The Last Horse
Trained—The Cholera Scare—Medicine Obtained—Vanished before Juvenile Curiosity—Ulysses Froze His Feet -
His Mother's Treatment—Self-reliance in the Family—I•
Excellent Discipline 79

VII.

BUILDING THE JAIL.

Mr. G. Contracts to Build Jail—Ulysses' Proposition—Buying a
Horse—The Animal's Name—Men Hired—Work Begun—
Men Gone—His Trouble—New Way to Load Logs—His
Father's Surprise and Satisfaction—Giving the Horse Credit
—An Interruption—Ulysses goes to Kentucky for Deposi
tion—The Letter—Runaway and Captain—The Captain's
Regard for the Boy—Arrives Home—Ulysses Buys Another
Colt—The Jail Finished—The Wagon Sold—Trying His
New Colt—Going to Aberdeen—The Fracas—Sells His
Colt on the Way—Suspicion Aroused—The Compliment—

His Return — Poor Talker, but Good Listener — Learning of Visitors — His Sharp Observation — Studied Men and Not Books — How it Helped to Make a Noble Man of Him .. 98

VIII.
AT WEST POINT.

Desiring to Go Up Higher—His Decision, and His Father's Acquiescence — Wanted an Education — The Wide Field He Opened — What a "Mississippi Trader" Was — His Father's Surprise — His Pecuniary Ability and Family — Desire to Go to West Point — How it Came About — Congressional Districts and Senators Nominate Cadets — Mr. Grant's Letter and Reply — How a Vacancy Was Made — The Application — More Trouble About His Name — Ulysses Receives the Appointment — Studies Hard to Prepare — Preparing Outfit — News of His Appointment Surprises People — Not Understood by Paul Devere — The Philadelphia Journalist — His Departure — The Bailey Tears — The Gap — A Week in Philadelphia — The Contingency Fund — Good Examination — West Point, Where and What — Course of Study — Poor Students - Discipline — Nicknames — Going Home — His Progress — A Noble Record — His Fine Horsemanship — A Popular Student — Application the Foundation of His Military Success 102

IX.
ON THE WAR PATH.

Graduated and Furlough — Jefferson Barracks — Size of Army — Near City of St. Louis — The Dent Family — Falls in Love with Julia — Opposition of Mr. and Mrs. Dent — Their Plea Against Betrothal — Furlough and Visit Home — Ordered to Red River — Unjust War — The Drunken Colonel — Grant Seeks and Finds Him in Court — The *Alibi* — General Taylor Dismisses the Drunken Colonel — Battle of Palo Alto — The Scene — Battle of Resaca — Balls Falling Behind Them — Battle of Monterey — Meeting an Old Georgetown Friend — Letter to His Parents — Taking the Old Mill — Forty Surrounded by One — Battle of Molino — Rapid Promotion of Grant — The Engagement at Chepultepec — Scaling Breastworks — Re-

port of Major Lee — Praise of Grant — In Less Than Twenty
Years He Surrenders to Grant — Promoted to Captain — A
Wonderful Feat — The Wild Boar — In Every Battle — General Scott — Two Horse Stories of Grant — The Readiest
Carver — Noble Record 117

X.
FROM SOLDIER TO CIVILIAN.

Returns to His Home — Matrimonial Intentions — In the Dent
Family — Married August 22d — Satisfied — Ordered to Detroit — A Change — The First-Born — Dominoes at Gore's —
The Surprise — The False Estimate — His Popularity — To
Pacific Coast and Vancouver — Lonely — Leaping the Battery
— Resigns — Becomes a Farmer and Builds Log House —
Hauling Wood — Death of His Mother-in-Law — Hon. H. T.
Blow's Wood — The Oyster-Man — Catching the Wood-Stealer — Goes into Partnership with Boggs — Sells "Hardscrabble" — Family in St. Louis — The Rich Lady's Visit — His
Business not a Success — His Conclusion — Applies for Engineership — Too Kind-Hearted — In Custom House — His
Wife's Support — His Exemplary Life — Removes to Galena
— In Leather Business — His Honesty — Kept Aloof from People — Lincoln and Douglas Clubs — Becomes a Republican. 130

XI.
CALL OF HIS COUNTRY.

Assault on the Flag and Call for Troops — Scene in Galena —
Grant's Remark — Meeting of Citizens — Rawlins, the Fighting Democrat — The Presiding Officer Weak — Washburne's
Patriotic Words — Applause — The Resolutions — The Speech
of Rawlins — Effect on Grant — His Decision — Meeting to
Raise a Company — Grant Made President — President of a
Meeting at Hanover — His Speech — Conversation on the Way
Home — Grant Predicts a Long War — Drills the Company,
but Declines to be Captain — Collins and Washburne — Washburne's Interview — Takes Grant to Springfield — Disgusted
with Office-Seekers — Governor Yates Employs Him — Musters in Regiments — Goes to Galena — His Modest Answer —
Applies to General McClellan — Appointed Colonel — His Re-

turn — Yates Inquiring of Book-keeper — The Regiment a Mob — Grant's Appearance — How he Disciplined Them — Popular — Visits Galena — Buys Outfit — Washburne's Opinion of Him — Marches Regiment Across the Country — In for the War 149

XII.

THE COMING MAN FORESHADOWED.

His Command — Punishing Whiskey-Drinkers — How to Serve a Boy — Asking Blessing at Table — Another Balloting — A Surprised Brigadier — Making up His Staff — Hillyer the Minute Man — Pilot Knob — Commands District of South-east Missouri — Grant at Cairo — Battle of Belmont — Moves on Paducah — His First Order — Dishonest Contractors Snubbed — Buell's Opinion of Grant — Order to Respect Private Property — Reduction of Fort Henry — Grant's Sagacity — Moves on Fort Donelson — Terrible Battle — The Turning Point — Scenes Described by Eye-Witness — The Negro — The Surrender — Grant's Famous Reply — Interview with Buckner — Scene at Nashville — Halleck's Order to Send Back Fugitives Ignored — Buckner's Complaint — Earning Promotion — Mrs Grant's Opinion of His Abilities 181

XIII.

MOVING ON THE ENEMY'S WORKS.

Made Major-General — Stanton's Rebuke of Timid Officers — Fresh Captures — The Enemy at Corinth 80,000 — Halleck's Bad Treatment of Grant — Absurd Charge of Drunkenness — Marching on Corinth — Grant at Savannah — Firing Sunday Morning — Breakfast Left — Hurrying up River — Order to Wallace — Grant Rides to the Front — Scene of Disaster — Sends Rowley to Grant — Latter Still Hopeful — Shot and Shell Falling about Him — Where Heaviest Firing Grant Was — Buell's Arrival — Fall of Rebel General Johnston — Dismay of Rebel Army — Union Gunboats Fire — The Crisis — Carson's Head Blown Off — Council of War — Urges Battle at Early Morn — The Army Victorious — Grant Leading a Charge — The Enemy Driven — Beauregard's Note — A Great Battle — False Charges against Grant — His Letter — His

Thanks to the Army — Halleck's Jealousy — Grant's Exemplary Conduct — Halleck's Timidity — Grant's Impatience — Logan's Rebuke — Halleck's Promotion — Grant's Onward Movement — More Military Skill — Phil Sheridan — Knocks Down a Soldier 184

XIV.

ON TO VICKSBURG.

Discipline of His Army — His Baggage a Tooth-Brush — A Brilliant Affair — Sherman's Assault on Vicksburg — a Gibraltar Indeed — Must Open the Mississippi — At Young's Point — Defenses of the City — Planning to Attack Vicksburg — Grant Defending Sherman — The First Canal — Second Canal — Other Failures — Council of War — Taking the Risk — Sherman's Visit to Thayer — Keeping Halleck in the Dark — I Shall Take the City — Grant Described — Letter of General Thayer — A Lady's View of Grant — Sherman Opposed Grant's Plan — The River-Men — Grierson's Wonderful Raid — The Army Starts Around the Swamp — The Memorable Night — Running Past the Batteries — The Exasperated Rebel — Crossing the River — Newspaper Men Captured — Onward with Little Baggage — Six Battles — Halleck's Telegram — Grant's Promptness — Building the Bridge — The Union Woman — Young Rebel Officer — Another Risk — Fred, his Son — Rebel Manufacturer Paying Tavern Bills — What Member of Staff Said — Major Penniman's View 203

XV.

SIEGE OF VICKSBURG.

Investing the City — Two Assaults on Works — The Seige Begun — Terrible Cannonading — Cave-Life in the City — Short of Provisions and Powder — Grant's Way of Getting Information — Conversation with a Rebel Picket — Grant's Example to Scared Men — Capture of Letters Between Pemberton and Johnston — Another Rebel Army in the Rear — Another Assault Planned — The White Flag Raised — Pemberton Proposed to Surrender — Grant's Reply — The Two Generals Meet — Grant's Letter after Conference — Orders Sherman to Fall on Johnston's Army — Grand Victory — Another Letter from Pemberton — Surrender July 4, 1863 — **Raising the Union Flag over the City** — Rudeness of Pemberton and Staff — The Newspaper Issued and a Joke — Amount of Grant's Capture — His Praise on Every Lip — Even Halleck Praised — Letter from Lincoln — His Modesty did not Surrender — Order against Extortion — Drove out Speculators — Soldiers Voting — Another Proof of Modesty — Views of Slavery — Port Hudson — Hurt at New Orleans — Wife and Children with him,   224

XVI.

GREATER THINGS YET.

Great Expectations — Editor of the *Chronicle* — Lincoln's Great Trouble — Critical Condition of Rosecrans and Burnside — Taking Command of 200,000 Men — Supercedes Rosecrans — General Thomas Brave — Arrival of Grant at Chattanooga — Rebel's Strong Positions — Jeff. Davis Exults — "Can't" not in Dictionary — Telegram to Sherman — Telegram to Thomas — The Pontoon Bridge — Grand Scene — Battle of Orchard Knoll — Of Lookout Mountain — Of Missionary Ridge — Fearful Fighting — Grant's Telegram — The Hot Pursuit — Deceit of Jeff. Davis — Relief Sent to Burnside — The Woman's Story — The Skillful Plan Successful — Universal Rejoicing — Resolution of Congress and Gold Medal — The Medal Described — Lincoln's Noble Letter — Grant's Address to his Army .   244

XVII.

THE ROLL OF HONOR.

Destroying the Rebel Army — Letter to Halleck — How Army Distributed — Results of Sherman's Raid — His Tour of Inspection — Honoring Him at Lexington — Public Dinner in St. Louis — The Serenade — Can't Make a Speech — At Washington — Made Lieutenant-General — Lincoln's Inquiry — Grant and the Presidency — His Letter About Becoming President — Halleck's Letter — Summoned to Washington — His Letter to Sherman — Sherman's Letter to Him — Ovation on Way to Washington — Scene at Dinner Table at Willard's — At the President's Levee — Lincoln Presents to Him Commission of Lieutenant-General — Grant's Reply — His Opposition to a

Ball — The Play of Hamlet, and Hamlet Not There — The Driver Couldn't Find Him — Appointed Commander of all the Union Armies — His Return — Joy in Washington . . 258

XVIII.
ON TO RICHMOND.

A Tangled Skein of Affairs — Difference between Grant and Halleck — Grant's View and "Balky Team" — Not a Book-made General — Remark of Sherman — Greater Responsibility on Him than ever Mortal bore — Order out of Confusion — His Common-Sense Plan — Mrs. Grant's View — Making Rawlins a Brigadier — March to Richmond Begins — The Enemy Encountered — Battle of the Wilderness — Second Day's Battle — Battle at Spottsylvania — Death of Sedgwick — Rumors in Washington — Dana's Midnight Trip — A Rebel Bribed — Lincoln's Address to the Country — Bloody Battle on 10th — Grant's Famous Report to Stanton — "Bull-dog Grip" — Battle on 12th — Capture of Rebel Generals — Eighth Day of Battle — His Plan to take Richmond formed at Vicksburg — The Stranger's Suggestions — Sheridan's Splendid Raid — Cold Harbor Battle — On to Petersburg 273

XIX.
FALL OF THE CONFEDERACY.

Telegram to Halleck — Confident of Success — Bombardment of Petersburg — Description by an Eye-Witness — Resolved on a Siege — Army of Discontents in his Rear — Letter to Quiet Them — Grumblers Still at Work — Early's Raid on the North — General Scott's Letter — His Gift to Grant — Death of McPherson — Grant's Sorrow — Letter from McPherson's Grandmother — Grant's Touching Reply — Honest Tears — The Faithful Sentinel and Cigar — Triumphs of his Best Generals — Getting Ready for Final Campaign — Confederacy on its Last Legs — His Team Well in Hand — Lincoln's Cheering Letter — Final Order — Striking the Last Blows — Lincoln at the Front — Three Day's Fight — The Auspicious Sunday — Jeff. Davis Called out of Church — Prepares to Escape — Fearful Scene in Richmond — Iron-clads Blown Up, and City Set on Fire - - Not a "Retreating Man" — Davis Fleeing — Negroes

Jubilant — Lincoln Goes into the City — Grant Pursues Lee —
Race to Danville — Grant's Letter to Sherman — Lee Cornered, No Escape — Grant Demands Surrender — Vain Attempt
to Break Union Lines — Lee's Letter to Grant the Day Before
— Grant's Reply — Lee Decides to Capitulate — Grant's Answer — The Terms of Surrender Arranged at Appomattox —
A Singular Fact — Terms of Surrender — Grant's Clemency
— Laying Down Rebel Arms — Grant's Rebel Cousin — Remarks of Conquered Men **287**

XX.

THE NATION'S GRATITUDE.

Great Rejoicing over Fall of Richmond — Greater Joy Still over
Lee's Surrender — Grant in Washington — Meeting of Cabinet
on 14th — Grant Left at Night — Lincoln Assassinated — Providence Saved Grant — Grant's Hasty Return — Severely Criticised for Lenity — Treatment of his Enemies Noble — Number of Prisoners — Grand Review at Washington — Nothing
Like it Before — Grant's Final Address to Army — Reception
at Fifth Avenue Hotel — Great Fair in Chicago — "Old Jack"
there — Rides "Jack" through Streets — Welcome to Union Hall
— Grant's Speech — Sherman's Speech — Grant's Humor and
an Amusing Incident — Relics Sold at Chicago Fair — Grant's
Tour to New England — Welcome Home at Galena — The
Scene — Arches and Mottoes — Removes to Washington —
More Honors 308

XXI.

BETWEEN WAR AND THE WHITE HOUSE.

Grant's View of Military Rule — Disagrees with Johnson — Declines to Go to Mexico — Sherman and Grant — Favored Negro Suffrage — Advice to Southerners — Supports Stanton and
Sheridan Against the President — Grant Becomes Secretary of
War — Order to Remove Sheridan Denounced — Removing
Civil Officers — Makes Great Improvements in War Department — Resigns — Lenient Terms Towards the South Necessary to Peace — Opposes the Arrest of Lee for Treason — Testimony Before Committee — His Views Prevailed — No Painting of Surrender in Capitol — Tender and Kind — What Gen-

eral Badeau Says — Report of His Southern Tour — Visits
New York Again — Large Gift — Left-hand Writing — What
Facts Prove — Absence of Jealousies a Sign of Greatness —
More Magnanimity — Two Great Souls Conferring — His
Praise of Sheridan — General Badeau's Estimate — Same
Traits Through Life — Stamped Out Army — Like Moltke. 323

XXII.
AT THE TOP.

Room at the Top — Eighteen Chances in a Hundred Years — Objected to Being President — Letter of John A. Andrew — Carried Every Vote in Republican Convention — Enthusiasm Manifested — Grant's Letter of Acceptance — Another Communication — " Let Us Have Peace " — Opposed Measures for Party Success — His Situation Difficult — His Inauguration and Cabinet — Changes in Cabinet — Johnson an Obstacle — From His First Message — His Indian Policy — The Church and Not State to Manage Them — Opposing Republicans — Annexation of Santo Domingo — His Civil Service Reform Opposed — Indian Policy Opposed — His Plan of Appointments — The Electoral Commission a Political Shiloh — His Study to Do Right — Examples — Party Against Him — Renominated by Acclamation — A Third Term — Generous to a Fault — Philosophy of His Success — Further Testimony of Creswell — Eulogy of General Devens 340

XXIII.
IN THE MOTHER COUNTRY.

A Foreign Tour Contemplated — Sixteen Years of Service — Departure Amid Honors — England Decided to Receive Him as a Sovereign — The Voyage — Deputation from Ireland — Enthusiastic Reception at Liverpool — Reception and Speech at Manchester — Lunch and Toasts — Speech of Bright — At Bedford — Arrival in London — Ceremony of Presenting the Freedom of the City — Speech of Lord Mayor, and Grant's Reply — Lunch, and Another Speech — A Third Speech — Splendid Fireworks — Banquet by Trinity College — Reception by the Queen at Windsor Castle — The Workingmen's Deputation, and Grant's Speech — Other Banquets — His Opinion of Racing — Worshipping in Westminster Abbey — Honors Multiply — Reception at Liverpool, and His Humorous Speech — Adieu 561

XXIV.

ON THE CONTINENT.

Off for Ostend — Incidents that Show Grant — Going to the Roman Camp — Reception at Geneva — Laying Corner-stone of a Church — Lunch, and Grant's Speech — Over the Simplon Pass — Napoleon's Engineering — Grand Scenery — The Descent, and " Gorge of Gonda " — Another Reception — Returns to Scotland — Freedom of Edinburgh Tendered — Grant's Speech — His Views of Hand-shaking — Freedom of the City of Glasgow — Ovation on the Town Moor of Newcastle — Description of the Scene in the *Chronicle* — Laying Another Corner-stone — Reception at Birmingham, and His Speech — " Grantism " — Goes to France — Reception by President Mac-Mahon — Other Receptions — Views Published in the *Figaro* About Grant — Editors Talk with Him — Banquet by Americans in Paris — Also by Mrs. Mackay — Also by a Banker — Off on the Steamer *Vandalia* 571

XXV.

TO THE ORIENT.

At Naples — Going up Vesuvius — Outgeneraled — Return — At Pompeii — The Guard and Sheridan — Opening a House for Grant — Excavating Beefsteak at Palermo — Christmas Dinner on Board — Description by Young — To the Orient — Reception at Alexandria — Reception by the Pasha — Dinner with Vice-Consul — Stanley, the African Traveller — Going to Cairo — Reception There — His Old Acquaintances Found — Grant's Praise of Stone — The Yankee Doodle Pony — Goes up the Nile — Reception at Sieut — Visits Thebes — Ruins — Reception at Thebes — The Relic Manufacturer — Statues of Memnon — Whipping Girls — Grandest Ruin in the World — At Keneh — Inside Life of the People — At Assouan — Buying Ostrich Feathers — The Result — Letter to Grant from General Gordon — Goes to See Him — Return to Cairo —

Goes to Joppa — Looking up a Tannery — Reception at Jerusalem — Visiting Sacred Places — Goes to Nazareth — Damascus — Constantinople 301

XXVI.
FLIGHT THROUGH OTHER COUNTRIES

The Sultan of Turkey — Gives a Pair of Fine Horses to Grant — Description of Them — Goes to Athens — What He Saw — On to Rome — Marvelous Sights — A Good Custom There — On to Venice — Reception There — Milan and Its Cathedral — Vinci's Great Painting — At the World's Exhibition in Paris — Goes to Holland — Visits Berlin — Meeting with Bismarck — The Salutations — The Conversation — About Sheridan — About the Emperor — Grant's Words About War — About the Union and Slavery — To Hamburg — A Grand Dinner and Fine Speech by Grant — From Hamburg to St. Petersburg — Visits the Emperor — Great Sights — Yacht Excursions — To Warsaw and Vienna — Public Library at Munich — Napoleon at Ulm — Letter from King Alfonso . . . 443

XXVII.
FROM SPAIN TO CHINA.

King Alfonzo's Welcome — Grant's Reply — Reference to the Death of the Queen — Castellar Thanked by Grant — Palace and Picture Gallery at Madrid — The Escurial Palace — Banquet in Lisbon — The Boston Lady — In Seville — Cadiz — Gibraltar — Welcome and Speech of Grant — Starts for Ireland — Banquet at Pau — Welcome and Noble Speech at Dublin — At His Daughter's — Ready to Visit India — Welcome at Bombay — At Agra, Visits the Tay — Honors at Jeypoor — Visit to Lucknow and Benares — A Cow Attacks Mrs. Grant — Degrees Conferred — In Burmah — Invitation from King of Siam — His Welcome — Another King — Finally the Real King and Grant's Bust — George Washington — Royal Dinner — Grant's Speech — Grand Temples — Reception at Canton — The Green Chair — Reception at Shanghai — At Pekin Rides in Emperor's Chair — Address from English University — Grant's Reply — Talks with the Prince and Viceroy — His Great Good to China — Confidence of the People in Him 416

XXVIII.
JAPAN AND HOME.

Visit to the "Great Wall of China"—Grant's Estimate of the Labor—Welcome to Nagasaki—March to Head-quarters—A Dinner of Twenty Courses—Reception at Tokio—Highest Honor—Emperor's Address—Grant's Reply—Address to Mrs. |Grant—Fourth of July—Address of Mr. Bingham—Breakfast and Review—Great Good Done to Japan—An Earthquake—Taking Leave of the Emperor—Grant's Address—The Emperor's Reply—Farewell Honors—Reception at San Francisco—Costly Decorations—At Palace Hotel—Honor by Chinese—Honors at Oakland—Five Thousand School Children—Twenty Thousand Children Greet Him in San Francisco—At Sacramento—Taking His Leave—Reception at Chicago—At Philadelphia—Magnificent Display—*Fêted* for a Week—Many Speeches Omitted—Goes to See His Mother 426

XXIX.
MISFORTUNE AND SICKNESS AT LAST.

A Busy Civilian—Interest in Public Questions—Mexico—Resides in New York—Poor—A Large Fund Raised for Him—His Friends Put Him Forward for a Third Term—A Special Partner with Grant and Ward—Borrows One Hundred and Fifty Thousand Dollars for Ward—Ward's Arrest—Effect on Grant—Universal Sympathy—Arrest of Fish—Turned to Literary Work—Mighty Will Power—No Parallel to It—News That He Must Die—A Nation in Sorrow—Crowds of Inquirers Before His House—Visit of George W. Childs—On the Retired List—Mrs. Grant's Words—Thought to be Dying—His Condition Explained—General Grant Dying—Great Sympathy—Scene at Second Attack—Mrs. Sartoris at His Bedside—Obeying Orders—Blessing His Grandchild—Mrs. Grant's Grief—Dr. Newman Sent For—Views of Doctors—Another Interview with Dr. Newman—Eight Hundred Letters of Sympathy—The Old Man Praying for Him—His Birthday Celebrated—His Condition—Tennyson's Ode on Death of Wellingtion 436

XXX.
HIS LAST JOURNEY.

Grant's Like Garfield's Last Journey — Where Mt. McGregor Situated — Journey on the 16th — Colonel Grant's Remark at Stony Point — Looking at West Point — The Effect — Just a Week — Two Telegrams Received — Peaceful but Failing — To Doctor Newman — The Catholic Priest — Grant's Words - Response to Twenty Mexican Editors — His Strength Rallies — Democratic Resolution of Sympathy — Ride in Bath-chair — "Last Day on Earth" — Family About Him and Prayer — Writes His Last Message — The Death Scene — Universal Sorrow — The President's Proclamation — Governor Hill's Message — Other Symbols of Grief — Telegram from Victoria and Others — The Nation Mourns — Grant's Last Message — Doctor Tiffany's Reminiscences — National Funeral — A Family Scene — Service at the Cottage — Doctor Newman's Sermon — Funeral Cortege Moving to New York — Lying in State at New York — Floral Tributes — Memorable Display — Route of Procession — Fifty Thousand Men in It — Its Sable Grandeur — What London Papers Say — Service at the Tomb — Rest. 451

TANNERY TO WHITE HOUSE.

I.

BALLOTING FOR A NAME.

THERE was joy in the little frontier town of Point Pleasant, Clermont Co., O., on the twenty-seventh day of April, 1822. It was a new, quiet settlement of pioneers on the banks of the Ohio, making for themselves and their posterity a home in the wilderness. A newcomer to such a settlement was an event of great interest; hence the smile of satisfaction that wreathed the faces of the people on the day mentioned, for there was a fresh arrival, "direct from Heaven," as many a mother loved to express it — a pledge that the young inhabitant had come to stay — an increase of *one* to the population of the town.

"Jesse Grant has a boy!"

The announcement spread from lip to lip and family to family, until the whole community were rejoicing, — men, women, and children, — over the arrival. James Monroe was President of the United States at that time, and had he put in an appearance on that day, instead of Jesse Grant's son, the general satisfaction would have been less, because he would have come to *see* and not to dwell, and because there was not a habitation in the township suitable for the reception of a President. His coming would have created more *fluster*, but less joy. On the other hand, the surroundings were well adapted to the reception of Jesse Grant's boy. While a famous visitor from Washington would have annoyed them, this one from the skies only made them glad.

"Weighs ten pounds and three-quarters!"

This important intelligence followed the first announcement, and was carried over the town until the weight of the baby was as well understood as his veritable existence.

"A bouncing fellow; weighs ten pounds and three-quarters!"

If it was repeated once, it was a hundred times, by the inhabitants of the town, together with other bits of information concerning mother and child, — all perfectly natural in a pioneer settlement, and proving as well the high estimate put upon the young parents by an honest community.

Jesse R. Grant and Hannah, his wife, were much beloved by the citizens of Point Pleasant. Seldom do a young couple establish themselves so quickly in the confidence and affections of a people. Intelligent, enterprising, industrious, and virtuous, they were a valuable accession to the little community. Here was still another good reason for the prevailing interest in young Grant's prosperity.

The child was but a few days old when the subject

of naming him came to the front. Whether the fond young parents could not find a name good enough for so promising a boy, tradition saith not; but the fact remains, that at the end of six weeks he was nameless.

"What is his name?" was the repeated inquiry made by callers.

"Have you named him yet?"

The inquiries were repeated until they became well-nigh annoying.

"Good enough without a name," kindly suggested one old lady; "but suit yourselves, and don't hurry; he won't use a name yet awhile." Her advice was comforting to the perplexed couple, who had come squarely up to this difficult problem of their married life. Indeed, they had courted, made a match, married, established a home, and made themselves valued citizens of Point Pleasant without the least trouble; but now, for six weeks, they had been wrestling with the serious difficulty of naming their first-born.

"We will decide upon a name when we go to father's," suggested Hannah to Jesse. "Pa will help us."

"May be," answered Jesse; "and may be that we shall be still more unsettled by multiplying counsellors."

Nevertheless, the subject was held in abeyance until they visited Mrs. Grant's parents, a short time thereafter. Her parents lived ten miles distant, to which place they came from Pennsylvania only two years before, bringing Hannah with them, who became Jesse Grant's wife one year later; evidently a plan of Providence for the special accommodation of Jesse.

It was a great day in the Simpson family, when they welcomed their first and only grandchild to their humble abode. To be breveted "Grandpa" and "Grandma," by the hearing of the ear, was sufficient promotion to gratify their ambition for the time being; but to set their eyes upon the bright-eyed cause of all their honors filled their cup of joy to the brim, and over-spilled.

There were present, in addition to Grandfather and Grandmother Simpson, and the parents of the child, two sisters of Mrs. Simpson, aunts whom Hannah dearly loved — six in all, well-to-do, worthy, honored people.

"What's his name?" inquired the elder aunt.

"Baby," answered his mother, while Jesse smiled that the old inquiry of his neighbors at home should be the first one there.

"Not named him yet?" responded the other aunt with considerable surprise.

"Not yet," replied Hannah. "Perhaps we can get him a name here, to-day."

"Names enough, if that is what you want," remarked Grandfather Simpson. "Leave it to me, and I will fit one to him before dinner."

Thus, very naturally and quickly, the conversation drifted to naming the boy. One thought that an honored ancestry should be remembered, and a name be selected from the long line of noble ancestors, so well known. Another preferred the name of some distinguished man living. Still another advocated a fancy name, and so on. The names suggested were more numerous than the debaters, and the prospect of getting a name for the child seemed more dubious, for a time, than it ever did at Point Pleasant.

"Let us ballot for a name," suggested Grandfather Simpson.

"And the name on the most ballots be chosen?" inquired Jesse.

"Yes, that, or the first name drawn out of the hat be adopted."

"I like that," remarked Grandmother Simpson. "Each one write the name of his or her choice on a slip, and drop them into a hat, shake up the ballots, and the first name drawn out shall be the child's name."

"If all agree to that," continued Mr. Simpson, "the child can have a name before dinner, as I said before."

Hannah, the doting young mother, hesitated for a moment. She did not know exactly about giving her blessed boy a name by ballot. The method was not quite civilized. But, after considerable discussion, it became evident that the baby would return to Point Pleasant as he came, nameless, unless there was an appeal to the ballot. Under these circumstances, Hannah consented; and the company resolved themselves into a sort of legislative body, for effective business. Pen, paper, ink, and Grandfather Simpson's hat were provided, when the balloting commenced, and was soon ended. The eldest aunt was appointed, by general agreement, to shake the hat, and draw therefrom the ballot that would determine the child's name forever. The interest culminated at this point; and the company waited, with bated breath, the result. Lo! the ballot which she drew bore the name ULYSSES, written in a bold, plain hand. All could see it. It was the handwriting of the child's father. The child was irrevocably named, and dinner was not quite ready. Grandfather Simpson looked disappointed, but remarks were not in order. The agreement was a fair one, and there was no appeal from the ballot. He only suggested that the other ballots be examined, which suggestion was adopted, with the following result:—

HIRAM	1
ALBERT	2
THEODORE	1
ULYSSES	2
	6

Grandfather Simpson cast the ballot for HIRAM, from respect to an honored ancestor. He had urged his claim for that before the vote was cast. The maiden aunt, who made a plea for a fancy name, voted THEODORE; it was a charming name to her. Hannah and the other maiden aunt cast the ballots for ALBERT; and it came about in this way: There was a very distinguished public man then living, by the name of Albert Gallatin, known throughout the country, and especially popular in the West. At that time (1822) he was resident Minister of our Government at Paris. It was quite natural for those who desired the child should bear a great man's name to vote ALBERT. He must have been a very remarkable man, if he did what political history claims that he did. For, in his fifty years of public service, he declined a seat in two Cabinets and the Vice-Presidency of the United States. Hannah showed her wisdom in desiring to name her boy for such a rare man!

Jesse and Grandmother Simpson cast the two ballots for ULYSSES; and the reason for it was rather romantic. Not long after Jesse and Hannah were married, a neighbor came into possession of a copy of Fenelon's "Telemachus." Books were very scarce at that time in the settlement, and they were loaned to the readers of the town. Jesse borrowed "Telemachus" and read it with the deepest interest. He was captivated by the character of the great ULYSSES. Grandma Simpson was visiting the newly-wedded pair at the time, and she read the book. She, too, admired the character of ULYSSES. From the day his boy arrived at Point Pleasant, Jesse had not ceased to urge the name of ULYSSES. No other name compared with it in his estimation. So that when the ballot was taken, he and his mother-in-law voted for ULYSSES as a matter of course.

"Well, Jesse," said Grandmother Simpson, "your boy will carry something home with him that he didn't bring."

"A name!" answered Jesse; "and my favorite one, too."

"And all are pretty well satisfied, I think," added Mrs Simpson.

If she could have looked into her husband's heart just then, that remark would not have been made; for Grandfather Simpson was greatly disappointed, though he spoke not a word of complaint; but his silence was of that peculiar quality that speaks. The reader will be thoroughly convinced of this when we state the important fact, that when the child was christened, subsequently, it was with the name, HIRAM ULYSSES GRANT; positive proof of his strong desire concerning the name! So that the doings of the grand council of relatives was partially upset by one of the best grandfathers who ever lived; not the only legislative action that has been nullified by secret personal influence.

We risk little in claiming that our hero is the only American who was ever named by ballot. In this he was a marked character from the outset.

The reason of so much excitement over the naming of a child is not quite clear to the author, for a baby was not a novelty in the Grant family at that time. We have carefully traced the genealogical record away back to the original ancestor, "Honest Matthew Grant," who set his feet on Nantasket Beach on the thirtieth day of May, 1630, ten years after the Pilgrim Fathers landed at Plymouth Rock; and we have found that the ancestral tree has yielded large crops of humanity. Grant families averaged anywhere from six to thirteen children each, so that a baby was never a novelty in that particular branch of the human family; and yet, a more remarkable demonstration was never made over a child than was made over Ulysses. There are not wanting those who behold in the fact the forecasting of future events; they call it "destiny."

This chapter would not be complete without some notice of the inheritance to which Ulysses was introduced at birth. That event occurred sixty-three years ago, when the nation was in its infancy. Ohio was then a new State on the frontier, comparatively a wilderness, so far away that Home Missionaries had not been sent thither. Two years before, the Home Missionary enterprise originated in Massachusetts, and one or more missionaries crossed the borders of New England into New York, to labor among the scattered pioneers. The whole population of the United States was less at that time than it now numbers west of the Mississippi River. Boston contained less than forty-five thousand inhabitants; New York less than one hundred and twenty-five thousand; Cincinnati was a bustling trading-post of less than ten thousand people, while Cleveland was a collection of log-huts, inferior frame-houses, and stores, accommodating a population of about six hundred.

Only two years before the subject of our narrative was born, Abram Garfield, father of our late lamented President Garfield, being seized with the "Ohio fever," emigrated from New York to that portion of the "Far West"; a young man of twenty years. He was married to Eliza Ballou fourteen months before Ulysses was born, and settled in what is now a part of Cleveland, living in a log-house, with three-legged stools for chairs, and greased paper for "stained windows." A few years later, Garfield removed his family into the wilderness, fifteen miles away, where he built a log-cabin on fifty acres of land, which he purchased for two dollars an acre. His nearest neighbor was seven miles away. Here our late President Garfield was born, eight years and eight months after the birth of Ulysses at Point Pleasant.

Our purpose in rehearsing these facts is to remind the reader that the subject of our volume was born at a time when, in that portion of our country, opportunities were few and small. True, the birthplace of U. S. Grant was somewhat more advanced than that of James A. Garfield, although it was in the same State. He was not born in a log cabin, nor far away from neighbors, nor where schools were unknown; nor was he born to an inheritance of poverty, for his father, through his industry and frugal habits, was well-to-do for that time and place. And yet, after a careful memorandum of the advantages which his boyhood shared, we are compelled to admit that his opportunities for social and intellectual improvement were small. Born in a frame-house of inferior appearance, as will be seen by the accompanying picture, taught in a log school-house by inferior teachers, associating with friends and neighbors of little culture, and whose inexorable condition of life was "work or starve," his early years were not especially flattered by hopes and promises.

II.

"CHIP OF THE OLD BLOCK."

WENTY years ago, more or less, Richard A. Wheeler, of Stonington, Conn., denied the usual claim set up, that Ulysses S. Grant was of Scotch descent.

"Not a word of truth in it. He descended from the most Puritan of Puritan stock," said Wheeler.

"His biographers ought to have found it out," suggested the friend addressed. "I supposed that there was no question about his ancestry."

"There has not been, because no one has taken the pains to investigate until I attempted it recently," answered Wheeler. "I was not a little surprised myself by the clearness of the Puritan, instead of the Scotch, claim."

"How about the ancient Scottish Clan, whose chosen motto was, 'Stand fast, stand firm, stand sure'?" inquired his friend. "That fits pretty well, any way."

"Very true; and that is all there is to it. Because the motto would be appropriate on Grant's shield, biographers catch at the story of the 'Scottish Clan,' and proclaim that his veins run with the best Scotch blood. I have nothing to say against Scotch blood, — the blood is good enough, — capital blood for a man to hold; but I tell you that is not the blood to which our great American General is indebted."

"Possibly not," responded his friend; "but I should like to hear what proof there is of your position. It is admitted, as I supposed, that little is known of General Grant's foreign ancestry, and that what little is known, points to Scotch origin."

"Well," continued Mr. Wheeler, "give me your ear for a short time, and I will tell you what I know about it. The year 1630 was distinguished for the large number of emigrants to this country. The fame of the 'New England Colony' awakened a wide-spread interest among the English people, and, during the year mentioned, seventeen ship-loads of families, with their horses, cattle, and furniture, were brought hither. One of these ships, — the *Mary and John*, — which sailed from Plymouth, England, on the twentieth day of March, brought one hundred and forty passengers, and a more interesting company never trod a ship's deck; for nearly all of them were young, married couples and young bachelors. Among the number was Matthew Grant, married of course; for the Grants always marry early and well. They landed at Nantasket, though Captain Scuibs agreed to take them to Boston. The result was that the passengers, under the leadership of Matthew Grant, brought a suit against the captain, and recovered damages for the violation of his agreement. Thus did the original Grant set his face like a flint against injustice and duplicity.

"This ship-load of colonists were thoroughly religious, according to the record, and found solid comfort, during their long voyage, in their Christian worship. One Roger Clap kept a diary on the way, in which he said: 'So we came, by the good hand of God, through the deep, comfortably, having *preaching and expounding the Word of God every day for ten weeks together, by our ministers.*'

"Matthew Grant and his fellow-passengers settled at Matapan, about four miles from the present city hall, Boston. Subsequently they changed the name to Dorchester, in memory of a town by that name in their own native County of Dorsetshire. Here they suffered for want of food. Roger Clap said, in his diary, 'The place is a wilderness. Fish was a good help to me and to others. Bread was so scarce that I thought the very crusts from my father's table would have been sweet; and when I could have meal, and salt, and water boiled together, I asked, 'Who could ask for better'?'

"Matthew Grant's wife, Priscilla, died when they had been four years in this country, leaving four children. The year after her death (1635), Matthew, and about half of the colony, removed to the Connecticut Valley, between Hartford and Springfield, settling where the town of Windsor now is. Here they were more exposed to depredations by Indians, but the land was more fertile.

"'Honest Matthew Grant,' as he was called, became the chief spirit in the rich Valley of the Connecticut. He was surveyor, town clerk, and recorder; and he filled various other positions of honor and trust, from time to time. A schism arose in the church, after a few years, about an old minister who came with the colonists from Dorchester. The younger members of the community thought he was too old and rigid to be their spiritual adviser, so they withdrew, organized a new parish, and called a younger minister. Matthew Grant opposed the malcontents from the start, and he refused, as clerk of the church, to enter their doings upon the records. The malcontents insisted that the record should be made; but Matthew stood by his guns, in Grant style; refused to budge an inch, and denounced their enterprise as the outcome of the growing impiety of the times. Finally, however, the record was made, but not by the unconquerable Matthew Grant.

"Ten years after the death of Mrs. Priscilla Grant, her husband married Mrs. Susannah Rockwell, a widow with eight children. He was forty-four, and she was forty-three. Mr. Grant loved children, and some thought that the children attracted him fully as much as the charms of their widowed mother. At any rate, he seemed to be perfectly happy when, in his new-made home, with his excellent wife, he found that the two broods together numbered twelve. He outlived his second wife fifteen years, and died at eighty years of age, in the family of his youngest son, John.

"Matthew's son Samuel left eight children when he died, the eldest of whom was named Samuel, for him. The last Samuel left nine children, at death, the eldest of whom was Noah, who, in turn, had a son born July 12, 1718, whom he named Noah; and this last Noah, with his brother, Solomon, proved themselves heroic soldiers in the French and Indian War of 1755, and both were officers; and both were killed in battle in 1756.

"The military Noah, just mentioned, had a son, Noah, who was born June 23, 1748, and became an officer in the American Army, in the war for Independence, and fought in the battle of Lexington. His wife died while he was in the army; and, at the close of the Revolution, he returned to his home in Connecticut, where he sincerely and deeply mourned the loss of his wife. Under the depression caused by his great affliction, he resolved to remove to Pennsylvania, where he settled in 1790, in Westmoreland County, near Greensburg.

"Two years after, he married Widow Rachel Kelley, by whom he had seven children, the fourth of whom was Jesse Root Grant, the future father of Ulysses S. Grant. When Jesse was five years of age, his father removed to Ohio, where Jesse was married, in course of time, as we have seen, and Ulysses was born.

"There you have briefly," added Mr. Wheeler, "the genealogy of the Grant family, traced back two hundred and fifty years; intelligence, honesty, industry, morality, and religion, prominent in all the generations; and not a few illustrious names on its roll of honor. Gov. Samuel Huntington of Ohio belonged to this family; also, Congressman Delano, Representative from Ohio; and Gen. Don Carlos Buell What say you to it?"

"Well, I don't see but you have made out your case," replied his friend; "and there is not much

Scotch about it, either. Our General does not need any Scotch blood; that is plain enough."

Noah Grant, the grandfather of Ulysses, inherited the intelligence, tact, and virtues of his ancestors, and not a little of their bravery. When he first made himself a home in Ohio, the Indians were troublesome. One of his neighbor's sons had an altercation with White Eyes, and shot him; and this aggravated their troubles. Noah Grant saw at once that, henceforth, peace was impossible unless the Indians were driven from that section, and he proposed a campaign against them. The proposition was popular with the inhabitants; and uniting their forces, the Indians were driven out. From that time, their most serious troubles were removed.

Jesse, the father of Ulysses, was not excelled by his ancestors in mental ability and tact for business. He was singularly practical in his views and methods, upright in all transactions with his fellows, and devotedly pious. He and his wife belonged to the Methodist Church, in which their example and influence were a tower of strength. Their home was thoroughly religious, and their parental lessons sound and elevating.

When Jesse was five years old, he saw his mother in tears one day, and his child-heart was touched. Running up to her, he called out, —

"Mamma, what you crying for?"

"General Washington is dead," she replied, with tears streaming down her cheeks. The tidings of his death had just reached the family.

"Was he any relation of yours?" inquired the

youngster, evidently thinking that it was not worth while to cry over dead men, except they were relatives.

Had he been mature enough to understand, Jesse would have accepted the honest grief of his mother as proof of that patriotism and loyalty which had come down from former generations of the Grant family, — "The mother's milk had been the milk of liberty."

He was but six years of age when he began to carry the grist to mill on the back of the old family horse. One day, on his return, he fell asleep, as the moderate beast walked along lazily, and fell from the back of the animal, bag and all. The fall awoke him suddenly to comprehend the novelty of his situation. He was two small to reload the meal, or to mount the horse himself. Should he leave the meal, and lead the old horse home, the hogs, running at large in every direction, would devour it before his father could return for it. What could he do? His fertile brain soon found an expedient. He saw a half-fallen tree near by, forming an inclined plane with its stump, on which the butt rested six or eight feet high. Drawing the bag of meal to the foot of the plane, and pulling it across the trunk, he gradually worked it up higher and higher, until he could push it off upon the horse's back; then he dropped himself upon the bag and drove home.

Jesse was ten years old when the Western Reserve was thrown open for settlement, and thither his father removed, settling in Portage County, near the present town of Deerfield. One year later his mother died, and the family was broken up. Jesse went to live in the family of Judge George Tod of the Supreme Court, twenty-five miles distant. Judge Tod was wealthy, for that day and place, and lived in much style. Jesse looked with wonder upon the shining spoons and dishes, and finally ventured to ask the son, David, —

"What are these spoons made of?"

"Silver."

"What are the bowls made of?"

"China."

"What did they cost?"

"I don't know; I'll go and ask mother."

The little fellow soon returned with the message,—

"She says that you will have to be very rich before you can own them, for the set cost eighteen dollars!"

"I don't care how much they cost. When I am a man I will own some just as good as them," answered Jesse.

This little David Tod became Governor of Ohio when Jesse's son, Ulysses, was leading the Union Army to victory over the late Rebellion.

At sixteen years of age, Jesse left Judge Tod's to learn the tanning business; and at twenty-one years of age, set up the business in his own name, at Deerfield. In four years he laid up fifteen hundred dollars, and was worth vastly more than that in the confidence and affections of the people.

Several years before, he promised himself to get married at twenty-five, and he never broke a promise to himself any more than he did to another. So, on the morning of his twenty-fifth birth-day, he awoke early, and said to his bed-fellow,—

"I have always promised myself a wife at twenty-five, and to-day I am twenty-five; but where to look for one is more than I can tell. But I am going to make a beginning to-day, anyhow."

"Not much of a job to find a wife, especially for you, Jess," replied his chum. "Enough girls who will jump at a chance to marry *you*."

"Do you really believe that?" responded Jesse.

"Of course I do — I *know* it."

The conversation proceeded on this line, while Jesse was arraying himself in his best suit, thereby showing that he meant business. Having completed his toilet, he sallied forth to inspect the tan-yard, and see that everything was right before breakfast. He boarded at the tavern; and when he responded to the call for breakfast, his landlady observed that he had on his Sunday clothes, and she said, —

"What's to be done to-day, Jesse?"

"Find a wife, if I can," replied Jesse, with the most serious air.

"Where are you going to find her? Not out of town, I hope," continued the landlady, scarcely thinking that the young tanner was in earnest.

"The Lord only knows, I don't; except I shall be under the necessity of going where there are girls." answered Jesse. "I am twenty-five years old to-day, and I always said that I would get married at twenty five, and I will."

"Well, if you didn't keep your word, you wouldn't be Jesse Root Grant," added the landlady, in a complimentary way. "I don't think you will meet with much trouble in finding a wife, unless you are a difficult young man to please."

Jesse satisfied her that he was serious in his intentions; and so she gave him some good advice, accompanied with words of encouragement, such as her motherly instincts suggested.

To make a long story short, we must say that Jesse had thought of a young lady in the neighborhood, on whom he first called; but, before he had time to make known the object of his visit, she volunteered a recommendation of her cousin, in the next house; adding, "She will make you a capital wife, Mr. Grant." The result was that an engagement was entered into with Prudence Hall, which engagement was subsequently broken by her, reminding Jesse of what his landlady said — "Marry for love, Jesse." So far, it had been a matter of business with him, and he did not get on remarkably well.

But he persevered, — the Grants were famous for perseverance, and Jesse was not a whit behind his illustrious predecessors in that reliable quality. Failure only stimulated his determination to succeed. He said that he would get married, and he would. It was this important element of character which he transmitted to his first-born son; who, forty years thereafter, declared, "I will fight it out on this line if it takes all summer."

But the battle was more than half fought then. He was nearer success than he thought he was. The slip which Prudence Hall gave him, proved an introduction to Hannah Simpson, whom he won and "married for love."

Jesse Grant could turn his hand to almost any thing. In addition to tanning, he run a slaughter-house, did something at teaming, and occasionally erected a building for other parties. Clear-headed and practical, his judgment and counsel were often sought. Possessing sharp observation, knowledge acquired by contact with men, and a benevolent spirit, he became a leading man in the community; and later, was elected the first mayor of the city. He was a ready, forcible speaker in town-meeting, and on other public occasions; and often wrote both prose and poetry for the *Castigator* — a paper published at the shire-town of the County. At one time, a "backwoodsman," who was out of money and shoes, addressed a letter to him in rhyme, through the *Castigator*. The letter began: —

> "Jesse R. Grant, my loving friend,
> I cannot go; and therefore send
> This little letter, and less news,
> To let you know I'm out of shoes," etc.

Through the same paper, Mr. Grant replied in rhyme, as follows: —

> "Backwoodsman, sir, my aged friend,
> These lines in answer back I send,
> To thank you for your rhyming letter,
> Published in *The Castigator*.
> The story of your worn-out shoes
> Is, to a tanner, no strange news;
> We often hear that story told,
> By those whose feet are pinched with cold,

"When they apply to get some leather,
To guard against the frosty weather.
That cash is scarce, they oft complain,
And wish to pay their bills in grain.
Others who wish to be supplied,
Will promise soon to bring a hide.

"Such pay by us is greatly prized,
But is not always realized.
Now, one thing here I must relate,
As written in the Book of Fate:
As you've grown old, you have grown poor,
As poets oft have done before.
And yet, no one of common sense,
Will charge that fault to your expense;
Or, otherwise, disprove the weight,
Than charge it to a poet's fate.

"Dame Fate with me, though, need not flirt,
For I'm not poet enough to hurt!
The world, 'tis said, owes all a living;
What can't be bought, then, must be given.
And though I have not much to spare,
I can, at least, supply a pair —
Or leather for a pair — of shoes,
That you may sally forth for news.
And when another pair you want,
Just drop a note to
                              J. R. GRANT."

He was educated by business, and not by schools
He studied men and things, and learned something
from them every day. Common sense, which is the
most uncommon kind of sense, was conspicuous in
his plans and work; and this quality kept constant
company with decision and principle.

As Ulysses advanced to youth and early manhood,
it became evident that he had inherited the noblest

qualities of his father. Though not precocious, nor very remarkable, except in certain lines, his ways often reminded others of his father. Frequently the remark was heard, "A chip of the old block"; and this was a just estimate of the son, with this difference, as the sequel will show, —

THE CHIP WAS LARGER THAN THE BLOCK.

III.

HOME AND MOTHER.

AN eminent scholar once said, "Good professors can make good scholars, but good mothers only can make good men."

John Adams wrote to his wife, after an interview with George Washington, "In reading history, you will generally observe, when you light upon a great character, whether a general, a statesman, or a philosopher, some female about him, either in the character of a mother, wife, or sister, who has knowledge and ambition above the ordinary level of women, and that much of his eminence is owing to her precepts, example, or instigation, in some shape or other."

Jesse Root Grant wrote of his wife (mother of Ulysses), "Her steadiness, firmness, and strength of character, have been the stay of the family through life." And a neighbor, with the best opportunities to observe and judge, said of her, "She was a very remarkable woman, modest and unassuming, amiable almost to a fault, kind and benevolent towards all, forgetful of herself, and a sincere Christian. She was always pleasant in her family, never cross or irritable, and labored to make her home attractive to her husband and children. She would not have a rod in the house, but governed her household by love. She once said to me,

"'Mothers make a great mistake in using the rod so much; there is no need of it. If a son or daughter cannot be controlled by love, I am quite sure they cannot be by the rod.'

"'But would you never use the rod?' I asked.

"'I never have used it,' she replied. 'I do not say that circumstances may never arise to make its use necessary; but so far I have not been placed in such circumstances.'

"'If you had some children to manage, you would find your theory lame,' I added; 'but your children are naturally obedient.'

"'No child is *naturally* obedient,' she instantly replied; 'all children want to have their own way and that is just as true of my children as it is of other folk's children. But I try to make them fee that their mother seeks their highest good in all that she does; and I know that I can accomplish this better by appealing to their hearts in love, than I can by stern authority.'

"Certainly," continued the neighbor, "her method worked well in her own family, and a more harmonious, happy home I never knew. The Grant children would do anything for their mother; and her boys were never racing about the streets in the evening; they seemed glad to be at home."

This is very important testimony, and furnishes the key to the home-life of Ulysses. The mother makes the home. There is no real home withou a good mother. She is its sun; and children, like planets, revolve around her. No matter how good and true the father is, the mother gives the moulding character to home. That was certainly true of Ulysses' home. Nor does what we have said respecting the qualities inherited from his father and grandfather detract in the least from this claim for maternal influence. Some of his best qualities were inherited from his mother, and those inherited from his father were more or less directed by her home influence.

Mrs. Grant realized that Georgetown was a hard place, and therefore a bad school for boys. There was much drinking, and consequent revelry and vice there. There was more or less gambling, also, together with the many temptations that usually follow in the wake of dram-shops and other places of vicious resort. She knew that some boys in the place had fallen victims to prevailing vices; and her sensible plan was to make home more potent to control her sons than the street or bar-room. In this she was entirely successful. Her boys were at home when many others were on the street and in the beer-shops. They were at home, where both example and precept enforced temperance, honesty, purity, and religion. Their home was more than a match for the liquor-shops and gaming-clubs of the village. But for this power of the home, the Union Army might not have found a successful general to lead it on to victory.

When Ulysses was two years old, his father was on the street with him on the morning of some gala-day. The son of a neighbor came along, a boy of twelve or thirteen years, with a pistol in his hand. Seeing Ulysses, he stopped and said,

"Hullo, Lyss, you here? Want to see my pistol?" And he proceeded to exhibit the pistol, and to explain to the child in petticoats how it would explode and make a loud noise.

"Would n't you like to fire it off, Lyss?" he continued. The child signified that it would afford him great pleasure; and so, turning to Mr. Grant, he pleaded, "Let Lyss fire it."

After a little parleying, Mr. Grant put the child's forefinger around the trigger, and told him to pull; when, lo! the pistol banged away, startling some of the bystanders, but not startling Ulysses in the least. Most children would have been terrified by the report, but the only effect upon Ulysses was to extort a shout of delight.

"Fick it again! Fick it again!" the child pleaded. The pistol was loaded again, and again Ulysses fired it, shouting with increased delight over its stunning report, one of the lookers-on remarking, as he saw the coolness of the child,

"He will make a general."

Mr. Grant was very much impressed by this scene; and the incident may be used to illustrate a difference between himself and wife. He was proud of his children, and often spoke of Ulysses' precocity; but Mrs. Grant never did. No one ever heard a word of this kind drop from her lips. She abhorred self-praise; and, next to that, was praise of her own children. Even when Ulysses commanded the Union Army, and victory had finally perched upon his banner, she would blush when he was highly praised in her presence. The journals which she read, teemed with praises of the conqueror; and nearly every man and woman with whom she conversed was equally emphatic in their expressions of admiration; but she could not get used to the praise of her son. No doubt that, in her heart of hearts, there was real joy over his success; she was human, and such must have been the fact. But her modesty and humility exerted such controlling power over her life as to prevent all external demonstration of such internal pleasure.

We can scarcely estimate the force of this quality exerted upon a family, year in and year out, through wedded life. Here is where the great modesty of the son, Ulysses S. Grant, originated. Who ever saw him indicate, by word or deed, that he had accomplished great things? When his grateful country laid its proudest honors at his feet, and when other nations vied with each other to swell his fame, who ever saw the least gleam of pride in his eye? When the Government fêted him, at the close of the war, in Washington, he suppressed his personal distaste, and submitted from a sense of duty; but when the ovation ceased, he could not withhold the exclamation, "*I am tired of this show business.*"

Little, however, as Mrs. Grant was interested in the pistol-firing, she was very much amused soon afterwards by the following incident: Ulysses was taken suddenly sick, and was so ill that the physician was called. Usually, Mrs. Grant doctored her own children, and was very successful in her treatment; but Ulysses' case now demanded the physician. Dr. Bailey came, examined the patient, and prescribed.

"I will leave some *powders* for him to-night," said the doctor, after having administered a dose.

At this announcement, Ulysses burst out crying.

"What is the matter, my child?" said his mother, with some surprise, for her two-year-old was not given to crying.

"I don't want to take *powder;* 't will blow me up."

Sick as he was, the child was obliged to hear considerable laughter at his own expense, while his mother comforted him by saying, —

"Dr. Bailey never carries the kind of powder that blows up people."

Ulysses recovered, not only from his sickness, but also from the fear of being "blown up" by powder; for, from that time, and all through the war, he never appeared to think that powder put his life in jeopardy.

It was genuine modesty, and not bashfulness, as his father said. In response to an inquiry in 1863, his father wrote: "When a child, and all the way up to the present time, he has been extremely modest and unassuming. Some called it bashfulness, but that was not the proper name, for those who knew him best said, that if he were required to meet a company of crowned-heads from Europe, male or female, he would approach them with as much ease and confer with them as free from embarrassment as he would meet his playmates in the streets."

A circus came to town when Ulysses was about

two years old, and his father took him, with his family, to witness the performance. Mr. Grant said, "Ulysses had a passion for horses almost from the time he could go alone," and it came out visibly on this occasion. The little fellow became intensely excited over the feats of horses and men, and when a beautiful pony appeared upon the course, and a boy rode him gracefully around the circle, he became almost wild with enthusiasm. He stretched out his little hands and pleaded for a ride. He could not take no for an answer, denial would break his heart, so he was held upon the tiny beast, and rode several times around the course, to his inexpressible delight.

Several years afterward, when he had become distinguished in town as a boy-rider, he was present at another circus, when a pony was introduced upon the course.

"Will some boy step forward and ride the pony?" inquired the manager, who had already exhibited the feats of a monkey on his back, the monkey being at last thrown.

"I will ride him," answered Ulysses, as he stepped forward. The audience, who knew him well, clapped their hands. The pony could not throw him, they thought, for they had seen him, again and again, dashing around the public square on the back of a vicious colt, whose feet, in front and rear, were alternately in the air.

"You are not afraid of being thrown, I suppose?" remarked the manager, as the boy mounted the animal.

"No, sir," answered Ulysses promptly, and he

never made a truer answer. Afraid of being thrown! — not he; it was the last thought to enter his head.

Away flew the pony, under the crack of the driver's whip, faster and faster, as round and round he sped, the audience testifying to their appreciation of the fun by their shouts and laughter. At length the pony leaped and kicked, throwing his heels high into the air, for the express purpose of hurling Ulysses to the ground; but he stuck his bare feet into the sides of the beast, clung to his mane, and looked, for all the world, as if saying to himself, "You can't do it." The audience clapped their hands, laughed, and shouted in wild excitement. Scarcely had their noisy demonstrations abated, when a trained monkey leaped upon the lad's shoulders for the purpose of hastening his discomfiture; but all in vain. Standing there, the monkey seized the hair of his head, holding on for dear life, as the pony darted round the course, kicking, plunging, and rearing, amid a still wilder demonstration by the spectators, some of whom cried out, —

"Stick! Lyss, stick! Good! Good!"

Not a muscle of Ulysses' face moved, not the least sign of fear appeared in his demeanor; but, rather, a calm, self-possessed, satisfied expression rested on his countenance, as if he felt sure of winning.

The pony was beaten. The manager confessed that the lad was too much for him; and the audience rewarded the young hero with rounds of applause. This incident is important only as showing an element of character which had not a little to do, thirty years and more thereafter, with Ulysses' triumphs on the field of battle. Here, as in more important events, it is proved that "the boy is father of the man."

Mrs. Grant did not enjoy these things. There was no merit in them to her, while there was danger, and, perhaps, moral exposure. Her boy was neither profane, nor disobedient, nor vicious; but she feared that he might become all of these by such appeals to his lower nature. But home influence guided what she feared was of evil tendency up to a high plane of life. In a corrupt home, such tendencies would undoubtedly lead to ruin.

IV.

THE LOG SCHOOL-HOUSE.

HEN Ulysses was nearly four years old, he began to attend school. At that time, most of the inhabitants lived in small, cheap, frame-houses; but the school-house was built of logs—such a structure as a few men would erect in a day.

Schools were poor, and as short as they were poor. A few weeks in summer, and as many more in winter, continued for a few years only, constituted the education of that day. As soon as Ulysses was able to render his father substantial assistance in the tannery, he attended school only the few weeks in winter.

The pioneer class did as well as they could to instruct their children. They did not undervalue education; but they did not see the necessity of so thorough and protracted culture as the people of Georgetown demand to-day. While many of them would have been glad of better schools, they were forced to accept such as they could get; and the same was true of their teachers. Georgetown would not now tolerate such uncultivated teachers as were employed then. It was the best the parents could do at that time.

Ulysses was a shy, slow, but reliable pupil all through his school-days. He was in no sense brilliant; and some teachers might have pronounced him dull. His indomitable perseverance, however, enabled him to perform his tasks surely. When he was seven or eight years of age, the teacher gave out an unusually difficult lesson in arithmetic.

"I can't do it, and I won't try," said one of the scholars to another.

"I shall try," answered the pupil addressed; "but I have no idea that I can master it."

"Lyss will put it through," remarked another boy, casting a patronizing look upon him. "His forte is in arithmetic, and he will dig away until he has got it; but I *can't* do it."

"Can't! can't!" responded Ulysses quizzically. "What does that mean?" and away he rushed to the teacher's desk to examine the dictionary. The boys looked on silently, awaiting to see what was up "Can't!" exclaimed Ulysses; "there's no such word in the dictionary," as he closed the volume. "It *can* be done."

His companions laughed; for their decided little schoolmate was unusually demonstrative for him. It was not exactly surprising to them; but it was rather unexpected.

"That is so, Hug," added one of the scholars, who admired Ulysses' pluck.

His usual nickname was "Lyss"; but sometimes the boys called him "Hug," from his initials "H. U. G." There was something in the boy's nature which caused them to think that the nickname

"Hug" was appropriate. At one time he was called "Texas," because his father visited that far-off part of the country, and when he returned, published a long account of his visit.

The discussion of the boys about the lesson occurred at recess, and the teacher heard it. So, when the recitation had proved a failure with most of the class, Ulysses and one other pupil excepted, he called attention to the conversation which he heard.

"No, there is no such word as *can't* in the dictionary," he said. "Ulysses is right; and he never would have mastered the lesson if he had believed with some of you boys — that he could not do it. Believe you *can*, and you *can*. It is half the battle to have confidence in your ability to accomplish a task. To *try* and fail, is vastly better than it is to *fail* without trying."

Ulysses was an illustration of a remark of the famous teacher of Rugby, Doctor Arnold. "The difference in boys is not so much in talent as *energy*." He meant that the boy with five talents and unconquerable force of character will make his way in the world, when a boy of ten talents and lack of *energy* will prove a miserable failure.

When speaking of nicknames, we should have mentioned another by which Ulysses was sometimes known, when a party wanted to be facetious. It was "Useless," and it originated thus:—

His mother sometimes indulged in dry wit; and when counseling him concerning the improvement of his time, in his early school-days, so **as to make** an honored man, she added, —

' I hope you will never give people a reason for calling you *Useless*, instead of Ulysses, Grant." His playmates derived some sport at times from the use of the nickname.

As we have said, Ulysses excelled in arithmetic. He was deficient in some branches of study, — perhaps below the average. He was a good speller and a fair reader. He engaged in spelling matches with considerable enthusiasm, and with credit to himself; but he shrank from declamation and debate. At one time there was a debating society in the school, but he could not be induced to participate. It was the same with declamation. No amount of persuasion could coax him upon the rostrum. A Methodist minister relates, however, that once, when he was stopping at Jesse Grant's house (this was the home of ministers who came to town), he remembers that his mother asked him to "speak a piece," and the boy responded by stepping into the middle of the room, making his bow, and reciting, with much force and fluency, —

"You'd scarce expect one of my age
To speak in public on the stage."

Ulysses was nine or ten years of age when his father invited a nephew in Canada to a home in his family, that he might attend school. The lad had no opportunity for schooling in his native place. In due time John came, and was duly entered as a member of the Grant family. He was about the age of Ulysses, and the two boys became attached to each other, although their mutual attachment did not prevent one serious collision.

Ulysses had read the life of Washington, and admired the great man's character. He had heard much, too, about the American Revolution, and the French and Indian War, because some of his ancestors were engaged in those contests. People of that' lay, throughout the country, rehearsed much more than now the heroic deeds of ancestors. The scarcity of books was made up by tradition, and lack of reading matter was supplied by talk. A military spirit prevailed at that day — the laws of the country requiring that it should be fostered. Military companies were familiar to Ulysses, and he often witnessed military drills. To attend the annual mil itary muster, with its grand display of all the companies in the region, was his chief delight. In addition to this, townships and institutions around him were named in honor of famous military characters: Scott was named for Gen. Winfield Scott; Ripley for General Ripley; and Brown County for Gen. Ethan Allen Brown; all of whom distinguished themselves in the war with England, in the year 1812.

In these circumstances, it was perfectly natural for Ulysses to talk much about Washington with his Cousin John. No doubt that he supposed his cousin was in full sympathy with him in his loyal spirit, although belonging to the British dominion; and it is quite evident that John was disposed to tolerate his patriotic deliverances until they became annoying; for John was loyal to his country, also. He was a genuine patriot, and possessed courage enough to defend his government whenever it became necessary. He surprised Ulysses one day, by replying to his praise of Washington, —

"Well, your great Washington was a rebel, any how. He fought against the King."

"What is that you say?" Ulysses inquired, with some earnestness, as if not quite satisfied that he heard correctly.

"I say that Washington was a traitor to his country, because he fought against the King."

"You say that again, and I will thrash you if you are my cousin"; answered Ulysses, in patriotic anger. "I am not the boy to stand by and hear Washington called a traitor."

"I do repeat it," rejoined John, whose loyal spirit was now fully aroused. "Washington was a rebel, and you can't deny it and keep truth on your side."

More quickly than the incident can be related, Ulysses took off his coat and grappled with his cousin. The latter withstood his ground like a faithful subject of the King, and held his own readily for some time; but the dogged perseverance of Ulysses proved too much for his English bravery, and finally he lay sprawling upon the ground.

"There!" shouted Ulysses, "call Washington a traitor, will you? I wouldn't submit to hear my own mother call him so."

John was not inclined to prolong the controversy, and Ulysses cooled off rapidly, so that the two cousins were soon on good terms again. But the affair was reported to Mrs. Grant by some one.

"How is this, Ulysses," she said, calling him into the house. "After all that you have heard me say about fighting, is it true that you have been fighting with your cousin?"

"I thrashed John," answered the lad, modestly.

"Your own cousin, too," continued his mother. "You know that I always promised to punish you for getting into a quarrel with any one."

"But John was to blame," pleaded Ulysses; "he called Washington a traitor, and I wouldn't stand it." And he proceeded to rehearse the affair in detail, showing that he did not administer the thrashing from revenge or malice, but on *patriotic principles.*

His father stood by, and was evidently delighted with his son's conduct.

"I don't think you ought to punish him," he finally interjected. "He did not fight because he loves fighting; he is not that sort of a boy. No one ever knew him to quarrel with a schoolmate before· and he did it now in defense of his country; and, to tell you the truth, I should not think much of a boy who would not defend the good name of his country." How clear that Ulysses was a "chip of the old block!"

Here the matter ended; and Ulysses never fought again *on principle* until he went into the Mexican War, and subseqently conquered the Rebellion.

A phrenologist came to town one winter when Ulysses was a school-boy, and gave a course of lectures. At the close of each lecture he allowed himself to be blindfolded, when the citizens set who· ever they pleased into the chair for examination. One evening a gentleman set **Ulysses in the chair**, after the lecturer was blindfolded. The latter proceeded to examine his head, and continued so long without saying a word, that a citizen inquired,

"Do you discover any special ability for mathematics in that boy's head?"

"Mathematics!" retorted the lecturer, as if that kind of ability did not cover the case. "You need not be surprised if this boy is President of the United States some day."

This remark was unexpected to most of the audience; and it did not increase the reputation of the phrenologist in Point Pleasant. They knew that Ulysses excelled in arithmetic, and that he was a boy of invincible will; but they could not see that these qualities were particularly suited to make him President of the United States.

School-boys engaged in ball-playing and various other games, for which Ulysses had some taste and tact. He was an expert skater and swimmer, usually bearing off the palm when there was a trial. He possessed a nice sense of honor and justice in his intercourse with his play-fellows, and this quality was accompanied by profound respect for his superiors.

He was engaged in a hotly-contested game of ball, into which he was throwing his best endeavors. By a fortunate hit, he sent the ball to quite a distance, and it went through a window in Doctor Bailey's house. Throwing down his bat, he rushed to the house, and entering, almost out of breath, he said,

"Mrs. Bailey, I have broken your window, but I am going right off for another **pane of glass for you, and have it put in at once.**"

He would stop the game of ball at once in order to do justly to others ; or, in other words, to right a wrong.

"No, indeed, you won't do any such thing, Lyss," replied Mrs. Bailey, who admired the manliness of the boy. "Go back to your game of ball, and we wil take care of the glass." And she fairly compelled him to relinquish his purpose of restoring the broken pane. Ulysses was a great favorite with her, and, indeed, with all her family, on account of some of his elements of character already mentioned.

We must not forget to record his talent for drawing with pen or pencil. He could beat every boy and girl in school in drawing animals, on slate or paper; especially the horse, which he loved so well. For naturalness and real beauty, his pictures of the horse challenged the admiration of even his teachers. It was when he gratified his talent in this direction in school-hours, so as to interfere with his studies, that his teachers objected. He was very apt to indulge this propensity at the expense of his standing as a scholar, and had to be watched, and sometimes reproved, in consequence.

One thing interfered very much with his progress in school; it was his love of horses. As soon as he was old enough to assist his father by driving a horse (and that was at five or six years of age), there were frequent demands upon his time to carry passengers, to haul a load, or to go upon some errand. He was not so fond of teacher or school, but that he would catch at a chance any time to ride or drive a horse. He was more ready to be absent from school for such a purpose, than his parents were to have him On this account, when he quit the log school-house forever, at about twelve years of age, he was deficient in all studies except arithmetic.

At fourteen, he spent one winter in Maysville Ky., attending school. Peter Grant, his uncle, lived and died there; and his widow invited Ulysses to spend the winter with her, and attend the public school, which was far in advance of the school at Point Pleasant. Two years later he attended the Presbyterian Academy at Ripley a few months, where he applied himself closely, and made marked proficiency in all the branches of study he pursued. This constituted all the schooling Ulysses enjoyed until he entered West Point.

We must stop here to call the reader's attention to the fact that Ulysses S. Grant was not educated in school. Some boys are too large to be squeezed into the narrow limits of a school curriculum. Their great natures protest against it. There is not room for them. Their development is actually hindered by the straight-jacket rules and systems that prevail. There was no school in the American Colonies large enough to educate Washington. Indeed, there was none large enough in Great Britain to educate him. Had he been sent thither, as his brother was, he might never have been qualified to lead the American armies, or to preside over the destiny of the nation when independence had been achieved. But he was educated in the field and forum. From the time he entered upon public service, at nineteen, he developed **remarkably fast**. Surveying vast tracts of land, and exploring the wild country, was a school. Every drill, siege, and battle was a school. All public service appealed to his large soul; and under its inspiring power, he developed into the great General and Statesman that he was. "First in war, first in peace, and first in the hearts of his countrymen."

The same was true of Lincoln. The severe discipline of life educated him. Poverty, hardship, obscurity, and work, were his daily teachers; the world was his school-room. Had he been shut up within the walls of the academy and college, he might never have become President, and the "Great Emancipator." His greatness required larger liberty, a broader field, and the study of stern, practical life. So Providence educated him outside of schools for a mighty leader.

Garfield never found but one teacher as great as himself. He outgrew every school he entered within a few months. In two years he was ahead of his college. He learned more by teaching others than his own teachers taught him. He was cramped and hampered even here! Providence called him out into the broader, grander, more exciting arena of public service; and he soon proved himself a greater man than his best instructors supposed him to be No school was great enough to educate him.

It was so with the subject of our narrative. His school-days did not forecast his future renown. No teacher would have prophesied that he would become, in any respect, the greatest man of his age. No instructor believed him to be a great man in embryo;

and it was because he was larger than his surroundings. He could not soar without leaving the nest. His nature demanded the discipline of battle and peril. Peace could not arouse his latent energies. The call, "*To arms!*" fired his soul. From that moment he grew mighty, until his victorious banner floated over a thousand battle-fields. He had found his place,—a regenerated nation had found him.

V.

THE TANNER BOY.

E have said that Jesse Grant was a tanner, and that Ulysses, his son, learned the business. His tannery was a small one; and, at that time, the leather business of the country was small. But Mr. Grant understood the business thoroughly, and was regarded as a first-class tanner.

The first work of Ulysses was driving the horse in the bark-mill. A horse ground the bark by traveling round in a circle, hitched to a pole that was attached to the sweep which he drew. The pole led the horse, and Ulysses applied the whip. The lazy old beast required considerable urging at times to keep from falling to sleep in his monotonous work. Our embryo tanner was the boy to quicken his pace.

Another boy stood at the hopper of the mill, and, with a hammer, broke the strips of bark (which were brought to the mill three feet long) into it. In due time Ulysses was promoted to do this work, which was less attractive to him because there was less horse in it. Step by step, from year to year, he acquired a knowledge of different parts of the business, until he could tan hides as well as he *tanned* rebels twenty-five years later. All his time out of school was not spent in the tannery; indeed, the tannery was not in operation all the time; and it was for this reason that Mr. Grant turned his attention occasionally to other business. He had other irons in the fire nearly all the time. Ulysses liked some of the irons better than he did the tannery. To tell the plain truth, he did not like the tanner's business at all. Teaming, farming, choring, skating, swimming, almost anything else which he did, was preferable to tanning leather. Even the log school-house had more attractions for him than the tannery. Any assistance that he could render his father with the help of a horse suited him exactly.

One day his father was going to Ripley on business, and he said to Ulysses, —

"I shall not be back until evening; see that the chores are done, and the rest of the time you can play." Mr. Grant believed that there was a time for play as well as for work, that is, for boys; but he would make work the rule.

His father had not been absent a half hour before Ulysses thought of the colt, a very promising young animal which had never been harnessed. He thought of the brush in the woods, also, for he had heard his father say that he should haul it up before long.

"Now," he said within himself," if I could take the colt and haul up the brush to-day, father would be mightily pleased."

Something else inside said to him, "But the colt was never harnessed, and suppose he should be scared, and kick and thrash about, and break the harness, and a leg, too, what would your father say?"

"Oh, Billy will never do that to me; he is gentle as a lamb," he argued silently, but thoughtfully. "I don't believe he will kick if the cart should strike his heels. Then, there is no business without some risk, as I have heard father say forty times. I'll take the risk."

And he did; and just here was one of the points of Ulysses' character which helped him win success in later life, especially in the war. He took risks, as we shall see hereafter.

The colt was taken out by his young master, who was then but seven years and six months old, to be initiated into actual labor. The lad was too short to reach the animal's head, so he inverted a half bushel, and, standing thereon, proceeded to bridle him. Docile and happy, the colt yielded to the appeal of kind words, and allowed the whole harness to be adjusted without objection. Cautiously Ulysses advanced to the more difficult part of the experiment, that of hitching Billy to the cart. But it was done successfully, the considerate beast not protesting in the least. And he started off as steadily as the old family horse would have done, worked all day without any refractory demonstration, and closed his first day's work with evident self-complacency. If the colt could have talked as distinctly as Balaam's ass, he could not have made it more evident that he meant to help Ulysses through that experiment, to prove that the wisest men must assume risks.

At the close of the day Ulysses had a pile of brush in the yard as big as the log school-house; and he was in his element. His mother enjoyed the result as well, although her venturesome son did no venture to consult her about using the colt. H knew very well that she would issue an order to arrest the plan, and an order from headquarters must be obeyed. It is equally true, no doubt, that if his experiment with the colt had proved a failure, he would have been court-martialled by his mother before the head of the family returned at night. But taking the risk turned out well, and all were happy.

It was dark when Mr. Grant reached home, but not dark enough to conceal the huge pile of brush. It was close by the carriage-drive.

"What's this?" he said, in a tone of surprise to Ulysses, who was on the spot awaiting his father's arrival.

"A pile of brush I have hauled to-day."

"A pile of brush!" exclaimed his father, "I did not tell you to haul brush."

"No; but I heard you say that you were going to haul it up sometime, and I thought if I hauled it to-day, it would be clear gain."

"But what did you haul it with?" inquired his father, wondering.

"With the colt and cart."

"The colt, bless you," replied Mr. Grant, with still greater surprise. "How in the world did you manage him? I should have thought he would kick the brains out of you."

"Well, you see he did n't; my brains are all right," answered Ulysses. "He behaved just as well as the old horse would."

Going into the house, the subject was renewed

with Mrs. Grant, and the conversation ended by Mr. Grant saying,

"Lyss will turn into a horse yet."

"If I do," retorted Ulysses, "I shall be worth more to you than that drunken journeyman in the tan-yard."

"I guess you are right there, Lyss," answered his father laughing. "Jack is a miserable fellow any way, and I am only waiting for a favorable opportunity to send him adrift."

Jack was a journeyman, a roving, drinking fellow from New York, who floated into the place, and Mr. Grant hired him. He was a good workman, but a man of dissolute habits. Soon afterwards, the opportunity to dismiss him, for which his employer was waiting, offered itself in this way. Jack was on a spree, and, getting out of money, he appropriated several calf-skins belonging to his employer, and offered to sell them to a shoemaker. The latter exposed him, and he was expelled from the tannery. He lingered about the place for some time, however, until Mr. Grant met him one day, and ordered him out of town.

' When I get ready, and not before," was Jack's laconic reply; at the same time drawing his jackknife upon Mr. G.

"You villain!" exclaimed Mr. Grant, seizing the fellow at the same time, and wresting the knife from him; "we will see whether you will go or stay."

"Here, Lyss, run and bring my cowhide." Lyss, who was with his father at the time, never moved his feet more nimbly than he did then, his father holding the wretched culprit with an iron grip, and occasionally shaking him up, until Ulysses returned with the cowhide. A more thorough basting was never administered to a mean man, than Jack got from the Georgetown tanner. He did leave town, and never returned.

Ulysses was a kind-hearted boy, and had a poor opinion of cowhides in general; but ever afterwards, for this particular cowhide he cherished profound respect. The proof was now overwhelming, that if Jesse Grant's son were nothing better than horseflesh, he would be more valuable to his father than the brute of a journeyman in the tannery.

There was more or less teaming to be done to and from the tan-yard; and, at eight years of age, Ulysses did it with a pair of horses. He enjoyed this hugely, for the occupation took him away from the tannery a part of the time, and provided him with that most enjoyable of all business — driving horses.

He took the whole care of the horses, also, though he could not harness them without mounting the half-bushel measure. It was a spectacle which strangers often stopped to enjoy, the sight of this eight-year old, who was rather small of his age, hauling hides, wood, bark, and other merchandise, with the tact and ability of a man.

"Lyss, how would you like to go to Cincinnati for some passengers?" inquired his father one day. "Day after to-morrow, three or four men will be there, who want to come here."

"I should like nothing better," answered Ulysses.

"Forty miles is a long way for a small boy to drive

a pair of horses, but I will risk you," continued his father. Another instance of the propensity of the Grant family to assume risks.

Ulysses drove his pair of horses to Cincinnati on the following day. Stopping over night, he returned with his passengers on the next day. His trip was so successful, that, afterwards, he frequently drove to Cincinnati, always stopping at the Dennison House. Here he became acquainted with the proprietor's son, William Dennison, the senior of Ulysses by six or seven years. Young Dennison became much interested in Ulysses, because he was a child-driver of a pair of horses from Georgetown. This William Dennison became Governor of Ohio thirty years thereafter, and subsequently he was a member of Abraham Lincoln's cabinet, when Ulysses was leading the Northern army in triumph. The boy-teamster and the tavern-keeper's son became *first*, when their more highly-favored companions were *last*.

Mr. Grant allowed his son some perquisites, so that he could accumulate a little money, to encourage him. Carrying passengers, doing odd jobs for neighbors, performing extra work — in these ways he made money for himself; and, at nine years of age, he had laid up twenty dollars. He loved a horse more than ever; and now he longed to have one of his own. It seemed to him the climax of all material things to own a horse.

"Father, may I buy a horse?" he asked one evening.

His father had not dreamed of such a thing; and the inquiry was unexpected.

"What can you do with another horse?" he answered.

"I want one for my own," replied the boy.

"Got money enough to pay for him?"

"Enough to pay for a *colt.*"

"Perhaps you could invest your money better," Mr. G. suggested; for he always looked at the economical side of all questions.

"I think it is the best way to invest my money," replied Ulysses. "A three-year-old colt will double its value in three years, and during the three years he will be bringing me in money by use."

"Perhaps so," answered his father, doubtfully; "but suppose he is taken sick and dies, or breaks a leg, or *your* neck — how then? There is *risk* in buying a horse."

"And I am willing to take the *risk*, father," said Ulysses, decidedly. There it was again, — willingness to take a risk!

"Well, just as you please, Lyss. I don't know that I have any serious objection; only don't get cheated in buying a horse," was Mr. Grant's final decision, rather pleased, on the whole, with the enterprise of his son.

Ulysses had already canvassed the subject without saying a word to any one. He had his eye then upon a colt, and knew exactly what it could be bought for — seventeen dollars. In less than twenty-four hours he had purchased the colt, and it was in his father's barn. A child, nine years old, the happy owner of a horse! And there never was a time thereafter when he did not own a horse.

A horse-trade by such a youngster created considerable remark in town. People who had thought Ulysses was a dull scholar, began to open their eyes. There was no other boy in the township who displayed so much talent for business. No other parents had sons to be trusted with so great responsibilities at nine years of age. Horse-flesh was contributing to the reputation of Ulysses. His bargain turned out to be a good one.

Within a few months Ulysses trained his three-year-old colt to be under perfect control. One day he surprised the villagers by riding around the public square at a breakneck speed, *standing* on the back of his well-trained beast. He had strapped a sheep-skin on the colt's back to keep his feet from slipping, and fearlessly assumed all the risks. He frequently performed this feat afterwards, until it was quite common to see him ride furiously in a standing posture.

At ten years of age, he surpassed every person in the county as a rider. Horse-traders, who wanted to exhibit the speed of their horses, frequently applied for his services as rider. Owners of sick horses, desiring to heat them through and through, as a remedy, employed him to race their animals for miles. Colts, to be broken, were submitted to his management. It was certainly a rare spectacle, to see men of mature years applying to a boy of ten to break their colts, and teach their vicious horses how to behave. It made him a marked boy in the region, although few prophesied that he would rise higher than a circus-rider, or horse-trainer.

His father had great confidence in him, and he had reason to trust him; for his integrity was undoubted. His yea was yea, and his nay, nay. He had no bad habits, and, like his father, discountenanced the prevailing vice of the community, — intemperance. Unlike many boys, he was never profane nor vulgar, and was always obedient to his parents, and proverbially trustworthy; and what is worthy of note, he was singularly ingenuous, as the following incident will show: —

His father wanted to buy a horse of Robert Ralston, who lived one or two miles away, and he sent Ulysses to make the purchase. Doubtless this plan was adopted for the discipline of the boy, or else as a matter of curiosity, to see how he would transact the business.

"Offer him fifty dollars," said Mr. Grant, in giving the young horse-buyer his instructions.

"But you don't expect to buy him for that?" interjected Ulysses.

"Perhaps not; but if he won't take that, offer him fifty-five dollars; rather than not get the horse, you may pay him sixty."

The boy started upon his important errand, intending to obey his father's instruction to the letter. In his own mind, he went through the operation of a bargain, agreeably to the program cited; but the whole plan was overturned by the first inquiry of Mr. Ralston. Ulysses made known his errand, when Mr. R. asked, —

"How much did your father tell you to pay?"

This question was not anticipated, and the little

horse-trader was confused for a moment; but his honest heart leaped to the rescue, and he answered,—

"Father told me to offer you fifty dollars, and if you would n't take that, to offer you fifty-five; and rather than have me come home without the horse, to pay sixty."

Mr. Ralston smiled at the frankness of the boy, and thought that he was stupid. Because the little fellow was more honest than he himself was, he supposed that Ulysses was not a born trader, and sought to take advantage of him. But he "counted without his host."

"Well, my price is sixty-five dollars," replied Mr. Ralston.

"I sha' n't give that," retorted Ulysses at once, seeing the dishonest purpose of the man; "sixty dollars is all the horse is worth. I shall go home without him."

The conversation was not prolonged; for Mr. R. saw that he had mistaken the boy, and taken his honesty to be verdancy. The bargain was closed at sixty dollars, and Ulysses drove the horse home.

So much outside work interfered somewhat with the boy's progress in the tannery, as it had done with his education in the log school-house. Nevertheless, in the ten or twelve years he served there, he had ample opportunity to become a good tanner

The facts of this chapter show that Ulysses possessed those three elements of character which a great English merchant said insure success — tact, push, and principle. The first is the ability to use one's powers, opportunities, and acquisitions to the best advantage. With it, a single talent will accomplish more in practical life than five talents can without it. Emerson put it facetiously in rhyme, thus:—

> "Tact clinches the bargain,
> Sails out of the bay,
> Gets the vote in the Senate,
> Spite of Webster or Clay."

The least promising of a group of boys may out strip the whole number by his tact. While the brilliant fellow without it makes a failure of life, he ascends to the top round of the ladder. Through tact, his dulness beats talent; the tortoise wins the race. We shall see that Ulysses did that; but not without push — energy, singleness of purpose, and perseverance. There was a quiet energy about him; we might call it determination — a quality which an English writer says "will do anything that can be done in this world; and no talents, no circumstances, no opportunities, will make a two-legged creature a man without it"; and not without principle, either. "Sheridan might have ruled the world if he had possessed *principle*," it was said. Ulysses would not lie even to save his father money. He was taught, that while wealth is not absolutely necessary, nor fame, nor even health, PRINCIPLE was indispensable. The lesson was drilled into his soul.

VI.

A NOTABLE TRIP.

ULYSSES was eleven years old when his Uncle Marshall died, six miles beyond Deerfield, Ohio, nearly one hundred miles distant. The widow was in great trouble in consequence, and Mr. Grant, whose sister she was, felt deeply for her.

"She must come here with her family, that I may look after her," he said, "I shall bring her right along with me when I return, if possible."

"As I cannot go with you, why not let Ulysses go?" suggested Mrs. Grant. "He can be of much assistance to you, if you move the family here."

"He can go; I would like to have him go with me," replied Mr. Grant. And it was so arranged, to the great satisfaction of the boy.

They hurried away so as to be present at the funeral. Going to Ripley, they took the steamer to Wellsville, and thence by stage to New Lisbon, thirty-five miles, traveling the last fifteen miles on horseback. The trip from Ripley to Wellsville was Ulysses' first ride on a steamer, and he enjoyed it thoroughly. Still, he was not so enraptured with the sail that he lost any interest in the horse. He would not have traded his colt for the steamer, with the river thrown in.

Widow Marshall was greatly comforted by the arrival of her brother, who made himself very useful at once in the final preparations for the funeral. This solemn occasion having passed, he disclosed his plan of removing her to Georgetown, to which she readily acceded. Her decision to remove made it necessary for Mr. Grant to remain two or three weeks at Deerfield. She had business to be transacted, household articles to sell, and various incidental things to be attended to, all of which required time. Selecting from the furniture what was the most valuable, like beds and bedding, crockery, and other articles, which could be easily transported, he sold the remainder at auction.

Mrs. Marshall owned a farm-wagon and a pair of horses, with which the goods and family were transported to Georgetown. A convenient seat was arranged for herself and children on top of the load, which was a heavy one. Her eldest son, James, who was about the age of Ulysses, rode on the coupling-pole behind the wagon—an expedient suggested by the latter, that they might relieve the horses by jumping off when going up hill or over hard places.

All things being ready, they started on Monday afternoon and traveled to Deerfield, six miles, where they stopped at the "tavern" over night. On Tuesday night they reached New Lisbon, the horses very much exhausted by their day's work.

"The load is too much for them," said Mr. Grant, "and we must hire another team here. If the horses give out it will cost us **more than** it will to hire a team now."

"I thought they would give out before we got here," answered Ulysses, whose sympathy for the jaded horses was stirred. "Another day with the load will finish them."

It was settled that another team should be engaged to convey a part of the furniture to Wellsville, where they would take the steamer, and run down the river to Maysville. After a good night's rest at the "village tavern," Mr. Grant chartered a wagon and pair of horses, and dividing his load, proceeded to Wellsville, where they arrived during the day. Here the hired team was dismissed to return to New Lisbon, the goods being transferred back to the original wagon, which was driven on board the steamer *Lady Byron*. Thence to Maysville by water afforded an opportunity for the horses to rest.

The steamer was obliged to stop several hours at Wheeling, for the repair of a broken wheel. Ulysses and his cousin strolled into the town, and while making observations about the City Hotel a gentleman came out and accosted them.

"Will you take my trunk down to the steamer?"

"Yes, sir," answered Ulysses.

"For how much?"

"A fi'-penny bit," replied the boy. This was six and a quarter cents, sufficiently small pay to show that Ulysses did not practise extortion. It was a full half-mile to the steamer.

"It is a bargain," responded the gentleman, evidently pleased to get his trunk down to the steamer for so little money.

The two boys took up the trunk, one at each end,

and bore it to the steamer, perfectly satisfied on arriving there that they had earned every cent of the pay

Now occurred the only deliberate act of mischief which we have found to record against our hero. There was no wharf built at Wheeling. The water came up nearly to the top of a wall, from which a loose staging extended to the boat. Over this the children of some French and German emigrants on board were running for amusement. Ulysses and James thought the amusement might be varied by an involuntary bath. Accordingly, the opportune moment was improved to move the planks so that the first boy who should step upon them again would fall into the water. Scarcely was the trap laid, when a little, chubby, three-year-old German, wearing a red flannel dress, ran upon the staging and tumbled into the water. A shout of alarm arose, and all on board rushed to the scene. One of the boat's crew seized the child by the hair of his head, and rescued him from a watery grave.

The two naughty boys, who were the cause of the accident, were more scared than the little Teuton in the water. Their thoughtless act came near ending in a tragedy, and they saw the guilt of it the moment the child dropped into the water. No one saw them set the trap, and so they kept the knowledge of it within their own breasts, which was worse for them. They were overjoyed, however, when the child was saved.

Ulysses always condemned himself for this thoughtless deed. It was wholly unlike him; there is nothing else of the kind in his life-record. Perhaps

James was the author of the plan, and Ulysses only yielded. Be that as it may, the incident proves that Ulysses was sufficiently human to have some mischief in him.

The steamer reached Maysville on Saturday, the party having consumed six days in performing a journey which can now be accomplished in less than six hours. They visited relatives in Maysville, and remained several days, when the horses were in a good condition to take them the remaining twenty miles, to Georgetown,

Ulysses enjoyed this trip, though he was glad to get home. It was a good school for him, and he learned some good lessons. He thought more of Georgetown than ever. The place where his Uncle Marshall had lived was isolated, away from school and church privileges, so different from Georgetown that the latter place seemed doubly inviting, and his home dearer than ever.

Mr. Grant's house was becoming crowded. His growing family required more room. He was able to build a larger dwelling, and pay for it. More than all, Mrs. Grant wanted a new house, and that alone was reason enough for building.

"A job for you, Ulysses," he said. "I shall build of brick, and you must haul the brick, and sand, and stone for the cellar."

"That I can do. I rather do that than work in the tannery," replied Ulysses.

"I thought so, and you will be of more service to me, hauling stuff for the house, than working in the tan-yard," added his father.

Mr. Grant decided to erect a spacious brick dwelling, two stories high, his old house becoming its L, and Ulysses began the work of drawing materials at once. Four or five months elapsed before the building was completed, and the family occupied it, and they were months of industry, fatigue, and progress to Ulysses. The interest of no one in the erection of the house was greater than his. He had interest in no outside matter during the whole time. In vain was he asked to hunt and fish, and engage in other pastimes. It did not trouble him at all to see other boys engaged in amusements while he was at work. His profound interest in the new house became the source of his highest enjoyment. The discipline of that season contributed much towards his manhood.

We have said that Ulysses turned aside for nothing while his father's house was building. There was a single exception, however. A citizen owned a fine horse, which he would have trained to pace, and he knew that Ulysses could do it. But the boy had become quite sensitive about training horses, for he was often called a "horse-jockey," jocosely it is true, but he was such a matter-of-fact boy, that even jokes became real to him in time. He had declined to train several horses for this reason, when this neighbor approached him. So the owner of this horse resorted to stratagem in order to secure his services.

"I will give you two dollars, Ulysses, if you will jump on my horse and carry a letter to Decatur for me to-day," he said.

"I suppose I can do it without hindering the work

on the house," replied Ulysses, "if the business is urgent."

"Well, it is urgent, and if you start very soon, you can get back before night," added the citizen.

Decatur was thirteen miles distant, and the owner of the horse thought that the animal could be taught to pace in that distance. Ulysses was soon ready, and when the neighbor handed him the letter, he said, as if it were a thought just suggested, —

"By the way, Lyss, do you suppose that horse could learn to pace?"

"Of course he can," responded Ulysses; "any good horse can learn to pace."

"Well, you try him while you are gone, and see what you think about it."

Ulysses dashed away as he was wont to do on horse-back, saying to himself, "Of course this horse can pace. I will prove it before I get back."

When he reached home at sundown, the horse was a good pacer, as Ulysses proved to the neighbor by riding up and down the street two or three times in his presence. Training the horse to pace had cost the owner but two dollars, and his letter was delivered, into the bargain. He would gladly have paid ten dollars for this successful training.

It was soon noised about the village, that a laughable trick had been played upon Ulysses, and many friends teased the boy much concerning it. At first he did not quite understand the jokes cracked at his expense, but when he really learned the facts in the case, he said that he would never train another horse for anybody, *and he never did.*

In this his decision of character was strikingly set forth. When he said he would do a certain thing, he did it; and when he said he would not do it, no amount of coaxing could induce him to do it. And in this particular case, his decision was doubly fortified by his aversion to being called a "horse-jockey."

About this time there was a cholera scare through out the West. The disease was feared more then than it is now. Its approach caused a general con sternation. Many people were superstitious in re gard to it, and they would catch at every straw that promised protection against its ravages. In many places it was making sad havoc, and there were some cases of it in Georgetown. At Maysville it prevailed alarmingly, and proved fatal in a majority of cases. Everywhere it created intense alarm. The author ities of Georgetown heard that a wonderful remedy had been brought to Maysville, and that the scourge was rapidly disappearing. They decided to procure the remedy, and appointed Mr. Grant to proceed to that city and secure a quantity of the medicine. Mr. Grant lost no time in going to Maysville, for he, in common with the whole population, stood in mortal fear of the scourge. He returned with an ample supply of the remedy, but the disease had disap peared when it was ready for use. It was stored in Jesse Grant's cellar.

The history of that cholera-medicine closed in this way: Juvenile curiosity was as active fifty years ago as it is to-day, and the medicine in question vanished before it. Ulysses was in the habit of staying at home from meeting often on Sunday afternoons;

and some of his companions were in the habit of keeping him company on these occasions. It was rumored that their conduct was not always of a strictly religious type, for they drilled themselves in athletic exercises, such as jumping, turning somersaults, and the like.

For some reason they had occasion to visit Mr. Grant's cellar one Sunday, and the cholera-medicine was discovered. Juvenile curiosity led them to investigate its flavor, and the stuff was found to be decidedly palatable. Each one imbibed, perhaps, more than once. On the following Sabbath afternoon, Mr. and Mrs. Grant being at meeting, they imbibed again. And this was repeated, Sabbath after Sabbath, until the medicine had entirely disappeared. Neither Ulysses, nor any one of his curious companions, ever had the cholera, though we might reasonably wonder why the remedy did not kill them. As it turned out, the medicine did them less injury, without doubt, than their Sabbath-breaking.

Sometime during the eleventh or twelfth winter of Ulysses' life, he froze his feet while skating. He strapped his skates too tightly, and his feet were frozen in consequence. Skating he enjoyed almost as well as teaming, so that he frequently indulged his passion in this direction with other boys. On this occasion the cold was intense, and the skating of superior quality. His feet were frozen before he fully realized that they were cold.

Reluctantly he quitted the sport and started for home, accompanied with the other boys. There was only one person in creation to whom he would have run in such a time of need, and she was his mother.

"Frozen my feet, mother," he announced on entering the house.

"Why, Ulysses, how did that happen? Sure they are frozen?" his mother answered.

"You can see for yourself," replied the boy, calmly.

Examination showed that they were badly frozen, and Mrs. Grant hurried to relieve him at once, remarking,—

"They must be attended to immediately."

One of the boys suggested that Doctor Bailey be called.

"Ma is my doctor," Ulysses responded, "I don't want any other."

Mrs. Grant seldom employed a physician. She had a whole *materia medica* of herbs, besides numerous other catholicons for every emergency. Pioneer women of the West were obliged to know much about the treatment of different maladies. Many townships could not boast of a doctor. In cases of severe sickness, a neighbor would be posted off twenty, thirty, and, perhaps, forty miles, to call one. Georgetown had a physician, but ordinarily Mrs. Grant relied upon her own knowledge and skill to restore the sick members of her family. This case was no exception.

She sent one of the boys to the barn for some hay, with which she smoked the feet thoroughly, and then bound slices of bacon upon them to extract the frost. Doctor Bailey would not have cared for the pa tient more promptly, coolly, and successfully than did Mrs. Grant.

The fact illustrates the self-reliant spirit that pervaded the home of Ulysses. Parents and children were trained to depend upon themselves. We have seen this element of character prominent thus far in Ulysses' young life. Not the spirit of conceit that overestimates one's abilities, but that manly confidence in self which enables one to make his own way in the world. When Samuel J. Mills said to a fellow-student, "You and I are little men, but before we die our influence must be felt on the other side of the globe," there was no conceit in his heart. I' was simply a self-reliant, Christian spirit asserting itself in view of the needs of a benighted world — the essential spirit that controls the being, and puts all the faculties upon the *qui vive*, so that a youth, under its power, will make the most of himself possible. Ulysses possessed this element of character; and so did his mother and father, too, as well as other ancestors far back in the family history. This quality was lifting him into a nobler life, even when some people thought he was dull.

VII.

BUILDING THE JAIL.

HEN Ulysses was twelve years old, his father contracted to build the County jail. Georgetown being the shire-town of the County, the jail was to be located there, making a very convenient job for Mr. Grant. A jail had become a necessity. As population increased, criminals increased.

"If you will buy Paul Devore's horse to work with ours, I will draw all the logs, brick, and stone," was the proposition of Ulysses to his father. "He wants to sell his horse."

"It will be the heaviest job you ever undertook," replied his father; "but if you think you can put it through, I can buy the horse."

"I can; and that horse will be a good match for ours," said Ulysses.

Paul Devore was the Georgetown attorney, whom thoughtless people called "Dave." He had a large, black horse, and Mr. Grant had another black one about the same size; the two would make a splendid pair. Such was the lad's opinion; and his father seemed to think it was correct, for he purchased the horse for fifty-five dollars, and Ulysses christened him "Dave," without discussion or ballot. The naming was done in honor of the attorney, though report said that the latter regarded it as an insult, and ever afterwards appeared to owe the boy a grudge. But the name suited Ulysses, who bestowed it upon the animal without ill-will toward any member of the human family; and the horse was certainly content to wear the distinguished honor.

The first thing to be done was to secure the logs, each one of which must be a foot square when hewn, and fourteen feet long. Eleven hewers and one scorer were engaged, and the work commenced in earnest. The woods were two miles from the site for the jail, and soon Ulysses had all that he could do. Rather proud of his pair of fine, black horses, he began his summer's work whole-hearted and resolute.

One morning he went to the woods, as usual, and no hewers were there. It was their business to load the timber; the boy was to drive the team only What could he do now? He called aloud, supposing they might be in the vicinity somewhere, but there was no response to his call. He was in trouble — never more perplexed in his life than he was for a short time on that morning. Should he return without a load of timber? That would be humiliating to himself, and disappointing to his father. He was accustomed to accomplish whatever he undertook. He looked about for a way out of the difficulty. He saw a half-fallen sugar-maple, with its top lodged in another tree. Its trunk slanted just right for him to haul the hewn logs up to a proper height upon it. Hitching "Dave" to the logs, one by one, he drew them up, resting one end of each on the inclined plane which the fallen tree formed. Then backing his wagon up to them, and fastening a chain to one, "Dave" drew it into the wagon easily; and so on until the load was complete.

"Nothing like trying," he thought, in his exultation, for he had good reason to congratulate himself in surmounting this difficulty; "how many times I have heard father say that!"

He was happier, and perhaps prouder, on his return with that load than he ever was before. His wits had done him good service, and his self-reliance and perseverance supplemented them well.

"Not one of the men in the woods to-day," he said to his father, as he delivered his load.

"How is that? Where are they?" his father asked with surprise.

"That is what I tried to find out; I almost split my throat calling for them," said Ulysses. "Perhaps they thought it was going to rain, and so stayed at home."

There was a drizzling rain in the morning, when Ulysses started for the woods, and a pouring rain was threatened; but the boy was not accustomed to stop work for so slight causes. Doubtless the threatening weather did keep the hewers at home.

"Well, that is singular; but who loaded the logs for you?" continued Mr. Grant.

"Dave and I loaded them."

"A pretty story, Lyss; now, tell me how in the world you got the logs loaded," responded his father.

It was not strange that Mr. Grant considered the claim of his son improbable, for it took four or five men to load the logs; and they accomplished it by taking the wheels off on one side, and letting the axles rest on the ground; then lifted the logs on with handspikes, raised up the axles with levers, and put back the wheels. It was not a probable story to him, that Ulysses loaded the logs, when he considered these stubborn facts.

"It is true, father, Dave and I did it," repeated Ulysses.

"It is not possible; it is incredible," re-asserted Mr. Grant.

Ulysses proceeded to describe the process of loading to his father, as we have already narrated, and when he was through the whole thing was clear and simple to him as A, B, C. He saw that his son had resorted to a plan which his hewers might thereafter adopt to the advantage of all concerned.

"Your wits did it this time, Lyss," remarked Mr. Grant.

"My wits would not have done it without Dave," the boy promptly answered. "Dave is a splendid beast."

He would not take all the glory to himself. He was too honest and just to rob even a horse of his laurels.

"Well, you can divide the glory with Dave if you wish," added his father; "the thing was well done, whether you do or not."

Mr. Grant enjoyed this feat, particularly because Ulysses' method of loading logs was vastly better than that adopted by the hewers. He advised them to use more wit and sweat less thereafter.

The work of Ulysses, hauling logs, brick, and stone, was not interrupted during the summer, except once. His father had a law-suit pending in the State of Connecticut, and the deposition of a man in Louisville, Ky., was indispensable. His hands were so full of business, that he could not spend time to go himself, so he wrote two or three times to different parties, but all in vain. He failed to secure the deposition.

"I can do the business," said Ulysses, when he heard his father deploring the necessity of going to Louisville.

"I am afraid not," replied Mr. Grant; "law business is not exactly in your line; it is more difficult than loading logs."

"Well, I can try, anyway," added the boy, taking advantage of his father's stereotyped counsel repecting the virtue of trying. "I should like to go, first-rate."

Strange as it may seem, it was finally arranged that this lad of twelve years should go to Louisville to transact that important business.

"Who knows but you may be taken for a runaway before you get there," suggested his father, who was not joking in the least; "but I can give you a letter to use when it is necessary."

He wrote a letter, stating that the bearer was his son Ulysses on his way to Louisville to transact business for his father. He feared that when he went on board the boat, the captain might not carry him without a pass of this kind.

It happened that, on the way to Louisville, he met with an acquaintance going thither, so that he had no use for his letter until he returned. He reached the city and transacted the business without the least difficulty; securing the deposition and additional papers necessary.

On taking a boat at Louisville to return, the captain declined to carry him.

"I don't know but you are a runaway," said the captain. "Who are you, anyway?"

Ulysses was more amused than scared, because he had the letter; without the letter, he would have been more scared than amused, in the circumstances. He told the captain who he was, and produced his letter.

"All right, my boy," responded the captain, after reading the letter. "You and I must get acquainted."

They did get acquainted, and became friends forever. The captain was curious to learn what the important business was which a twelve-year-old was sent to accomplish; and he finally drew it all out of the boy. By the process of extracting this knowledge, he found that he had made the acquaintance of an uncommon youth. That a father should send a son, twelve years old, such a distance to transact important business, and that, too, among strangers, was evidence to him that the son must be a miniature man. He became so much interested in his young passenger, that, on learning he had relatives at Maysville, he invited him to go there without any charge.

It is sufficient to add, that the mission of Ulysses was very successful; and his father, in consequence, was enabled to conduct his suit to a favorable issue.

Before the jail was completed (in December), Ulysses bought another colt for himself, — a beautiful bay mare, three and a half years old. The animal had never been harnessed; and her general appearance indicated that she never would be without a tussle. She was high-spirited and fractious.

When the jail was finished Mr. Grant sold his wagon to a citizen of Aberdeen, who happened to be in Georgetown on business. He was to deliver the wagon at Aberdeen, twenty-one miles away, the purchaser leaving his horse to pair with another for that purpose.

"You must take the wagon over," said Mr. Grant to Ulysses; "it will be an interesting trip for you."

"I can make it interesting by harnessing my new colt beside the Aberdeen horse," replied Ulysses.

"I think I should not undertake to harness your colt yet — at least not on this trip," advised his father.

"I think she will keep sober beside another horse. I will risk her," answered Ulysses. "It is a good opportunity to begin with her."

The young colt was harnessed beside the Aberdeen horse without much trouble. A saddle was put into the wagon; for Ulysses would ride the colt back, after the wagon had been delivered. She was already broken to the saddle, but was nervous and frisky. All things ready, Ulysses drew the reins on his span, when, much to his surprise, the colt started off as sedately as an old horse, and for ten miles behaved herself with the utmost propriety. All at once she began to prick up her ears and snort, as if frightened. Ulysses had scarcely discovered the cause, which proved to be the smell of a slaughter house near by, when she began to rear and kick furiously. The more he tried to quiet her, the more she kicked, until she cleared herself from the harness. The resolute driver leaped to the ground, seized her by the head, and held her until she became quiet, during which time he took in the situation, and resolved what to do.

Putting the saddle upon the fractious colt, he jumped on her back and rode hurriedly into Ripley.

"Are there any horse-buyers in town?" he inquired of a man on the street.

"Yes, there is one here, certainly," the citizen answered. "He is collecting horses to transport to New Orleans. He was over yonder [pointing] at the stable a half hour ago."

"Thank you," said Ulysses, and dashed away to the stable. Seeing a man standing at the stable door, he inquired, —

"Are you buying horses?"

'Yes; got any to sell?"

"My horse is for sale."

"What do you ask for him?"

"Sixty-five dollars, and the use of him or some other horse to take my wagon to Aberdeen."

"Well, I like the appearance of your mare; she is a smart beast, I should think; but your price is rather high."

"Not for as valuable a mare as she is. Examine her, — such horses are scarce."

"I will give you sixty dollars and risk it," said the horse-buyer.

"No, I can't take that ; she is worth more."

"I 'll split the difference then," continued the man.

Ulysses hesitated a moment, canvassing his situation, and then replied, —

"Agreed ; I will close the bargain."

When the buyer was about to pay the money, he hesitated a moment, and said, —

"Look here, little fellow, you are pretty young to be selling a horse. How do I know that it is all right?"

Evidently the buyer was surprised that a mere boy should be selling a horse, and his suspicion was aroused that he might be disposing of what was not his own.

"If you suspect there is any dishonesty connected with the trade, I think I can satisfy you," Ulysses answered, in a way so manly as to impress the stranger.

"No, no; not exactly that. But you are the first small boy I ever bought a horse of, and I have bought a great many ; and I wondered if everything was right about it."

But Ulysses desired to remove all suspicions, and he ran over the way for Captain Knight, whom he knew, telling him what he wanted.

The captain left his work, and went to the stable with his young friend. Accosting the stranger, he said, —

"You've bought a horse of Ulysses; it is all right. Any trade you make with him is just as straight as it would be if you made it with his father."

"His father couldn't have done it better," replied the stranger; "and when he is as old as his father is now, he will be head and shoulders above him."

Ulysses paid no attention to the stranger's compliment, and it did not inflate his pride at all.

"Now for a horse to drive to Aberdeen," he said; "I shall have to hurry."

"There is a good, reliable beast you can take," the buyer said, pointing to one in a stall. "You can depend on him every time."

The stranger had no suspicions now. When he hesitated about closing the bargain, doubtless he thought of the horse he was to provide for the drive to Aberdeen. Was it a trick to get pay for the horse sold, and get another horse into the bargain? But all such unjust, though not unnatural, suspicions were dissipated by Captain Knight; and Ulysses drove the horse to Aberdeen, and rode him back to Ripley on the following day. From Ripley he went by stage to Georgetown.

Ulysses was unlike his father in conversational powers. He was not much of a talker; but his father was. He was a capital listener, however. From the time he was three or four years of age he enjoyed the society of his elders, because their conversation afforded him pleasure. He would sit for hours, drinking in every word of their conversation; this habit continued with him into manhood. He was constantly learning through the ear. By the time he was twelve or fifteen years of age, his father was the foremost man of the town; deeply interested in public affairs, and able to discuss them. He became quite a politician, in the best sense of the word, and could support his views well on public occasions. Of course, the visitors at his house were kindred spirits, an influential class, intelligent and wel. posted. Much of Ulysses' knowledge acquired in his early life, was derived from this class by listening. He always knew more than most people gave him credit for. That was true during his whole life. He never told all he knew to others. He pondered it in the silence of his own mind. In this way, he derived more satisfaction from it than was possible by retailing it.

Another element of Ulysses' character, which has cropped out all along thus far, was *Observation*. We mean by this just what one of his neighbors meant, when he said, "Ulysses keeps his eyes peeled." He might have added, also, that he kept his *mind* "peeled," for he saw with his *mind*, as well as with his eyes. This was the kind of observation which he possessed — the highest and best known. This transforms the farmer into a geologist, the blacksmith into a linguist, the shoemaker into a statesman, the printer into a philosopher, the clerk into a merchant-prince, the mill-operative into a United States Senator, and the Tanner Boy into a great General and President of the United States.

We have seen that, while Ulysses did not read many books, he did read "men and things." Patrick

Henry's advice to young aspirants for the legal profession was, "Study men, not books." That is what Ulysses did. He observed the *tendency* of acts, good and bad, and he chose one and avoided the other. He saw that vice hindered and virtue helped young and old in many ways. He satisfied himself that his wisest course was to husband his resources, to improve his time, to be acquainted with the business of life, to do the right thing at the right time, to be equal to emergencies, to know men and even horses. Herein his keen, sharp *observation* assisted him through life, in school, on the play-ground, in the tannery, at home and abroad, in peace and war, in private and public life. The boy was like the man in this regard, and *vice versa*. If he had been a disciple of Hugh Miller he could not have put his advice into practice more directly than he did. "Learn to make right use of your eyes; the commonest things are worth looking at; even stones and weeds, and *the most familiar animals.*"

VIII.

AT WEST POINT.

ULYSSES was not satisfied with his position as he grew older. His dislike to the tannery rather increased than diminished from year to year. He aspired to something higher. His spirit grew impatient within its narrow limits; it would soar. Point Pleasant had ceased to be all the world to him. There was a larger, wider field of thought and action which he would enter. It was not an idle dream to him; it was a deep, earnest conviction, which could not be suppressed. Now and then he gave utterance to his desires, though not as forcibly as he felt; but, chiefly, he pondered these things in his own heart. At length, however, the way opened for him to express his mind. His father said to him, —

"Ulysses, I have been thinking that you had better go into the beam-house to work."

The son had never worked there, and he never wanted to, for it was the dirtiest and most disgusting part of the business. The hides were cleaned there. A knife, with a handle at both ends, was used to scrape off flesh, hair, and dirt. The whole thing was repulsive to Ulysses, and the thought of working in such a place he could scarcely endure. And yet, his reply was that of an obedient son. It was,—

"Father, if you say I must go into the 'Beam house' to work, I shall go; but my whole soul is against it. I will work at the tanning-business until I am twenty-one years old, if you say so, but not one day longer."

"Why, my son," replied Mr. Grant, "I did not know that you were so bitterly opposed to this business."

He did not know it, because Ulysses had not said much about it. He had felt vastly more than he had expressed.

"I do not want you should follow this business if you feel so about it," continued Mr. Grant. "Unless you intend to make it your business for life, it is not best that you should work at it another day."

"Well, that is the way I feel, father," added the son, "and I have felt so a long time; I never did like the business, and I want to go into some other."

"What business do you want to follow?" inquired his father.

"Best of all, I should like to get an education; next to that, I would be a farmer, or a Mississippi trader."

Here was an unexplored field opened by a single reply. It was the first definite knowledge Mr. Grant had that his son desired an education. Few people in Point Pleasant would have anticipated such a revelation. Most of them would have expected to hear that he wanted to become a boss horse-dealer. He was not understood. He was greatly misunderstood. Looking back from our present standpoint, we should say that he was a standard human puzzle to his neighbors. He knew much about farming, and he could be a farmer with satisfaction to himself, showing that his new attitude was not prompted by pride or vanity. He was a born-trader, so that the life of a "Mississippi trader" he could choose readily. Such a trader carried truck up and down the Mississippi River on a flat-boat Abraham Lincoln did this business, for a time, in his early manhood. Ulysses could do it as well.

"I should not care to have you become a 'Mississippi trader,'" answered his father; "it is a life of great exposure, and there are many temptations connected with it. You would come in contact with a class of the meanest men, though you need not be mean because they are. Your desire for an education is as gratifying to me as it is unexpected."

"I have been thinking about it a good while," continued Ulysses. "I could not see exactly how it could be brought about, and I do not see, now, how it can; but I desire an education all the same."

At this time, Mr. Grant's property was estimated at eight or ten thousand dollars, but he had five children besides Ulysses, viz.: Simpson, Clara, Virginia, Orville L., and Mary Frances. Should he educate Ulysses, he would be doing more for him than would be possible for him to do for the others, and he could not justify himself in doing that. He said,—

"I will spend money more freely for education than for almost anything else, but if I spend it on you, I shall have little to spend on your brothers and sisters."

"I know that," responded Ulysses; "but I have been thinking about West Point, where Doctor Bailey's son is."

"Would you like to go there?"

"Nothing would suit me better, father; and I shall do the very best I can, if I go."

"Well, I think we can bring that about, and I will attend to it at once," added Mr. Grant, in a tone which indicated the matter was settled in his own mind.

Ulysses' desire to go to West Point Academy came about in this way: His near neighbor, Doctor Bailey's son, was there, so that the school had been talked about more or less. He was well acquainted with its general character, and knew that young men were educated there at the expense of their country. Perhaps no one supposed that he was adapted to a military life. Perhaps he, himself, did not think so; but he desired an education, and there he could be well educated, although it would take on the military character, and his father would have no bills to pay.

Each Congressional District could keep one young man at West Point all the while, and George Bailey was supposed to be the cadet from that particular District, so that it would do no good for Mr. Grant to apply to his Congressional Representative. Each Senator, also, could appoint one cadet, as Mr. Grant learned, so he wrote to Senator Morris, inquiring if he had a cadet vacancy to fill. He received the following reply: —

"I have not. There being no application for the cadetship, I waived my right to appoint in favor of a Member of Congress from Pennsylvania. But there is a vacancy in your own District, and doubtless Mr. Hamer, your Representative, will fill it with your son."

This correspondence exposed an unpleasant fact. As we have said, George Bailey was supposed to fill the place, but he had been expelled for what might be regarded a trivial offence—alleging illness as an excuse for being absent from recitation, when he was not ill. He was so mortified at his expulsion that he did not return home, but went to Illinois, and his parents and friends had kept the affair secret. But now the facts were made known, and there was a vacancy for Ulysses, if he could secure the appointment. Mr. Grant wrote immediately to Hon. Thomas L. Hamer, a Representative from his District at Washington. Mr. Hamer received the letter on March 3, 1839, a few hours before the close of the session. Mr. Hamer despatched a note to the Secretary of War, asking for the appointment, and immediately wrote to Mr. Grant :—

"I received your letter, and have asked for the appointment of your son, which will doubtless be made. Why did n't you apply to me sooner?"

When Mr. Hamer applied for the appointment, he did it without recurring to Mr. Grant's letter, and so made a blunder in the name, giving it Ulysses S., instead of Hiram Ulysses. By that name he was appointed and recorded, and by that was known at West Point. He made several unsuccessful attempts to get back his baptismal name, but all to no purpose. National red-tape was altogether too mighty for his noblest efforts, and he finally gave up in despair, accepting the name accidentally given to him by his Congressional Representative, and wore it through life.

Never did another mortal have such a time in getting and keeping his name, and losing it after all, as our tanner's son. There seemed to be some direful fatality attending it, so that he bore a name for forty-five years, which neither he nor his parents meant he should bear; and yet, no one was to blame, and no one intended to do him a wrong. This fact is in complete harmony with much that was so puzzling about Ulysses' early life. It was the Nation's name that he took when he became a cadet, which means *son* — son of the Nation — and the Nation is not sorry. It is better that his name should go down through the ages without being encumbered with Hiram.

Ulysses secured the appointment in March, 1839, a month before his sixteenth birthday; and he was a happy boy.

"I have laid up enough money to pay the bills," said Ulysses to his mother.

"I thought the Nation paid the bills," answered his mother.

"The government requires a deposit of sixty dollars, so that I can have something to get home with, in case I don't pass an examination," replied Ulysses "Then my outfit of shirts, flannels, towels, etc,, and my fare, will take the remainder. But I am satisfied;

when I get there, there will be a respectable distance between me and the tannery."

"You will have occasion to use that sixty dollars in getting back home," responded his mother, "unless you improve the few weeks to come in hard study."

"I comprehend that truth fully; and I am going to see if Mr. Summers will hear me recite," said Ulysses. "A few weeks with him will give me a pass to West Point."

Mr. Summers was a popular teacher in Georgetown, and Ulysses arranged with him to study up to the very day of leaving. And he applied himself closely to his studies, making decided progress, and proving that there was more of the scholar in him than his father had supposed.

His mother was equally busy in preparing his outfit. He must leave on the fifteenth day of May, so that her work crowded every moment.

The news that Ulysses had been appointed cadet in that Congressional District, spread through the town quickly. It was unexpected. Few supposed that he wanted to go to school. Some wondered how so dull a boy could get the appointment. Paul Devore, the attorney, who remembered that Ulysses named his horse for him, said, —

"Lyss going to West Point? Why in the world did Hamer not appoint a boy who would do credit to the District?"

If he was honest in his remark, and that was all he knew about Ulysses, his ignorance should be forgiven, and the ignorance of all other citizens of

Georgetown who understood the human nature of Ulysses no better than they did Hebrew or Greek. A journalist of Philadelphia, who was born in Georgetown about the time Ulysses was born in Point Pleasant, wrote as follows about his becoming a West Pointer; and his words show what the prevailing feeling was at home when the news of his appointment came. The journalist's letter was written since the war.

"A brother of the General was a fellow-'devil' in the printing-office in which we were then the younger imp, and through him we became acquainted with Ulysses, or 'Lyss,' as he was called by the boys. He was then a stumpy, freckle-faced, big-headed country lad of fifteen, or thereabouts, working in his father's tan-yard; and we often stood by his side and exercised our amateur hand, under his direction, in breaking bark for the old bark-mill down in the hollow. Though sneered at for his awkwardness by the scions of noble Kentucky, who honored Georgetown with their presence, Ulysses was a favorite with the smaller boys of the village, who had learned to look up to him as a sort of a protector.

"We well remember the stir created by the appointment of the tanner's son to a cadetship at West Point The surprise among the sons of our doctors, lawyers, and store-keepers was something wonderful. Indeed, none of us boys, high or low, rich or poor, could clearly imagine how Uncle Sam's school-masters were going to transform our somewhat *outré*-looking comrade into our *beau ideal* of dandyism — a West Pointer. But the rude exterior of the bark-grinder covered a wealth of intellect, which, of course, we youngsters were not expected to be cognizant of. Modest and unassuming, though determined, self-reliant, and decisive then as he still seems to be — we mistook his shy, retiring disposition for slowness, and, looked up to as he was by us all, we must confess there was much joking at his expense as we gathered of evenings in the Courthouse Square."

The departure of Ulysses was the first breach in the Grant family, and it was a large one. But there was bravery there; and, for the cadet's sake, all determined that tears should not disclose how badly they felt. So their faces were as smiling as that May morning, when he bade them good-bye, and ran across the street to say "good-bye" to Doctor Bailey's people. He was somewhat put back, however, when he would have a cheerful parting, by Mrs. Bailey and her daughter bursting into tears. He was confused for a moment. Doubtless Miss Bailey was the first girl who ever shed a tear over him. His fluster was excusable. Recovering his equilibrium in a moment, he said, —

"Why, you *must* be sorry that I am going. They did n't cry at our house"; and off he hurried.

"They did n't cry at our house." No, but they wanted to badly. Jesse Grant himself would not have been more missed by his family. Take away from a household such a trusty, handy, driving, loving, faithful member, and nothing can be found to fill the place. There is a *gap* there, and it continues to be a *gap*. For a week or two, a *gap* was about all there was of the Grant family. In the morning, at night, at breakfast, dinner, and supper, the *gap* appeared. The *gap* which Ulysses left behind him was **not so great as death occasions, but it was next to it.**

Mrs. Grant had relatives in Philadelphia, and Ulysses always had a strong desire to go there, and now was the favorable opportunity for him to spend a week in the "Quaker city," of which he had heard so much. It was so arranged on planning his journey, and relatives were written to in that metropolis.

A more delightful time Ulysses never had than he spent in Philadelphia. Everything was new and attractive to him. From morning until night, day after day, for more than a week, he walked the streets, wondering, enjoying, spending his money and running over with interest. He had seventy five dollars when he left home, including the sixty dollars he would be required to deposit at West Point; but when he concluded his visit at Philadelphia, he had remaining but little more than enough to carry him to West Point.

On reaching the Military Academy, and responding to his name, he replied to the inquiry about his deposit money in case he should not pass the examination,

"I intend to pass examination."

Of course he had no need of sixty dollars to deposit for such a contingency. He would annihilate the contingency; and he did. He passed the examination without the least difficulty, and entered upon his four-years course of study with high hopes.

West Point is situated on the west bank of the Hudson River, fifty-two miles from New York City It occupies a beautiful plateau, and is world-renowned for its attractions The military school was established there in 1794 by the recommendation of Washington.

The course of study, when Ulysses entered, embraced a thorough English education; the modern languages, particularly French and Spanish; chemistry; experimental philosophy; ethics; constitutional, military, and international law; mineralogy and geology; together with drill in infantry and artillery tactics; the use of rifled, mortar, siege, and seacoast guns; small sword and bayonet exercise; construction of field-works and fortifications; and the fabrication of munitions and material of war. Within the last twenty-five years, changes have been adopted for the improvement of the institution, until now it is said to be second to no American college in thorough instruction and discipline.

After a class is admitted, each one is examined separately in regard to family connections, particularly as to the occupation and pecuniary circumstances of his father. The student is limited to three answers, viz.: "indigent," "moderate," or "affluent." This examination is conducted by the adjutant at his office, so that the result cannot be known to the students, lest the rich should impose upon the poor. It has been found, however, that a majority of the students are the sons of "indigent" parents. Another fact is publicly stated, that a majority of students dropped out or expelled during the past history of the institution, have been the sons of rich men.

A rigid examination of each student as to his physical condition is considered indispensable, and many applicants are rejected. A student must be five feet high. Ulysses measured five feet and one inch. If he had been one inch and a quarter shorter, he would have been rejected, and the United States would have lost a great general. Young Grant grew several inches during his college-course, and measured five feet and eight inches when he was graduated.

The students are awakened at five o'clock in the morning by the drum-beat; and, from that time, the drum calls them to every duty as well as to their meals. They are drilled five days in the week from March to November, and encamp in tents like an army, during July and August, performing in rotation the duties of sentinel night and day, while subject to all the regulations and discipline of an army in the field. They are drummed to bed every night at ten o'clock, from the time they enter until they are graduated. They study five hours in the morning; then dinner; roll-call at one o'clock p. m.; then drill from two to four; then recreation until ten o'clock, except dress parade at sundown.

The government of the institution is firm and autocratic. And yet the aim is to make each student feel tha he stands upon his honor — that he is something more than a student; he is a soldier and gentleman qualifying himself to serve his country. Ulysses was just the youth to regard such a rule to the letter. It was no self-denial, but a real pleasure for him to come under such a regulation.

Ulysses was nicknamed "Uncle Sam" by his fellow-students, because he was grave and reliable. All the students were nicknamed; one was called "Dad" because his hair was prematurely gray;

another "Doctor" because he had studied medicine still another, for some unrecorded reason, was called "Bullhead"; and yet another "Jeremy Diddler."

During the four-years course, students can go home but once — at the end of the second year. Ulysses went home after an absence of two years, and after the first joyful salutation, his mother said,

"Why, Ulysses, how much straighter you have grown!"

"That is the first thing they taught me," he replied.

Everybody took notice of his great improvement in manners, culture, and conversation. He was less retiring, much more manly, and his general bearing was that of a gentleman.

Many false stories have been told about his trouble with fellow students; how he was ridiculed and insulted, until he thrashed the offenders and taught them better. As a matter of fact, he never had any trouble with students, and he was treated kindly by them. Indeed, he became popular with them for his many good qualities; and no student ranked higher for sound judgment than he. Often, when questions of dispute arose, a student would say,

"Well, let us leave it to Uncle Sam."

As a scholar he did not excel, though he was thorough, and never slid over a lesson without understanding it. In mathematics he was superior to most of his class. In all branches of study, he exhibited decided ability to get at the root of the matter. Indeed, he sought to master his lessons, although he was slower than many in accomplishing it. When he was graduated, he stood number twenty-one in a class of thirty-eight, which was remarkably good standing, when we consider that he was very poorly prepared for college in comparison with most of his classmates. Notwithstanding this discouraging odds against him, by application and perseverance, he maintained this creditable standing. His class numbered a hundred at the beginning of his course, and more than half of them dropped out or were expelled, before the expiration of the four years. Yet young Grant, with all the drawbacks from lack of early culture, stood number twenty-one! That was a noble record!

In horsemanship he surpassed all. He was considered the best rider the institution ever had. He could ride the most vicious steed, and ride standing sitting, or lying down. The most powerful horse known in the whole region was "York," ugly as sin, and brilliant as he was ugly. Only two students had pluck enough to ride him — Grant and Clouts. Grant delighted to mount him, and ride him upon the "dead run," and leap the fifth bar, about six feet from the ground. Hamilton said to him one day, after he had taken the highest leap ever taken at West Point on the back of York, —

"Grant, you will get killed some day by that beast."

"Well, I can't die but once," answered Grant. He did not appear to possess the slightest fear, or even to think there was any danger.

Grant won the confidence and esteem of his teachers for his amiability, purity, fidelity, and commend able application to his daily tasks. He won the respect of his fellow-students, also, for his generous, fair-minded, straight-forward conduct in school and on the campus. His classmates might have been surprised at his success in the field; but none of them were sorry. Rather, they rejoiced in the glory which he won in so many bloody conflicts.

There can be no question that Grant laid the foundation of his great generalship at West Point. There is no proof that he was a born military genius. People who knew him were surprised that he entered a military school; but a few only construed his choice into taste or tact for military life. We think the secret lies here. He entered West Point with a high aim, which could not be sustained without rallying the noblest forces of his being. APPLICATION was indispensable; and this demanded singleness of purpose, industry, thoroughness, and a whole group of virtues. Sir Isaac Newton said, that his success was due, not to genius, but to "continued application"; and that has been true of successful men in all departments of work. It was certainly true of Grant at West Point. He learned the great business of his life there. The ability to lead a million men, and to plan and execute mighty campaigns, had its origin there. True, the first two years of the war gave him experience, which proved a higher education to him; but that would never have been without the four years of APPLICATION at West Point.

IX.

ON THE WAR PATH.

GRANT was graduated at West Point in June, 1843, receiving ninety days' furlough, according to the custom, which time he spent at home with his friends in Ohio. He was appointed brevet second lieutenant in the Fourth Infantry, stationed at "Jefferson Barracks," near St. Louis. To that post he repaired, after having had a particularly good time with relatives and friends for ninety days.

Here began his real army life. At that time, the army of the United States numbered but seven thousand five hundred men, scattered over the country, to garrison forts and to protect settlers on the frontier from the depredations of Indians. "Jefferson Barracks" was designed to protect the scattered whites from the violence of savages. Of course, soldiers had little to do in time of peace. It was a dull, monotonous, lazy life, especially when barracks were far away from civilization.

"Jefferson Barracks" being near the city of St. Louis, the soldiers found congenial society and pleasures in that town. Grant found additional enjoyment, also, in the family of Col. Frederick Dent,

who lived four miles from the "Barracks." He
was in tne twenty-second year of his age, and there
was a daughter in this estimable family three years
younger. She was accomplished and beautiful,—
the most attractive young lady Grant had ever seen;
that is, if results are an index. The city of St.
Louis had no attractions for him so long as the
Dent family was accessible. To be a doorkeeper in
the latter was preferable to the tents of wickedness
which abounded in the city. Very fortunate for
Grant that affairs took this turn; for not a few
soldiers were led into evil ways by the temptations
of the city. On the other hand, Grant was led up,
up, up, by the love of the Dent household. He had
never manifested the slightest sensibility to the
charms of girlhood; but he was here led up gradually to the high plane of true love; and his affection was reciprocated. The young couple struck up
a bargain, somewhat to the annoyance of the parents, who could not discover large promise in the
future of a young second lieutenant in the "Jefferson Barracks."

"You know nothing about his history," her mother
said to her infatuated daughter. "He is really a
stranger to you."

"But he is a graduate of West Point," the daughter replied. "If he was an unprincipled, good-for-nothing young man, he could not have taken a
diploma there; and certainly he appears to be a
worthy young man."

"I grant that his appearance is that of a steady,
honest young man," responded Mrs. D.; "but ap-

pearances are often misleading. It is better to wait and learn facts."

Her father felt as deeply upon the subject, and, possibly, more than the mother, had been hoping that his daughter would marry greatness or a fortune. He could discover neither of these in store for her if she married an unknown army officer

"Wait, Julia, and not take up with a man who is not your equal," he said. "You can do better; and you are young yet. Do not take a step for which you will be sorry all your life-time."

Opposition availed nothing. It is said that "love will go where it is sent," and it did in this case; and t not only went, but it stayed. The engagement was consummated and confirmed. The two lovers determined to wait for each other, whether the time might be long or short.

Grant had been at "Jefferson Barracks" nearly two years when he received a furlough, and started for his home in Ohio. On the same day that he reached home, he was notified by letter that his regiment was ordered to Red River. Stopping with his parents but one day, he returned to Missouri, bade his betrothed good-bye, and moved with his regiment towards the war-cloud. War with Mexico was imminent — an unjust war on the part of the United States, because it was waged in the interest of slavery; but the army had to obey orders, right or wrong. Hostilities were delayed, however, and the regiment was encamped nearly a year at Ecore, on the Red River; then moved, and for a time rendezvoused near New Orleans, where the colonel

of the regiment made himself obnoxious by drunk·
enness. Sometimes the police of that city arrested
him, and locked him up. At one time, Grant went
to search for him, and found him in the police court,
awaiting his call for trial for "drunkenness and dis·
orderly conduct." Grant took a seat by his side;
and before the case was reached, he heard the tramp
of soldiers in the street, and very soon the com·
mand, —

"Halt! Ground arms!"

The young lieutenant hurried to the door, where
he found a squad of his own company.

"Boys, what does this mean?" he inquired.

"Well," answered the corporal, "we heard that
the colonel had got into an ugly scrape with those
rascally police, so I have brought up a squad to
prove an *alibi*."

"It is too late; you may march back," answered
Grant, laughing.

At Corpus Christi, subsequently, General Taylor
became so thoroughly tried with this dissolute
colonel that he said to him, —

"You have my permission to resign."

"That is not practicable," answered the colonel,
who had partially recovered from a debauch; "I
have spent all my property, and have no other
means to live by. Military life is the only one I am
acquainted with, and I am too old to learn any
other."

"You are not too old to be decent, and not dis·
grace your uniform; but we shall see about that,"
replied General Taylor.

The colonel was removed; but in view of his long service, President Polk reinstated him.

But war was inevitable; and Grant fought the first battle of his life at Palo Alto, where the tall grass of the prairie was set on fire by burning wads, and, under cover of the smoke, Grant's regiment and Ringgold's battery flanked the enemy on his left, and forced him to change his line of battle. It was a new experience to Grant, to see comrades falling at his side. Captain Page had his lower jaw shot off by a cannon ball. The head of another soldier near by was blown off. A bayonet was thrust into the mouth of another, and it pierced through the neck and came out on the other side, and he was left for dead on the field; but, strange to say, he entirely recovered.

Another battle was fought on the following day at Resaca de la Palma. Captain McCall, with Grant and one hundred picked men, engaged the foe. Grant and his regiment were in the hottest of the fight. It was here that an officer entreated General Taylor, who was under a hot fire, to retire to a place of safety, to which the brave General replied, —

"No, we won't go back; but let us ride a little forward, *where the balls will fall behind us.*" The Mexicans were completely routed in this battle.

Subsequently, Grant was appointed acting-assistant quartermaster — a very honorable position, requiring the best business capacity.

Soon followed the assault on Monterey, where two of Grant's messmates, — Hoskins and Wood, — fell while cheering on their men. Grant was not under obligations to fight, because he was quartermaster; but he was in the thickest of the battle fighting with more bravery than ever. He wrote to his parents when he was "*en route* to the City of Mexico,"—

"My new post of quartermaster is considered to afford an officer an opportunity to be relieved from fighting; but I do not and cannot see it in that light. The post of danger is the post of duty in war. That is the way Warren looked at it, you remember, when he asked General Putnam where he would send him in the battle of Bunker Hill. 'I shall send you, Mr. President,' replied Putnam (for you recollect that Warren was the President of the Continental Congress at that time), 'to a place of safety.'

"'No, General,' said Warren quickly; 'send me where the fight may be the hottest, for there I can do the most good to my country.'

"So I feel, in my position as quartermaster. I do not intend it shall keep me from fighting for the flag when the battle comes."

On the day after the battle of Monterey, Grant met an old friend of his boyhood, from Georgetown. He was captain of an Ohio company of volunteers. They sat down together and talked over the days of *auld lang syne*. The Captain said he was going to be married on his return after the war was over. Grant confided to him an account of his own engagement, disclosing the fact that his betrothed had offered to release him from the engagement, because her father had become pecuniarily embarrassed; but Grant did not hanker for such release. The girl had captured him, after taking all the approaches by storm, and a more willing captive never figured in history. The two old friends parted, by each promising to name his first son for the other. More than twenty years afterwards a son of the Ohio Captain was graduated at West Point, by the name of Ulysses Grant White.

The battle of Molino del Rey, Sept. 8, 1847, was one of the most sanguinary contests of the Mexican War, and here Grant so distinguished himself for bravery that he was promoted to the first lieutenancy of infantry. Congress proposed to confirm this as a brevet appointment, but he modestly declined the honor, preferring, as he said, —

"To reach the position by regular gradations of service."

In working their way up to Chepultepec, it was necessary to capture an old stone powder-mill, several hundred feet long. It was crowded with Mexicans, who had fled into it for refuge. Grant left his commissary-wagons to engage in the fight, and it was here that he saw Robert Anderson fall, shot through the shoulder. This was the Anderson who subsequently commanded at Fort Sumter, when the rebels fired upon it. In this charge upon the mill, too, he stumbled over the body of his friend Dent, who was wounded in the thigh. Stopping to learn whether his old friend was dead or alive, he discovered a Mexican adjusting his musket to fire at Dent; but seeing Grant, and noticing Lieutenant Thorne near by, the Mexican suddenly wheeled about to run his bayonet through the latter officer, when Grant shouted, —

" Look out, Thorne ! look out ! "

Quicker than we can relate it, Sergeant Robinson thrust his bayonet through the Mexican's body, while Thorne put a bullet through his head. In a twinkling, Grant, Thorne, and Robinson rushed into the mill, and drove the frightened Mexicans from room to room, until the building was cleared, and they passed out on the back side. Forty or fifty of the enemy were on the top of the building, and to reach them, Grant turned up a cart against the mill, and climbed the shafts to the roof. To his surprise, there he found an Irish soldier, with musket in hand, keeping guard over the terrified Mexicans, whom he had alone captured. The prisoners still bore their arms, and yet yielded to their single-handed captor without a contest. Grant took away their arms.

The terrible battle of Chepultepec quickly followed, in which Grant not only displayed great courage, but decided military skill as well. He pursued the fleeing foe toward the San Cosmo Gate, but was stopped at a cross-road by a volley of musketry from a breast-work. Taking a half-dozen men, he led them around to the rear on the run, where he found Captain Brooks, who had come up with his cannon and fifty men.

" Captain," shouted Grant, " we can carry the works by storm. Shall we do it ? "

" Forward ! " answered the brave Captain.

In five minutes, Grant and Brooks had taken the enemy in the rear, and were over the breast-work, driving the startled Mexicans at the point of their bayonets. On the following morning the capital of Mexico surrendered. Grant received honorable mention for his exploits in official reports. Major Lee said, —

"At the first barrier the enemy was in strong force, and stood his ground well. We had to be very cautious how we came up under his raking fire, for he enfiladed us the whole length of the line. So up we went, slowly creeping along, until the head of the battalion was within short musket-range of the barrier. At this point Lieutenant Grant came up handsomely, pushed forward with our men, and drove in the enemy's flank."

Major Lee made special mention of Grant in his report, thus: —

" Second-lieutenant Grant behaved with distinguished gallantry on the 13th and 14th."

General Garland, also, said, "I must not omit to call attention to Lieutenant Grant, 4th infantry, who acquitted himself most nobly on several occasions, under my own observation."

It is worthy of note that the Major Lee, who reported as above, became commander of the confederate forces in the late War of the Rebellion, and finally surrendered his sword to Grant at Appomattox. Little did the Major dream, when he wrote so kindly of young Grant in his report, that he was speaking of his future conqueror, in the bloodiest civil war on record, and that to him, in less than twenty years, he would be forced to surrender his sword, the most humiliating act of his life

General Worth, too, made special mention of Grant's bravery and skill, in his official report of the battle at Chepultepec; but one other officer was mentioned. For meritorious conduct in this engagement, he was promoted to a captaincy in the regular army, and Congress confirmed the appointment at its next session, in 1849.

Perhaps the most remarkable feat which Grant performed in the Mexican war was his perilous ride for ammunition, at the battle of Monterey. The detachment engaged found themselves, towards night, with scarcely any ammunition, and their supply was a mile away, with General Twiggs.

"Who will volunteer to go for ammunition?" said the commanding officer, who would not order any one of the rank or file to go, on account of the perilous undertaking.

"I will go," responded Grant, stepping forward promptly.

The illustration shows how the feat was performed. In his frontier soldier-life he had learned much of horsemanship from the Comanche Indians. This knowledge, added to his previous skill in this line, made him the best horseman in the army. He had a well-trained animal, and he went behind a house to get ready for the fearful ride, then dashed forward as represented by the cut. Clinging to the side of his beast, on the side opposite the enemy, with one foot thrown over the saddle, and holding on upon the horse's mane, the animal just flew over the ground, through a shower of deadly missiles the whole distance. A bullet could not hit the rider without passing through the horse, but that the latter was not riddled through and through with balls before accomplishing half the distance was indeed miraculous. He found the General, who at once issued an order to forward the ammunition, but before it started the detachment engaged came rushing back, being unable to hold their position. They had gallantly marched forward into a dangerous position, which they were forced to abandon. Grant said, —

"I am reminded of the man who caught a wild boar. Friends, coming up, congratulated him upon his success, when he replied, —

"'Yes, I did pretty well in catching him, but now I wish somebody would come and help me let him go.'"

Grant was in every battle of the Mexican war except that of Buena Vista. He was at the capital of Mexico when it fell, the final event of the war. He beheld the flag, under which he had fought, unfurled over the national palace. The claim of the United States to the territory of Texas was established, and sealed with blood. The result was that Mexico ceded to our government that portion of our country which we call California and New Mexico.

Several facts should be recorded here. The most difficult part of the Mexican war was to supply the army, and here was one reason for Grant's position as quartermaster. He had ability for the position. General Taylor, who distinguished himself in that war, wrote to the Government, "Fighting and whipping the enemy is among the least difficulties we encounter; *the great question of supplies* necessarily controls all operations."

Gen. Winfield Scott was commander-in-chief of our forces in the Mexican war; and he remarked, when he first learned of Grant's rising fame in the War of the Rebellion, "I remember a little Lieutenant by the name of Grant who won laurels in the war with Mexico." At Vera Cruz, General Scott was walking the trenches, when the soldiers rose up to look over the parapet at his noble form.

"Down, down, men; don't expose yourselves," Scott cried.

"But, General, *you* expose yourself," one replied.

"Oh, well," answered Scott, "Generals can be made out of anything now-a-days; but men can't."

Coppée, who was with Grant at West Point, tells this story of him in Mexico: —

"He was an admirable horseman, and had a very spirited horse. A Mexican gentleman with whom he was on friendly terms, asked the loan of his horse. Grant said afterward, 'I was afraid he could not ride him, and yet, I knew if I said a word to that effect, the suspicious Spanish nature would think I did not wish to lend him.' The result was, that the Mexican mounted him, was thrown before he had gone two blocks, and killed on the spot."

Another officer relates the following: —

"One day he came to see Colonel Howard, who was in command of the castle of Chepultepec. The Colonel's quarters were inside of the fortress, which was surrounded by a high, broad earth-work. Grant rode up to the slope outside, and, after riding around the castle two or three times, and seeing no post to hitch his horse to, deliberately spurred the animal down the broad, but long and steep stone stairs that led into the fort. When Colonel Howard came out of the castle and saw Grant's horse tied at the door, where, perhaps, a horse had never before been, he said, in astonishment, 'Lieutenant, how in the world did you get your horse in here?' 'Rode him in, sir,' quietly replied Grant. 'And how do you expect to get him out?' 'Ride him up the steps instead of down, answered Grant; and, mounting the animal, he rode him to the foot of the stairs, and, with Grant on his back, the intelligent brute climbed like a cat to the top, where Grant, waving his hat to Colonel Howard below, disappeared like a flash over the breast-works."

Without doubt Grant was the readiest learner among the West Point graduates in the Mexican war. He said that, at Palo Alto, he learned how it was that Napoleon made such a fearful agency of his flying artillery. It was chiefly an artillery fight; the bugles sounding and the banners flying, while the cannon-balls literally plowed up the earth under the very feet of the foe. He went into that war an unknown, humble soldier, with no friend or military officer to aid him in promotion. By his own unassisted efforts, the display of his native courage and skill, he worked his way up, and came out of that contest, after several promotions, with his name on his country's roll of honor.

X.

FROM SOLDIER TO CIVILIAN.

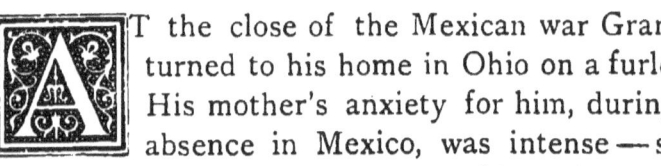T the close of the Mexican war Grant returned to his home in Ohio on a furlough. His mother's anxiety for him, during his absence in Mexico, was intense — so intense that her hair turned gray. She welcomed him almost as one from the dead. Mother and son were happy in each other's society, to say nothing of the joy that sprang up in the whole family over his return. The hardships and perils of war gave him a new relish for the quiet and rest of home; so that his few weeks there vanished like a tale that is told. Before leaving, however, he made known to his mother that he should enter into matrimony on reaching Missouri.

"A wise thing, Ulysses," was his mother's glad endorsement of his intentions.

On returning to St. Louis, the Dent family extended to him a most cordial welcome. It was their son, Miss Julia's brother, whose life Ulysses saved at the capture of the old powder-mill near Chepultepec. All opposition to the young Second Lieutenant of the "Jefferson Barracks" had disappeared. Their daughter was engaged to CAPTAIN Grant, a hero of the Mexican war. All were happy now; and the sound of the marriage-bells could be heard.

Grant went to claim his bride; and the wedding was appointed on the twenty-second day of August. This was in the year 1848, so that Grant was twenty six years and four months old on the day of his marriage.

The wedding was a lively one, as all weddings ought to be. Many friends of the Dent family from far and near were present, and many friends of Captain Grant, also, from St. Louis and the "Barracks"; Grant was in his element. He was enjoying the rewards of victory; not the triumph of arms in Mexico, for that was a small affair in comparison with the victory of true love. He was satisfied; and that is much more than was true of Alexander after he had conquered the world.

His regiment had been ordered to the northern frontier, with headquarters at Detroit; so that he took his wife there, and commenced housekeeping in a cottage near the garrison. He was still quartermaster of his regiment; but another officer, who wanted the position, secretly plotted for it, and, by intrigue and deception, secured it, and Grant was sent to Sackett's Harbor. But the matter was laid before General Scott, who ordered him back to his old position.

When Grant selected his cottage for housekeeping, a citizen said, —

"A bad neighborhood, Captain. I'm afraid you will find disorderly neighbors there."

"No matter." replied Grant; "if home has a hell

outside of it, it ought to be a heaven within." So far as we know, Grant never changed his opinion.

In the spring of 1850, Mrs. Grant returned to her father's house, where their first-born son was given to them. Captain Grant relinquished the cottage, and boarded with Capt. J. H. Gore; and he continued to board there after Mrs. Grant returned with little Fred, who was named for Grandpa Dent. Grant was no more of a talker then than he has been since. He was so silent, that neither Captain Gore, nor Mr. Bacon, who owned the house in which Gore lived, understood him. Bacon frequently spent the evening at the Gores', where he played dominoes with Grant, and interviewed him about the Mexican war. And yet, when the fame of Grant was spreading over the country in the late civil war, Bacon did not recognize that he was the same Captain Grant with whom he played dominoes. Finally, however, something arose which hinted to him that they might be identical, and he was heard to say, thoughtfully,—

"Grant, Grant; was not that a Captain Grant who boarded with Captain Gore in my house? I can hardly believe it — that silent, bashful little fellow."

"Let me see," he continued, after musing awhile; "he cut his name with a diamond-ring on a pane of glass in his chamber, so Gore said. I will find out."

So he proceeded to Captain Gore's, where he found inscribed on a pane of glass, ULYSSES S. GRANT. The hero of Donelson, Henry, and Vicksburg, was the very man with whom he and Gore played dominoes. Grant, the Silent, was a veritable surprise to his old friends at Detroit, as well as to those of Ohio, who were supposed to know him better yet.

Some of the lighter duties of the quartermaster, Captain Grant allotted to a sergeant; and one day a clerk of Major Sibley said to the sergeant, —
"Why in the world have they put that lieutenant in as quartermaster and commissary? Is it because he knows less than any other man in the regiment?"

"He is the ablest and best officer in the Old Fourth," answered the sergeant, in a burst of indignation. "He knows the duties of a soldier better than any other man in the regiment."

This was the honest testimony of one who knew Grant well; and every other soldier who knew him was ready to confirm it.

Captain Grant and his family endeared themselves to the people of Detroit, to such a degree that there was general regret when his regiment was ordered to Sackett's Harbor. To this day, citizens speak of the pleasure it afforded them to see him ride through their streets on his favorite "Cicotte mare," which was subsequently sold for fourteen hundred dollars. Here, as everywhere, his passionate love for a fine horse was prominent.

His regiment was ordered from Sackett's Harbor to the Pacific Coast in June, 1852; thence, the regiment removed to Fort Vancouver, on Columbia River, Washington Territory. This was the 'dreariest location he had ever found, far away from civilization, and therefore lacking all the social advantages to which he had been accustomed. To add to his loneliness and hardship, he left his wife behind him, to remain at her father's during his absence. The thought of living in that part of the country for any considerable length of time made him wretched; and he could not think of ever bringing his wife there to dwell: it would be inflicting sorrow upon her. Yet, he was not so homesick as to lose his admiration for a horse. An officer tells the following: —

"One morning while sitting with some comrades in front of the officers' quarters, we observed Grant riding on his fine horse toward Major Hathaway's battery, which was in park about two hundred and fifty yards distant. As Grant drew near the guns, and we were observing the motions of his fine animal, we saw him gather the reins, take a tighter grip on his cigar, pull down his hat firmly on his head, and seat himself securely in the saddle. 'Grant is going to leap the battery,' cried two or three of the officers, and we all stood up to see him do it. He ran his horse at the pieces, and put him over the four guns one after another as easily and gracefully as a circus rider."

Grant sent in his resignation to take effect July 31, 1854, saying to a comrade, —

"Whoever hears of me in ten years, will hear of a well-to-do old Missouri farmer."

He returned to Missouri, and adopted the life of a farmer. His wife's father had made her a present of sixty acres of land, situated about four miles from St. Louis, on which he built a log-house. He drew the stone for the cellar, cut and hauled the logs, split the shingles, and put up the house, except, according to the prevailing custom, the neighbors turned out to raise it. Inside and outside it was an humble abode; but it was a happy home.

He knew little or nothing about farming. What little he learned of the business in his boyhood, he had lost during his years of military life. For this reason he found a difficulty in supporting his family; and he added the sale of wood to his business, cutting and hauling it to market. He drove a fine pair of horses in hauling wood, and never rode himself on the load, even though he was hauling it ten miles. On being asked why he did not ride, he answered, —

"The horses have enough to draw without carrying a lazy rider."

In 1856 his wife's mother died. She had become very much attached to her soldier son-in-law; and she appeared to have a more accurate estimate of his abilities than many of his friends. She once had a dream, which she interpreted as meaning that Grant would some day rise to great distinction; and she died in this belief.

When he was elected President of the United States, there were old customers of '57 and '58 in St. Louis who voted for him. They remembered him as the wood-vender, wearing a soldier's blue overalls and slouched hat, always driving a nice pair of horses. The following incident is related by a friend: —

"He used to supply Hon. Henry T. Blow, of St. Louis, with wood. Mr. Blow was elected to the Thirty-ninth Congress, and on one occasion went with his wife to one of General Grant's popular receptions. Mrs. Blow wondered if General Grant would recognize her as an old acquaintance and customer, under the different circumstances of their relative situations in life. Well, Mrs. Blow had not been long in the General's house before he came to her and said, —

"'Mrs. Blow, I remember you well. What great changes have taken place since we last met!'

"'Yes, General,' said Mrs. B., 'the war is over.'

"'I did not mean that,' he replied; 'I mean with myself. Do you recollect when I used to supply your husband with wood, and pile it myself, and measure it, too, and go to his office for my pay?'

"'Oh, yes, General; your face was familiar in those days.'

"'Mrs. Blow, those were happy days; for I was doing the best I could to support my family.'"

He was on his way to Massachusetts while President. In the city of New York a man rushed up to his carriage from the great crowd on Broadway, and reaching up his hand, called out enthusiastically, —

"How do you do, General? How do you do?"

General Grant took his hand and shook it mechanically, all the while scanning him, as if trying to make out who the man was. Evidently he was an old acquaintance, and his countenance looked familiar. Just as the man was turning aside, the President located him, and he said, —

"Oh, I remember you; you kept the best oysters in St. Louis. I used to call there often to get a plate."

In the winter of 1856 or '57 he discovered that some party was stealing his wood two miles distant, and he resolved to find out who the thief was. On a bright moonlight night he secreted himself in the woods to await results. He did not wait long before he heard a team approaching. Soon appeared the strapping great fellow who leased the adjoining farm, and stopped his team close by Captain Grant's hid ing-place. The thief proceeded to chop down a tree, cut it up, and load it, when he started for the main road. Grant took a circuit, and came out on the main road to intercept him, which was soon accom plished.

"Halloo, Bill! Going to St. Louis with your wood, I suppose?" Grant said.

" Yes," answered Bill, somewhat disconcerted.

" How much do you ask for it?"

" About four dollars."

" Well, I will take it. Bring it over to my house."

" No, I can't do that; the wood is promised to a man in town."

" But I must have it," insisted Grant. "There's no use in hesitating ; you must haul this load to my house, and pay me twenty dollars for what you have cut and carried off before. That won't be more than half-price, you know."

" If I don't, I suppose you will sue me before the 'Squire?"

" No, we won't trouble the 'Squire or the public, but settle the whole thing here and now."

" Well, I'll do it," wisely concluded the thief; "but don't say a word to anybody about it. I will never take any more."

The wood was driven to Grant's house, the money

paid, and the thief dismissed, the Captain all the while ready to laugh over the comical turn of affairs.

Grant carried a load of corn to St. Louis one day, when he met Harry Boggs, who married Mrs. Grant's cousin.

"Good morning, Harry," said Grant in his usual familiar way. "I have been wanting to see you. Father Dent is trying to persuade me to go into business with some one, and he speaks of you. He thinks I could soon learn the details, and that my large acquaintance among army officers would bring enough additional customers to make it support both our families."

"I have worked hard to build up the business," answered Boggs, "and I do not want a partner unless he can increase it, but I think you can. Come and see me the next time you are in town."

The result was a partnership, under the name of BOGGS & GRANT, to collect rents, negotiate loans, buy and sell real estate, etc.

Grant was not able to board at a hotel, or even a respectable boarding-house, so he hired an unfurnished room of Boggs, and took his meals out. There was no carpet on the floor, and no chair in the room, except a very poor one, which held the wash-bowl. A second-hand bedstead, on which was laid one poor mattress, occupied one corner. This was all the furniture. He occupied this room, through the business-week, for two months, walking home on Saturday nights, to spend the Sabbath with **his family.**

At the expiration of two months he exchanged the log-house at "Hardscrabble" for a small one in St. Louis. The buyer failed to meet his pledges, litigation followed, and it was not until two years after the close of the war that Grant recovered "Hardscrabble." He purchased, also, Wishtonwish and the Whitehaven House, together with six hundred acres of land in the vicinity. Captain Grant, himself, christened his farm "Hardscrabble," because he had to scrabble so hard there to support his family.

An incident occurred after Grant removed his family to the city, which shows how poor he was. A gentleman of considerable prominence in St. Louis, who had made the acquaintance of Captain Grant, and liked him much, advised his wife to call upon Mrs. Grant. Accordingly, she embraced the first opportunity to make the acquaintance of the Captain's wife. On her return, she said to her husband,—

"Why did you send me there?"

"Because I thought it would be a good place for you to go. I like Captain Grant; he is a fine man."

"And Mrs. Grant is a fine woman, without doubt," replied the lady; "but they must be very poor, indeed, for the house is very shabbily furnished. I have not been into such a poverty-stricken place for many a day."

"Well, poverty is no sin. Captain Grant is highly esteemed by our leading men, although they do not regard him as having special capacity for business. If I were you I should not avoid Mrs. Grant because she is poor."

This was excellent counsel, and the gentleman's wife was wise enough to accept it, and the result was a friendship between the two ladies, true and strong, which has continued to this day.

Captain Grant won many friends in St. Louis by his genial, honest, straight-forward way of doing business, but he did not increase the income of the firm largely. Boggs visited Philadelphia and New York City to interest capitalists to invest their money in Missouri at ten per cent. He arranged with one in each city, and returned to loan their funds, to the amount of four hundred thousand dollars, at ten per cent. But the securities they were able to offer did not satisfy the eastern capitalists, so the project was a failure.

When Captain Grant had been in company with Boggs nine months, he said to him, —

"It is quite evident that my best efforts do not increase your business as we expected. It is not right for me to embarrass you by continuing the partnership to your disadvantage. The business will not support two families, that is clear."

"It is not your fault, however," answered Mr. B., who meant to be as magnanimous as his partner was. "I think you have done the best you could; but there is one good thing about it, if you have not made much money, you have made many friends."

"How would it do for me to apply for the vacant county engineership?" inquired Grant. "That is a good position; salary is nineteen hundred dollars a year."

"Capital! capital!" replied Boggs; "if you say

the word, I will prepare a petition, and get the leading men of the city to sign it."

Mr. Boggs did as he promised, and supplemented Grant's letter of application with a petition signed by forty of the leading business men of St. Louis, but political considerations decided the matter, and Grant's petition was rejected. In the meantime the copartnership of Boggs & Grant was dissolved.

Some parties claimed that Grant was "too kind-hearted to make a successful collector."

'How is that?" inquired a friend. "I don't exactly see how that sort of a heart should interfere with the collector's business."

"Well, it did, and his commissions were smaller because of it. You see, all sorts of excuses were rendered to him for not paying bills. Many debtors were really poor, and when they told their pitiable stories of want and suffering, his heart yielded at once, and he said it would be too bad to force payment. Sometimes, instead of pressing his claim, he actually gave parties small sums to relieve their wants. Do you see it now?"

"Yes, it is tolerably plain, and such a collector could n't be very popular with creditors."

"But he *was* popular with *debtors*, I assure you."

About that time a vacancy occurred in the Custom-house, and Captain Grant's friends secured him the situation without any difficulty. But a month had scarcely passed before the collector died, and this threw him out of employment again. It seemed as if every avenue to success was closed against him Still, while he was somewhat cast down, he was not in despair. Mrs. Grant came to his rescue every time. She was a remarkable woman, intelligent, self-reliant, hopeful, and cheerful. In her Captain Grant found both counsellor and comforter, when otherwise he might have yielded to despondency and said, "There is no use in trying." But, in her presence, he was under the necessity of being resolute and plucky, so he hoped against hope. Her sympathy, devotion, and true love were ever a reserve-force to him in battling with misfortune.

In March, 1860, Grant removed to Galena, Ill., to fill a clerkship for his brothers, who were in the leather trade. He had made a host of friends in St. Louis, and they were sorry to lose him. He was so exemplary, although not professedly a Christian man, that he was respected by all who knew him. He never used profane or vulgar language, thus maintaining the habit of his boyhood. He never told coarse stories, but was pure and dignified in his conversation. He never spoke evil of any one, but had a kind word for all. He smoked, but did not use intoxicating liquors. On his leaving the army, he became a total abstainer in self-defence. At Fort Vancouver, away from his family, lonesome and depressed, his habit of moderate drinking grew into partial excess; but he had the good sense to see it, so that, on returning home, he resolved to adopt total abstinence. His decision was often severely tested in St. Louis, where the drinking customs were universal. But he maintained his integrity with himself in this, as in other things, and always declined the proffered cup. All these things, and more, we need not mention, endeared him to a large circle of influential people in St. Louis, none of whom had the least idea that in five years from that time he would be the most famous man in America.

His father had been in the leather business with his brothers, in Galena, but he had retired with a competency; still, however, retaining an interest therein. The sign over the door remained, "J. R. GRANT."

Captain Grant devoted himself to business closely, although he was not much of a salesman. His brothers, Simpson and Orville, attended chiefly to customers. He loaded and unloaded leather, bought hides, weighed stock, kept books, and did many other things equally necessary. One day the clerk of the court sent to the store for leather to cover a desk. Captain Grant shouldered a roll of leather walked up to the court-house, cut off what was needed, and tacked it on. Rowley, the clerk, looked on, and said to himself, "A handy man," little dreaming that the most remarkable man of the times was repairing the desk. WITHIN EIGHTEEN MONTHS GRANT WAS A MAJOR-GENERAL IN THE FIELD, AND ROWLEY A CAPTAIN ON HIS STAFF.

Western currency was much depressed at that time, and the firm bought large quantities of pork and shipped to New York to pay eastern bills, and save the great price of exchange. A farmer brought a load of pork one day, and wanted gold instead of notes for it, that he might pay his taxes. The gold was offered him at a rate which Grant considered high.

"I think that is more than the banks charge," he suggested modestly, out of the honesty of his heart.

"Have you inquired?" one of the firm asked.

"No, but the gentleman can run over to the bank and see for himself."

The suggestion was adopted, and the farmer saved twelve dollars by Captain Grant's scrupulous honesty. Some people very ridiculously ascribed his failure in business to this noble virtue.

Grant sought no acquaintances in Galena. He found his society at home, chiefly with his wife and four children. He was less talkative there than he was in St. Louis. He was a stranger, poor, and unknown; and therefore debarred from familiar intercourse with the people, were he disposed to mingle with them. His wife was "tied down" to her family. She did her own work, dressed plainly, and accepted her situation cheerfully. Few of the people knew what a prize the town had in her until the outbreak of the war.

A neighbor says of Grant,—

"I first encountered him coming down the hill toward the store with Orville. He wore a blue overcoat and old, slouched hat, and looked like a private soldier. He had not more than three intimates in the whole town."

He kept himself so much aloof from citizens, except as he met them in business, that even Hon. Elihu B. Washburne, his fellow-townsman, did not know that such a man lived in Galena, until the presidential election of 1860.

Each town had its Lincoln and Douglas-clubs,—

Republican and Democratic. A few Democrats knew that Grant's sympathies were with Douglas, although he could not vote in Illinois. So they elected him president of their club.

"I do not want the position, and I will not accept it," he said. "I am not a voter; I never voted but once in my life; and besides, I desire to attend to my business and not dabble in politics."

Douglas spoke in Dubuque before the election, and Grant went to hear him.

"How did you like him?" some one asked

"He is an able man, and very eloquent; but I was disappointed; I don't like some of his ideas; if I had the legal right to vote I should be more undecided than ever."

Rowley was a Democrat and tried to convince Grant that he was a voter, whereupon his brother Orville interrupted by saying, —

"You let Ulysses alone, Rowley, if he were to vote, he would vote our ticket." Grant's brothers were Republicans, in favor of Lincoln, and so was his father.

"I don't know about that," replied Captain Grant; "I never voted but once, and then I voted against Fremont."

"You ought to be ashamed for voting for Buchanan," replied Orville.

"I didn't; I voted against Fremont. I thought it would be a misfortune to the country if he should be elected. Otherwise, I have never meddled with politics. I don't like t' , position of either party."

Grant could never ,: ฯ politician. He disliked

chicanery and log-rolling in politics as in everything else. This was one reason why he did not enter into politics with interest. He did not like Buchanan, who was the Democratic canditate for President in 1856; but he liked him better than he did Fremont, the Republican candidate, and as he called it, "voting against Fremont."

But Lincoln was elected, and Douglas was defeated. The demonstrations of joy over the result were enthusiastic in Galena, and Grant participated in them to such an extent, that Republicans claimed him. From that time his attitude towards his country was not questioned.

The following extract from a letter which he wrote to a friend in St. Louis, shows where his sympathies were, —

"It is hard to realize that a State or States shoul commit so suicidal an act as to secede from the Union, though from all the reports, I have no doubt but that at least five of them will do it. And then, with the present granny of an executive, some foolish policy will doubtless be pursued which will give the seceding States the support and sympathy of the Southern States that don't go out. The farce now going on in southern Kansas is, I presume, about at an end, and the St. Louis volunteer General Frost at their head, covered all over with glory. You will now have seven hundred men more in your midst, who will think themselves entitled to live on the public for all future time. You must provide office for them, or some of them may declare Missouri out of the Union. It does seem as if just a few men ha produced all the present difficulty. I don't see why by the same rule a hundred men could not carry Missouri ou of the Union."

XI.

CALL OF HIS COUNTRY.

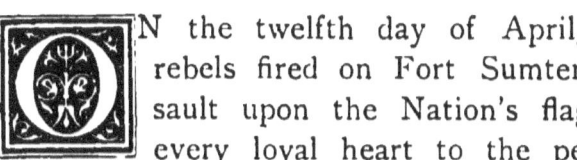N the twelfth day of April, 1861, the rebels fired on Fort Sumter. This assault upon the Nation's flag awakened every loyal heart to the perils of the hour. President Lincoln issued a call for SEVENTY-FIVE THOUSAND volunteers. The whole North blazed with patriotic fire.

Galena was wild with excitement, and Captain Grant was no less excited than his neighbors. Indeed, all loyal men forgot the distinction between Republicans and Democrats over the insult to the old flag.

"I thought I had done with soldiering," said Grant. "I never expected to be in military life again. But I was educated by the Government, and if my knowledge and experience can be of any service, I think I ought to offer them."

A meeting of citizens was called at the courthouse the following evening. They assembled with banners and music, among the number several prominent Democrats. John A. Rawlins was there, a young lawyer of large ability. In the antumn before he stumped the State for Douglas, and was one of the electors on the Democratic ticket. His soul was on fire over the attack on Sumter.

"Assault on Liberty, Union, and Free Government," he said to a fellow Democrat. "We must fight."

"It is all done by the Abolitionists," replied his Democratic friend. "Better leave it for them to fight out."

"I know no party now, Republican, Democratic, or Anti-slavery," roared Rawlins. "It is enough for me that the South has fired on our flag."

"Well, you'll find that you will injure our party if you side with the Republicans," continued his friend.

"Any party ought to be injured when it declines to defend the flag," added Rawlins with vehemence. "I propose to join heart and hand with true and loyal men to defend the country."

The war-meeting was crowded; Mayor Brand was elected president. Though he was a Democrat, it was supposed he would prove loyal to the flag in the crisis, but he was timid and irresolute. On taking the chair, he made a brief speech, in which he indirectly claimed that Republicans had plunged the Nation into present difficulties, and he hoped that some compromise would make it unnecessary for the North to wage war against the South. He had scarcely taken his seat, when Hon. Elihu B. Washburne sprang to his feet, and exclaimed, at the top of his voice, —

"Any man who will try to stir party prejudices at such a time as this is a traitor."

The sentiment created the greatest furor of enthusiasm, and the hall rang with cheer on cheer; the band struck up "Yankee Doodle," men threw up their hats, and the wildest excitement followed, in which Rawlins and most of his brother Democrats joined.

As soon as quiet was restored, Mr. Washburne arose and presented a series of resolutions, in which a union of all parties to support the Government and defend the flag was recommended, as well as the immediate organization of military companies. The resolutions closed with the following : —

" Finally, we solemnly resolve, that having lived under the stars and stripes, by the blessing of Almighty God, we propose to die under them."

Another wild scene of excitement followed; cheering, shouting, the band playing, the banner waving, and hats flying, until many were fairly exhausted by their patriotic efforts. As soon as the enthusiasm abated, another shout went up, —

" Rawlins ! Rawlins ! Rawlins ! " The call was repeated from every part of the hall, until that gentleman responded by pushing his way through the crowd to the platform.

Such an ovation as he faced the audience ! Peal on peal of honest applause ! It was several minutes before he could speak. Then he went on for forty minutes, portraying the greatness of the American Union, and the necessity of uniting heart and hand in its defense, denouncing the assault upon the flag as treason, and calling upon loyal men, without distinction of party, to stand shoulder to shoulder in conquering Rebellion. He closed his impassioned speech with the following words: —

"I have been a Democrat all my life, but this is no longer a question of politics; it is simply Country or no Country. I have favored every honorable compromise, but the day of compromise is passed. Only one course is left for us. WE WILL STAND BY THE FLAG OF OUR COUNTRY, AND APPEAL TO THE GOD OF BATTLES!"

Still another burst of loyal feeling, greater even than what had been heard, rang out, longer and louder, lasting till the audience had strength to shout no more. Captain Grant was captivated by Rawlin's speech. He had never made the acquaintance of the speaker, but from that time they became intimate friends. Subsequently, Rawlins became Grant's favorite staff-officer.

On his way home, Captain Grant said to his brother Orville, —

"I think I ought to offer my services to the Government."

"I think so, too," replied his brother; "and if you will go, I will stay and take care of the store."

Two days later a meeting was called to raise volunteers, and the somewhat famous and numerous John Smith family was represented on that evening. John E. Smith arose, when the time of the meeting arrived, and calling the meeting to order, said, —

"I nominate Capt. Ulysses S. Grant for chairman of this meeting."

The motion was carried unanimously, and loud applause followed. A large number of the audience had never seen the Captain, and most of them knew nothing of him until he declined to be president of the Douglas Club.

Grant made his way to the platform, with hat in hand, and broke his silence for the first time in Galena, by making a brief, patriotic speech, in which he imparted the needed information in regard to organizing a military company. He proceeded to business at once.

The rolls were opened, and A. L. Chetlain, who became major-general during the war, was the first to enlist. Nine or ten others signed the roll that evening, and within a week the company was full, and two hundred applicants were rejected.

On Saturday morning, Rowley called at the leather store, and said to Grant, —

"Captain, there is to be a meeting at Hanover this afternoon, to raise a company, and Rawlins and I are going. Won't you go with us?"

"Yes, I think I will," answered Grant. "You and Rawlins come around after dinner, and Orville and I will take the ponies and drive over."

Accordingly, the four men drove to Hanover, and Captain Grant presided at the meeting, which was held in a school-house. Rawlins made a rousing speech, followed by brief remarks by others. Then, the first time in his life, the Captain was called upon for a speech, and he responded as follows: —

"I don't know anything about making speeches, that is not in my line, but we are forming a company in Galena, and mean to do what we can to put down the Rebellion. If any of you feel like enlisting, I will give you all the information and help I can."

Many loyal men responded to his appeal, and the meeting proved a successful one. On the way home the party conversed about the attack on Sumter, and the ability of the South to carry on a war.

"I guess the seventy-five thousand men, which the President has called for, will stop such work," remarked Rowley. "There is more bluster than fight in the South, I think."

"I don't agree with you, exactly," answered Grant. "This is a bigger thing than you imagine. I think those fellows will fight, and mean it. Uncle Sam has a heavy job on his hands, and if I am needed I shall go."

"Look here, Captain," interrupted Rawlins in a jesting way, "suppose we get up a company for the war, longer or shorter; you shall be captain, and Rowley and I will toss up to see who will be first- and second-lieutenant."

"This is not mere fun," replied Grant; "we shall find it serious business before we get through. No one can tell how long the war will last — it may be six months, and it may be six years. But war is inevitable now. The South has declared war against the United States Government, and the Government must defend itself. That is the only alternative."

Grant appeared to have a just idea of the magnitude of the war even then. He knew that West Point had educated a large number of young men from the South, and that most of them would cast in their lot with their respective States, so that the South ern Army would have able commanders. He knew that Southerners were brave and desperate, and would fight to the bitter end. Knowing these things, he was satisfied that a long and bloody war was before the country.

Captain Grant drilled the company formed at Galena several days, and the members wanted he should become its captain; but he declined, perhaps, because Chetlain desired the position. The latter was elected.

There was a peace Democrat in the town by the name of Collins, who met Mr. Washburne one day on the street, and addressed him rather abruptly, thus, —

"A pretty set of fellows your soldiers are to elect Chetlain for Captain."

"Why not?"

"Well, Chetlain is well enough as a man, but he has had no experience at all," repled the Democrat. "To take such a man when Captain Grant could be had was not very wise."

"Do you know Grant's history?"

"Certainly; he is the son of the old man Grant — Jesse Grant. He was educated at West Point, and went all through the Mexican war. Although he was one of the youngest officers in the war, he distinguished himself in several battles by his skill and bravery."

"Is that so!" responded Washburne, becoming greatly interested. "We shall need that class of men to lead our armies. I must see him."

Mr. Washburne embraced the first opportunity to

have an interview with Grant, and he was very favorably impressed by his appearance.

"I left the army expecting never to return," Grant said. "I am no seeker for position, but the country which educated me is in sore peril, and, as a man of honor, I feel bound to offer my services for whatever they are worth."

"Captain," rejoined Washburne with deep emotion, "we need just such men as you are in this war, — men of military education and experience. The Legislature meets next Tuesday, and several of us are going to Springfield. You must go with us, for your services will certainly be wanted."

"I will go if you think it is best," was Grant's final decision.

An hour afterwards Grant said to Orville and Simpson,—

"I guess you will have to get along without me hereafter. Mr. Washburne wants me to go to Springfield at once with him, and I think I must. Uncle Sam educated me, and though I have served him through one war, I am still his debtor He will want all the help he can get, and I think he will want me."

His brothers heartily supported his decision, and he went with Mr. Washburne to Springfield.

Capt. John Pope had charge of military affairs at the Capital, and in spite of his noblest efforts, everything was in confusion.

"No head nor tail to anything," said Grant; and it was so. The scramble for positions was confusing —a dozen for every post of honor. Mr

Washburne and others urged Governor Yates to give Grant a position without delay; but so many were pressing their claims, that the Governor was bewildered. Besides Grant was more silent than ever, being altogether too modest to press his own claims. The scramble for office disgusted him, also. He was shocked that loyal men should enter into such a contest for position.

"This is no place for me," at length he said to Washburne, "I will go home to Galena. I will not be an office-seeker, and I can't afford to stay here idle."

"Hold on a little, Captain," replied Washburne. "Can't do everything in a minute. Red tape must be cut. Have patience and things will come about right."

It was only by coaxing and promising that Grant could be prevailed upon to remain at Springfield. If nobody wanted him, he was the last man to force himself upon the attention of officials. He had already offered his services to the War Department at Washington, by letter, and no notice had been taken of his offer. His name had been sent, also, to the Governor of his native State, Ohio, and there had been no response; and now it looked to him as if there were three office-seekers in Springfield to every office to be filled. That disgust should crowd hard against patriotism in his soul was not strange.

However, by persuasion and skillful explanation, Washburne succeeded in keeping him at Springfield until the first of May, when Governor Yates asked him.

"How many men and officers are there in a company and regiment; do you know?"

Probably neither the Governor nor Council could answer the question, so that the Governor doubted whether this West Pointer could; at least, his question implied as much.

Finding that Grant could answer his intricate question, the Governor took him into his office, where the latter found "confusion worse confounded." There was scarcely a printed blank for anything. Grant went to work ruling paper, and preparing necessary forms. He was not under the necessity of consulting books for needed information; it was all in his head; and in a few days Governor Yates saw the tangled skein of military affairs adjusted, and experienced great relief in his own mind. He had found a prize unexpectedly in his clerical assistant.

Captain Pope, who had charge of Camp Yates, had leave of absence for a few days, and Grant was appointed to fill his place. On the return of Pope, Grant was employed to muster in several regiments. It was now the last of May, and he went home on a visit, having been absent six weeks. On his way back, a friend said to him,—

"Captain, why do you not go in for the command of an Illinois regiment? You are entitled to one."

Grant's reply was characteristic; modesty, his ruling virtue, pervading it clear through.

"To tell you the truth, I would rather like a regiment; but there are few men competent to command a thousand soldiers, and I doubt whether I am one of them."

Grant knew himself no better than other people did at some points. He doubted whether he was competent to command a thousand men; and yet, in three years, he commanded a MILLION, and appeared to do it with ease.

In June, Grant left Springfield to visit his father in Covington, Ky., just across the river from Cincinnati. As General McClellan's head-quarters were in the latter city, Grant called twice at his office to tender his services, thinking the General might give him a place on his staff. Doubtless, for this reason he went to visit his father; but he failed to see McClellan, though he saw the same sorry scramble for office that he had witnessed in Springfield. He had remained in Springfield until every regiment was mustered in without getting a position, and now it was not at all strange that he concluded his services were not wanted, and was deciding whether to go home and resume business or not. Providence, however, and not politicians, was hedging up his way. The "God of battles" had an appointment waiting for him. It would come in the right time and place.

Governor Yates forwarded the following telegram to him at Covington at the last minute,—

"You are this day appointed Colonel of the Twenty-first Illinois Volunteers, and requested to take command at once."

This was like a message from the skies; it was unexpected, but no less acceptable on that account

Colonel Goode commanded the Twenty-first when he left Springfield — what had happened?

Returning at once, he found that Colonel Goode had been dismissed for incompetency, and that his regiment was in a state of insubordination. Some of the men had deserted, and all were dissatisfied. Grant took command at once. He learned, also, on his return, that Governor Yates conferred with the book-keeper of the Grants in Galena before sending the above telegram. After all the opportunities to learn Grant, which the Governor had enjoyed, he evidently did not know him. His manhood appears to have been as great a puzzle to Yates as his boyhood was to his neighbors. For Governor Yates said to the book-keeper, —

"What kind of a man is this Captain Grant Though anxious to serve, he seems reluctant to take any high position. He even declined my offer to recommend him to Washington for a brigadier-generalship, saying he didn't want office till he had earned it. What *does* he want?"

"The way to deal with him," the book-keeper replied, "is to ask him no questions, but simply order him to duty. He will promptly obey."

This reply furnished Yates with the key to Grant's character; and hence the telegram. The book-keeper was God's messenger to put the Governor on the right track. Grant had found his place. From that he would go forth, "from conquering to conquer."

Governer Yates was reported as saying, sometime during the war, —

"It was the most glorious day of my life when I signed Grant's commission."

Colonel Grant took command of his regiment under the most unfavorable circumstances. The men were more like an armed mob. They were ragged and insubordinate. Expecting that the Government would provide them with uniforms, they had worn their poorest clothes to camp. As the uniforms were not then provided, the reader can imagine what a dilapidated appearance they presented. No officer, who had not been through great tribulation, would have had pluck enough to undertake the discipline of such a crew, but Grant was equal to it. Providence had been training him for that work many years. He had been educated by one tribulation after another, greater and greater, until now he was prepared to command the "Twenty-first Illinois Volunteers."

Some of the regiment claimed that they looked as well as their Colonel did, but the claim was not altogether valid. There was an approximation to truth in their claim, as we judge from General Smith's description of the new Colonel. General Smith accompanied Grant to the camp, and he said of him, —

"I went with him to camp, and shall never forget the scene when his men first saw him. Grant was dressed in citizen's clothes, an old coat worn out at the elbows, and a badly damaged hat. His men, though ragged and barefooted themselves, had formed a high estimate of what a colonel should be, and when Grant walked in among them, they began making fun o' him. They cried in derision, 'What a colonel!' and made all sorts of fun of him. And one of them, to show off to the others, got behind his back and commenced sparring at him, and while he was doing this another gave him such a push that he hit Grant between the shoulders."

On the morning after Colonel Grant took command, roll-call was an hour behind time.

"Return to your quarters," was the Colonel's brief reprimand, not waiting for the morning report. As there was no report, there were no rations during the day, and a hungry set of fellows they were at night, and nearly as mad as they were hungry.

At the first dress-parade several officers appeared without coats. The Colonel surveyed them from head to foot, contemptuously, and then said, —

"This is a *dress*-parade; officers are expected to wear their clothes. Dismiss the men to quarters."

That was all he said. The men laughed as they marched back to their quarters, satisfied that the Governor had now provided them with a *commanding* officer, with whom no one could trifle.

"He knows what he is about."

"He means business."

"Can't scare or deceive him."

These and kindred remarks showed that the regiment appreciated the new condition of affairs, and they rapidly came into good discipline. In one week the change was surprising, and in time it became one of the best regiments in the field. Soldiers respect a commander who knows his business, and whom they cannot over-ride. Grant's men learned to respect him. Indeed, they learned to love him, and became so enthusiastic for their leader, that they all re-enlisted *for the war*, although they had been mustered in for thirty days only.

Before taking the field Colonel Grant visited Galena to bid his family good-bye, and get money to buy an outfit. If some of the swords, badges, and horses, presented to him a few years later, had been given to him then, the gift would have been a double blessing, for he was poor. But he wrote his note for three hundred dollars, Collins, his father's old partner, endorsing it, and he drew the money from the bank. With the money he purchased a uniform, and a horse with proper equipments.

He called on Mr. Washburne before leaving Galena, and had a long talk about the Rebellion and how to conquer it. Grant expressed his views freely, and so intelligently, that from that day Mr. Washburne regarded him as "the coming man." He was never surprised at his successes, and was about the only man in the country who expected much of him. Several times thereafter, when official inefficiency or ignorance attempted to supersede him, Washburne fought for him as the ablest general in the field.

When Colonel Grant returned to Springfield Governor Yates said to him, " I would send another regiment, if I had transportation."

" Order mine, and I will find transportation,' replied Grant, with a decision that impressed the Governor wonderfully. How the new Colonel could find transportation, unless he brought it down from the skies, was more than Yates could tell. But there was that about Grant's reply which satisfied

him that transportation was sure. The Governor
did not stop to think that the soldiers had legs, and
could use them. He did order the regiment to
Mexico, in Northern Missouri, where the enemy was
making trouble.

"All right!" said Grant to the Governor; "I shall
march my regiment directly across the country to
Missouri, leaving railroad trains for those who come
after us."

"As you elect," answered the Governor, laughing
at the Colonel's simple method of transportation.
"I see that you are a practical man, and such men
are the ones we want in the field."

The regiment raised no objection to the long
march. Evidently they saw it would do no good.
Perhaps some of them thought it would give them a
good opportunity to commit depredations on the
way; at any rate, quite a number of them tried it.
The first night out, the Colonel had several of them
tied up by their thumbs for stealing. Before reaching their destination, all were fully convinced that
obedience to orders was the only way to keep the
peace with their determined Colonel.

Colonel Grant marched his regiment across the
country, really because he thought it was the best
way to drill them. A week's march, with all the
incidental experience of field-life, was exactly what
his men needed. The wisdom of his measure was
never questioned after the experience. The march
worked them into the service finely. In one week
the regiment went into camp at Mexico, Mo Col
onel Grant was now fairly equipped for the war

XII.

THE COMING MAN FORESHADOWED.

ENERAL POPE commanded in Northern Missouri, and Grant was put in charge of a brigade. On a raid, some of his men obtained whiskey, and became intoxicated. As soon as he discovered the trouble, he ordered the regiment to halt, and he searched every canteen, pouring all the whiskey he found on the ground. He tied the drunken men on the baggage-wagons, and severely reproved the officers for allowing such freedom.

An officer applied to him, asking him how to deal with a young soldier, a mere boy, from an excellent home, who was forming the habit of drinking and gambling. Grant's reply was tender:—

"The army is a hard place. It will ruin a great many young men. Talk to him, and try to teach him more self-control. Do everything to counteract the evil influences of camp-life, but do not punish him till you find it absolutely necessary, for that brings a sense of degradation."

There was a chaplain in the mess at head-quarters, and Grant said to him,—

"Chaplain, when I was at home, and ministers stopped at my house, I always invited them to ask a blessing at the table. I suppose it is quite as much needed here as there, and I shall be glad to have you do it whenever we sit down to a meal."

There was a special session of Congress in July. At the time, Illinois had sent thirty-six regiments into the field. President Lincoln sent a printed request to the senators and representatives of the State, to recommend four soldiers for brigadier-generals. Washburne nominated Grant, then followed Hurlbut, Prentiss, and McClernand. Grant received every vote, and he was the only one who did. He was started off, when he came into the world, by ballot, and now a ballot gave him another send-off. Since that time, ballots have had much to do with his remarkable experience. He has been balloted for more than any other American, we think.

Grant knew nothing about the balloting that was going on in his behalf. He had little time to read papers, or to lay plans to go up higher, because he was thoroughly absorbed in present duty. But his chaplain brought a St. Louis paper to him, which contained his appointment, before his commission was received.

"Good morning, Colonel. There is a bit of news in this paper that will interest you, I think," said the chaplain.

"What is it?"

"You have been made a brigadier-general."

"You are joking," replied Grant.

"Read it for yourself; there it is."

Grant took the paper and read the announcement, then replied,—

"I had not the slightest suspicion of any such thing. It was not brought about by any request of mine. I guess that it is some of Washburne's work."

He had commanded the Twenty-first Illinois Volunteers but two months, and now his connection with it was broken. He was going up higher. Leaders were beginning to know him. The mystery of his life was wearing off.

Major-general Fremont commanded the department, and he sent General Grant to Pilot Knob, where an attack was threatened to the Union forces; but the enemy not appearing, Fremont ordered him to Jefferson, the capital of the State, which was in imminent peril. Here he invited his old friend Hillyer, of St. Louis, to take a place on his staff. Hillyer was a lawyer of considerable prominence, without any hankering for the honors of military life; but, by appointment, he met General Grant at the Planter's House in St. Louis.

"Hillyer, you must go upon my staff," he said. "I have kept the steamer waiting three hours for you; got a horse all ready for you, and you must go. I must be off in a hurry to Cape Girardeau."

"Why, sir, I have n't even enlisted. Such a thought never entered my head until I received your telegram," answered Hillyer.

"Well, it has entered now, and you can enlist on the way; we can make that all right."

"But I 've got no clothes, and no money; my wife expects me home to tea, and my business needs attending to. I do not see how it is possible," urged Hillyer.

"I see," added Grant. "In time of war we are all minute-men. I owe you fifty dollars, and here it is (passing the money to him); that is all the money you will need. As to clothes, we can make out a suit among us. We are ordered to the field at once, and expect a fight with Jeff Thompson. If you survive the battle, I will give you leave to come home and fix up your business."

"But I have just taken a beef contract; I can't attend to that, and be on your staff, too." This was a contract to supply a quantity of beef for the army.

"Of course you cannot do both," said Grant; "so give up your beef contract, and come along with us."

"Well, I'll meet you at the steamer," Hillyer said, at last, and rushed out. He turned over his contract to a friend, ran home to see his wife, and hurried to the steamer, in time to sail with Grant — a minute-man, indeed!

"Have you a commission for me?" Hillyer inquired, when the steamer was under way. "A staff officer without a commission can't be of much use."

"Not yet," General Grant answered; "but Fremont promised me that he would appoint you. You are a staff-officer all the same, however."

"What is my rank?"

"I cannot say positively, but it will be the best I can get for you, of course. For the present, we will call you captain."

There was very little red-tape used in making this staff-officer, and yet he was well made. The new general understood his business, so that there would be no trouble about the arrangement.

The command reached Pilot Knob, when Jeff Thompson, who believed that "discretion is the better part of valor," fled at his approach, taking his army with him.

Just then General Fremont was superseded by General Halleck, who appointed Grant to take charge of the District of South-east Missouri, with headquarters at Cairo. To the latter place he repaired at once, and Hillyer, on leave of absence, hurried home to see his wife, and arrange his business for a long war.

Grant was soon settled in his head-quarters at Cairo. C. C. Coffin, the war correspondent of the *Boston Journal*, speaks as follows of him, showing the great contrast between him and General McClellan:—

"Having credentials from the Secretary of War I entered the head-quarters of the commanding officer, and found a man of medium stature, thick set, with blue eyes, and brown beard closely cropped, sitting at a desk. He was smoking a meerschaum. He wore a plain blue blouse, without any insignia of rank. His appearance was clerkly. General McClellan, in Washington, commander-in-chief, was surrounded by brilliant staffs, men in fine broadcloth, gold braid, plumed hats, and wearing clanking sabres. Orderlies were usually numerous at head-quarters."

"Is General Grant in?" was the question directed to the clerk in the corner.

"Yes, sir," said the man, removing the meerschaum from his mouth, and spitting with unerring accuracy into a spittoon by his side.

"Will you be kind enough to give this letter to him?"

But the clerk, instead of carrying it into an adjoining room to present it to the commander-in-chief opened it, ran his eye rapidly over the contents, and said,—

"I am happy to make your acquaintance, sir; Colonel Webster will give you a pass."

A more astonished man than Coffin was not found in Cairo just then, to find himself conversing with Grant. "The last shall be first."

The rebels were strongly fortified at Columbus, and their guns commanded the fort at Belmont. Grant resolved to destroy that fort; and, taking with him three thousand men, he steamed down the river under cover of night, and the next day, by desperate fighting, under very unfavorable circumstances, the enemy was driven from the fort with heavy loss, leaving all sorts of camp-furniture behind, to which the torch was applied. It was a fierce battle, and nearly five hundred Union soldiers fell in it. General Grant was in the thickest of it, and his horse was shot under him; mounting another, he led his gallant army to speedy victory.

The enemy sallied out from Columbus in large force to intercept their return. An officer rode up to General Grant, and said,—

"We are surrounded, General!"

"Very well," replied Grant, with the utmost coolness; "then we must cut our way out as we cut our way in. We have whipped them once, and I think we can do it again."

They did cut their way through thirteen rebel regiments of infantry, and two squadrons of cavalry, and returned to Cairo.

General Grant learned that the enemy had taken possession of Paducah, with the design of making it a stronghold. It was all-important that the Union forces should hold it as a strategic point. Grant telegraphed to his commander-in-chief for permission to drive out the enemy, and take possession of the place. At once he prepared an expedition, and no reply to his telegram being received, he telegraphed again : —

"I am ready to go to Paducah, and shall start should not a telegram arrive preventing the movement."

He waited until ten o'clock that night, and no answer came. He said to his staff, —

"Come on, now; I will wait no longer. I will go to Paducah if it costs me my commission."

With three regiments and a light battery, Captain Foote, of the flotilla, co-operating with him, he was in Paducah the next morning. The rebels fled without firing a gun. Had his expedition been delayed a single day, the place could not have been entered without a bloody fight, for a large rebel force was on its way there. Grant performed the feat at the *risk* of losing his commission ; another instance of the advantage accruing to him by assuming a *risk*.

Rebel flags were flying from the tops of many houses, but they were speedily exchanged for the stars and stripes Here, General Grant issued his first order, characteristic, and clear as the note of clarion:—

"PADUCAH, KY., Sept 6, 1861.
"TO THE CITIZENS OF PADUCAH:

"I am come among you, not as as enemy, but as your fellow-citizen; not to maltreat you, nor annoy you, but to respect you and enforce the rights of all loyal citizens. An enemy in rebellion against our Common Government has taken possession of, and planted his guns on the soil of Kentucky, and fired upon you. Columbus and Hickman are in his hands. He is moving upon your city. I am here to defend you against this enemy, to assist the authority and sovereignty of Government. *I have nothing to do with opinions*, and shall deal only with armed rebellion and its aiders and abettors! You can pursue your usual vocations without fear; the strong arm of the Government is here to protect its friends and punish its enemies. Whenever it is manifest that you are able to defend yourselves and maintain the authority of the Government, and protect the rights of loyal citizens, I shall withdraw the forces under my command.

"U. S. GRANT,
"*Brigadier-General Commanding.*"

When it is known that Kentucky claimed to be neutral, and that Grant led this expedition without authority from his superior officer, the foregoing order must be regarded as one of the most ingenious documents of the war. Written on the spur of the moment as it was, it is significant proof of Grant's readiness for any emergency.

Leaving a force large enough to hold the town, the General returned to Cairo, and immediately directed his attention to Fort Henry.

We should say here, however, that General Grant repudiated all army contractors, who were trying to fleece the Government; and there were many such. He read them at a glance, and turned them off abruptly, while he rendered efficient aid to honest men. His course brought down upon him the wrath of some of these contractors; and they spread abroad false reports as to his habits, repeating them from time to time. There was not the slightest foundation for these stories; malice created them, and time demonstrated their cruelty and falsity.

Through a Southern journal it came out, about this time, that rebel officers in Richmond discussed the ability of Northern generals to conduct a great war. Their opinions were not at all complimentary to our officers generally; but General Buell said, —

"There is one West Pointer, I think in Missouri, little known, and whom I hope the Northern people will not find out. I mean Sam Grant. I knew him well at West Point and in Mexico. I should fear him more than any of their officers I have yet heard of. He is not a man of genius, but he is clearheaded, quick, and daring."

Buell was right; so much had been proved already.

General Grant's men, or some of them, were inclined to disregard the laws of civilized warfare by appropriating what did not belong to them in the enemy's country. This brought out the following order from him: —

"Disgrace having been brought upon our brave fellows by the bad conduct of some of their members showing, on all occasions, when passing through territory occupied by sympathizers of the enemy, a total disregard of the rights of citizens, and being guilty of wanton destruction of private property, the General commanding desires and intends to enforce a change in this respect. . . . .

"It is ordered that the severest punishment be inflicted upon every soldier who is guilty of taking or destroying private property, and any commissioned officer guilty of like conduct, or of countenancing it, shall be deprived of his sword, and expelled from the army, not to be permitted to return," etc.

To the honor of General Grant be it said here, that he adhered to both the letter and spirit of the foregoing order to the end of the war. A more humane and thoughtful man never led an army.

Fort Henry was doomed. Captain Foote (now Commodore) co-operated with General Grant in an expedition to reduce this stronghold. With eight gunboats he proceeded down the river to attack the fort in front, while General Grant marched his army across the country to attack it in the rear. The day of assaulting the fort was agreed upon ; but a heavy rain had converted the soil into mud, so as to delay the land force ; and besides, the commodore found, in reaching the fort, that everything was favorable for immediate attack, and he bombarded it at once, without waiting until the assigned time of attack arrived. When General Grant reached the fort, the Union flag was flying over it, and it was immediately passed over into his hands.

Here, again, the superior wisdom of General Grant appeared General Halleck did not yield to the re quest of General Grant to move on Fort Henry, until Commodore Foote interceded. But General Grant's desire for immediate action arose from the fact that the enemy was erecting another fort just across the river from Henry. Waiting until that was completed would have given the rebels great advantage.

Grant lost no time in preparing an expedition to reduce Fort Donelson, which the South considered impregnable. Donelson was only twelve miles distant, built to blockade the Cumberland River, as Henry was to blockade the Tennessee.

With fifteen thousand men and eight batteries, General Grant started for Donelson. It was on the morning of Wednesday, February 12th. He came within shooting range of the fort before night, but Foote did not arrive till the next day. The fort was garrisoned with twenty-one thousand men, and General Floyd was in command. The engagement commenced soon after the arrival of Foote. The battle was a terrible one. Beginning on Thursday, it was renewed on Friday, and continued all day Saturday, with the odds against the Union army at three o'clock P. M. of the last day mentioned.

At that time, General Grant, who had been to the flag-ship to confer with Commodore Foote, who was wounded, and his fleet disabled, returned to find his army badly demoralized, a portion of it on the retreat, and the whole scene one of discouragement.

Grant stopped for a moment considering what to do, when he overheard a soldier say to another, —

"They are too much for us this time. They are so strong that they know they can lick us. But they are figuring on it that it may take several days' fighting."

"How do you know that?" asked the comrade.

"Why, they've got their knapsacks on, and their haversacks are full of grub."

He referred to a group of rebel prisoners near.

"Are their haversacks full?" asked General Grant, who had heard the conversation.

"Yes."

"Let me see one," he added hurriedly.

Quick as thought one was passed to him, and lo! it contained three days' rations. The fact disclosed to Grant's quick judgment the exact state of affairs at the fort. He turned hastily to his officers, and said, —

"Their purpose is plain. Men defending a fort and making a charge don't carry three days' rations; it means they are trying to get away! They have been trying to cut a way out, and the desperateness of their situation would not permit them to hesitate now if they were not badly injured. The party that now takes the offensive will win."

Added to the demoralized condition of the troops, the weather was bitter cold, and part of the time for two days, a chilling sleet had been falling. But Grant resolved at once to take the offensive, and recover the lost ground. He despatched an order to General Smith, one of the oldest officers, whose hair was long, and white as snow, to storm and capture the works in front.

"Tell General Grant that I will do it," was the answer the war-worn veteran sent back.

An eye-witness shall tell the rest of the story: —

"The Second Iowa was to take the lead. He formed it into two lines thirty paces apart, and taking his place between them, cried, —

"'Forward!'

"Far away to the right the guns are booming, telling that Wallace is meeting the foe.

"'Forward!'

"They go with a dash.

"The artillery pours a hot fire into the rebel works as they climb up the steep hillside and burst into view on the hill where the rebel outworks are planted.

"Gallant Smith's eyes flashed with delight. It was the kind of fighting he loved. And the men he led caught something of his enthusiasm and never faltered more than he, when the pattering shower of bullets grew into a terrible hurricane of grape and canister as the enemy caught sight of them.

"The ridge is reached.

"A pause now to form the lines, during which Smith rides along and says, —

"'Boys, I am here because fighting is my business, and the Government sent me. But *you* volunteered for this kind of work, and I expect you to go in and do it!'

"And he added, —

"'Now, then, we've got some stiff work before us! But we don't dare be defeated, and not a man must shrink And I won't ask you to do what I don't dare do myself. Do you understand that? By the Lord Harry, I mean to be the first man to step over the rebel works, and I expect you to be close behind to support me; and I don't want a shot fired — we must take it at the point of the bayonet!'

"The lines formed, he gave the order to advance, leading himself with the color-bearer beside him.

"It is a terrible scene.

" The flagstaff is almost shot it twain.

"Fourteen bullets pierced the emblem itself, and one — two — three — four — five color-bearers go down! But a sixth is not wanting, the glorious stars and stripes are not allowed to trail in the dust!

"Smith now drops behind the advance, and hat in hand, and white hair streaming in the wind, shouts encouragement, inspiring them with new heroism.

"Once a withering fire halts them for a moment.

"'I'm here, boys! — I'm here! — you can go where I can!' and the wavering men no longer shrink when they see the white hair dancing in the wind, and see the hat now perched on the point of Smith's sword.

"'Forward again!'

"'Forward — and over the works!'

"Without firing a shot they reached the protecting ditch, poured down it, climbed up, then over the parapet by twos, by threes, in squads at last! Swift and deadly work the flashing bayonets — flashing and bright at first, but soon stained with blood — perform, and then the rebels begin to quiver and quake. It is a hand to hand struggle, a duel to the death! The rebels suddenly become seized with a panic, and their own batteries are turned on them as they desert the works in mad haste, and the air is rent by wild shouts of joy as the rebel colors come down and the glorious stars and stripes wave in their stead above the works.

"Our batteries come rapidly forward. Steaming horses drag in the guns on the run, and quickly manned, they soon are pouring iron death, keeping company with the captured pieces, into the precipitately fleeing enemy.

"The position is commanding, and an enfilading fire is poured upon the flanks and faces of the works.

"Four hundred of Smith's gallant column have fallen, but the blow struck is a decisive one. Grant's tactics and Smith's gallantry have turned defeat into victory.

"Darkness ended the fight."

Before light on Sunday morning General Smith sent a negro, who had just come in from Fort Donelson, to General Grant's head-quarters. The negro claimed to be the servant of a rebel officer.

"Dey's been a-going all night," he said.

"What! leaving the fort, and running away?" inquired Grant. He suspected they might do that.

"Yes, massa."

"Tell us the truth now, for many lives may depend on your information. If you deceive us we shall hang you."

"All right, massa; if I's don't tell the truf I'll hang. I's just come from de fort, and dey's been a-going all night."

It was found, on the next day, that Floyd transferred the command to Pillow, the second officer in command; and the latter, in turn, passed it over to Buckner, the third officer in rank. Then Floyd and Pillow escaped on five rebel steamers, taking with them three or four thousand soldiers.

On Sunday morning, General Buckner sent a letter to General Grant, asking for terms. The following is a *fac-simile* of Grant's famous reply, the effect of which was felt to the close of the war:—

Hd. Qrs. Army in the Field
Near Donelson, Feby 16th 1862

Genl. S. B. Buckner,
Confed. Army,
Sir:

Yours of this date
proposing Armistice, and appointment of
Commissioners to settle terms of Capitulation is just received. No terms except un-

an unconditional and immediate surrender can be accepted. I propose to move immediately upon your works.

I am sir, my respectfully your obt- servt,

U. S. Grant
Brig. Gen.

The surrender was immediate and unconditional; and the fall of Donelson electrified the whole North; for it was the first great victory of the contest. At the same time, it filled the South with alarm.

As soon as Grant received Buckner's unconditional surrender letter, he jumped upon his horse, and with his staff, rode over to Buckner's. Fighting being over, they shook hands like friends.

"If I had been in command," said Buckner to Grant, "you would not have reached the fort so easily."

"No," replied Grant; "but if you had been in command, I should have waited for re-enforcements. I knew Pillow would never come out of his works to fight."

Just then General Smith arrived. Buckner was an old acquaintance; they were together at West Point.

"That charge of yours last night was a splendid affair," remarked Buckner, as he shook hands cordially with him.

"Yes, yes," answered the veteran; "the men did well — they did well. But it was no affair of mine; I simply obeyed General Grant's orders."

The papers being signed, the conference ended. Grant was in favor of moving directly on to Nashville, and telegraphed to Halleck for permission; but the latter vetoed the measure, — a great mistake.

Early on Sunday morning the journals of Nashville issued extras, with the intelligence, in flaming letters, —

"Enemy Retreating — Glorious Results — Our

Boys Following and Peppering Their Rear — A Complete Victory!"

The bells rang out more cheerily than ever, calling the people to worship; but, within ten minutes, the news came, —

"Fort Donelson has fallen! The whole garrison captured by the Yankees!"

Consternation took the place of joy. Instead of going to meeting, the people ran through the streets in wild excitement. Alarm bells were rung. A train of cars was made ready as quick as possible to carry citizens away. Every other vehicle was pressed into the service; and the inhabitants fled from their homes, as if fearing the "Yankees" would show them no quarter.

The prisoners were sent to Cairo in charge of Union officers. General Grant sent the negro, who brought him information on Sunday, with the officers, notwithstanding the order of General Halleck, to exclude them from the lines. At first, he was inclined to obey the order; but, finding the ex-slaves loyal and helpful, he disregarded the order on military principles. Thousands of slaves came into the lines for protection, and were allowed to remain.

On Monday night General Buckner rushed into Grant's head-quarters, and throwing himself into a chair, the following conversation took place: —

Buckner. — "Put me in irons, General; put me in irons!"

Grant. — "What do you mean?"

Buckner. — "Your troops are simply robbing my

men. They are stripping them of everything. They are taking the officers' arms, which, by your agreement, they were to retain. They are even stealing their blankets, and declare that is by your orders."

Grant. — "This compels me to say things which I hoped to avoid speaking of, because I wanted to save your feelings. Your men have committed the grossest outrages. I know you can not approve of them, and I suppose you could scarcely prevent them. But on the morning of the surrender, one of your officers, growing angry in discussion, shot Major Mudd, of the Second Illinois Cavalry, in the back. Your soldiers have stripped my dead, and left them naked on the field, while it was in your possession. They have taken every blanket from prisoners, and been guilty of many other things which I do not feel like detailing. The weather is cold, and my troops need these blankets. By the laws of war they are entitled to them; for in an unconditional surrender, everything belongs to the victors. They are to remain in the field. Your men are going to Cairo, where the Government has plenty of supplies, and will see them properly cared for. Our soldiers, falling into Confederate hands, have been almost starved, and are kept in the foulest prisons. Yours receive here the same accommodations and fare as my own. I have simply disarmed them, because I don't want my officers assassinated. They can get their side-arms again by applying for them at Cairo."

About this time, a friend wrote to Grant that

President Lincoln was willing to make him major general. Grant replied, —

"I do not want promotion until I earn it."

He was now piling up proof of his wife's words :—

"Mr. Grant has great natural ability. He would fill any public position well, if he only had the chance."

Friends heard this remark in the days of her adversity, and smiled. They overlooked it on the ground of a wife's blinding affections. Even when his promotion to major-general was announced, a relative said to her, —

"Ulysses may do very well as a brigadier; but he better be satisfied with that, and not attempt to rise higher." Mrs. Grant replied, —

"There is no danger of his reaching a position above his capacity. He is equal to a much higher one than this, and will certainly win it if he lives."

Mrs. Grant, Elihu B. Washburne, and President Lincoln, were almost the only persons, outside of his own command, who understood and appreciated Grant even now. The conundrum of his boyhood was not yet solved.

XIII.

MOVING ON THE ENEMY'S WORKS.

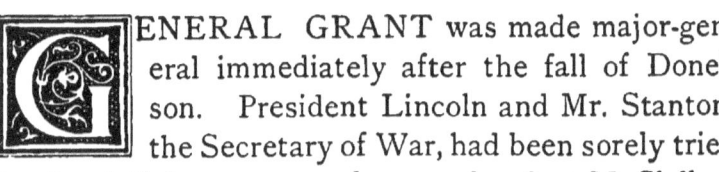

ENERAL GRANT was made major-general immediately after the fall of Donelson. President Lincoln and Mr. Stanton, the Secretary of War, had been sorely tried by the dallying course of generals; first McClellan, and then Halleck; and General Grant's method of "carrying the war into Africa" just suited them. Secretary Stanton issued the following congratulatory address to the country upon the glorious victory at Donelson, evidently intending to rebuke over cautious generals by his praise of Grant : —

"We may well rejoice at the recent victories, for they teach us that battles are to be won now, and by us, in the same and only manner that they were ever won by any people, or in any age, since the days of Joshua, by boldly pursuing and striking the foe. What, under the blessing of Providence, I conceive to be the true organization of victory, and military combination to end this war, was declared in a few words by General Grant's message to General Buckner: '*I propose to move immediately on your works.*'"

The fall of Fort Donelson forced the enemy to abandon Columbus, which they called the "Gibraltar of America." Also, the Union army took immediate possession of Island No. 10 and New Madrid. But the third great battle was at hand. The two great Confederate Generals, Johnston and Beauregard, had concentrated *eighty thousand* troups at Corinth, converting it into another "Gibraltar," as they thought, with the design of raiding from that point, and sweeping the Union army of the West out of existence.

General Halleck, a vascillating and over-cautious commander, ambitious and conceited, thought to take all the glory of the third victory to himself. Jealous of General Grant, whose praise was now on all loyal lips, he took command of the army in person, after the preliminary organization had been perfected, reducing Grant's rank, and ordering him to watch at Fort Henry; at the same time placing Sherman in command at Cairo. True, Grant commanded the "District of West Tennessee," but the change was brought about in such a way, that even General Sherman regarded it as the act of a jealous superior officer, to degrade Grant before the country. Halleck wrote to Washington that General Grant was insubordinate, proving that the change mentioned was a blow at Grant. He had manhood enough to give no credit to the reports about Grant's intemperance, for he knew that the latter was a total abstainer, and he publicly expressed the absurdity of such a charge, after the fall of Donelson, by issuing the following bulletin from his head-quarters, in St. Louis : —

"If Grant's a drunkard, and can win such a victory, I shall issue an order, that any man found sober in St. Louis, to-night, shall be punished by fine and imprisonment."

President Lincoln, also, who learned that Grant was a total abstainer, through Washburne, and to whom complaints were made, with the request that Grant be removed for intemperance, exposed the foolishness of the charge, by saying, —

"Do you know what kind of liquor Grant uses?"

"Why, no," answered the complaining party; "I don't know as that makes any difference."

"Well, I was only thinking if I knew what kind of liquor he used, I would recommend it to some other generals."

When preparations to march on Corinth were completed, General Grant was at Savannah, General Wallace at Crump's, with his command, five miles above, and the remainder of the army, thirty-five thousand, encamped on the south bank of the Tennessee River, in five divisions. General Sherman was near Shiloh Meeting-house, three miles from the river, holding the front. General Buell was on his way, with forty thousand men, to re-enforce Grant.

It was Saturday night, April 5, 1862. On retiring, General Grant said, —

"We will move our quarters to Pittsburg to-morrow. We must breakfast early, and while our traps are being got on board, ride out and have a talk with Buell before we go up the river."

The General understood the designs of Johnston and Beauregard, but he did not expect an attack before Monday or Tuesday. He never dreamed that, at that moment, the flower of the rebel army, led by two of the most famous Southern generals, were silently resting on their arms, only three or four miles away, awaiting early dawn to fall upon the Union army and crush it.

General Grant was out of bed before daylight on Sunday morning, and ordered the boats to get up steam, and the horses to be saddled; then sat down to breakfast. Before they were half through, a noise like distant thunder startled them.

"That's firing," said Colonel Webster.

"Yes," answered Grant, "it sounds very much like it."

At that moment his favorite orderly rushed in, exclaiming,

"General, there is terrific firing up the river."

All sprang up and hurried out the door. The roar of cannonading increased. The earth seemed to tremble under the shock of battle.

"Where is it?" inquired Webster nervously. "At Crump's, or Pittsburg Landing?"

"I am trying to determine," answered Grant, with the utmost coolness. "Very heavy, is n't it? I think it's at Pittsburg Landing." Turning quickly about,—

"Orderly," he said, "take the horses right on the boat, and tell the captain to make ready for starting at once. Come, gentlemen, 't is time to be moving."

The breakfast was left on the table, Grant buckled on his sword, and, with Webster's help, hobbled down to the boat. A few days before the General's horse fell, injuring one of the rider's limbs quite seriously.

"I have been looking for this," he said, "but did

not believe the attack would be made before Monday or Tuesday."

Perfectly self-possessed, Grant dictated orders, one after another, and sent them hither and thither. His order to General Buell was, —

"Hurry up your re-enforcements as quickly as possible."

The roar of battle increased, as the General and staff steamed up the river. A negro said it sounded like "the wrath of God." At Crump's, General Wallace was standing upon the guard of his steamer, and Grant called out to him, —

"General, have your baggage and camp-equipage moved right down to the bank, and your men ready to march at a moment's notice."

"They are already under arms," replied Wallace.

Grant went ashore at Pittsburg Landing, was helped upon his horse, and, with his staff, galloped hurriedly to the front. Here a scene of disaster met his eye, which would have appalled any General but himself. The encampment of the advance line was in the hands of the enemy. General Prentiss' division was destroyed. Even the divisions of Generals Sherman and McClernand were greatly demoralized, and had been driven back two miles. Many soldiers were running in terror from the field to the river, to get under the protection of the gunboats. The army was made up of raw recruits, and such a terrific assault upon them at the outset, overcame them. Almost any General but Grant would have said that the day was lost, and ordered retreat.

It seems that the rebel army, having twice the

number of the Union forces, rushed upon the latter, in three divisions, early in the morning, when many of the troops were fast asleep. The attack was a fearful one, and as sudden and unexpected as it was terrific. No doubt that Generals Johnston and Beauregard expected to destroy Grant's army by their first mighty swoop upon them; and but for the coolness and bravery of the commanding officers, such would have been the tale.

General Grant took in the situation readily and posted away his orderlies with messages in every direction. Rowley was sent to Sherman.

"General Grant sent me to see how you are getting along," he said.

"Tell him if he has any men to spare, I can use them; if not, I will do the best I can. We are holding them pretty well just now — pretty well — but it's a hard fight."

Rowley noticed a white handkerchief tied around Sherman's hand, and he inquired, —

"Why, General, are you wounded?"

"Well, yes," he replied, looking at his hand; "but that don't hurt me half so much as this thing on my shoulder, which I suppose has n't left any mark whatever."

A spent ball had struck his shoulder-strap, his horse had been shot under him, and his face was besmeared with powder and blood. Yet he was dashing about in the thickest of the fight, animating his soldiers, who would have quailed before the foe and run from the field, but for his inspiring presence and example

Rowley said to General Grant, on his return, —

"General, this thing looks pretty squally, don't it?"

"Well, not so very bad. We've got to fight against time now. Wallace must be here very soon."

General Grant and his staff passed near a rebel battery, which opened upon them. The first shel' struck just in front of Grant.

"We must ride fast here," he said, spurring up his horse, without taking any other notice of the danger. The words were scarcely out of his mouth before another shell struck under his horse.

"Pretty loud call that, for my horse's legs," he remarked.

"I think it is a pretty loud call for *your* legs," responded Rowley.

They rode behind a house and stopped for con sultation; but shells soon crashed through the roof, scattering the shingles about them.

"The old building don't seem to be very good shelter; suppose we move on," remarked the General.

Scarcely had they begun to move forward, when a bullet struck the General's scabbard and threw it into the air. The sword dropped out, and was never found.

They found a portion of our troops in the woods, fighting from tree to tree. Now and then a rebel shouted, —

"How about Bull Run?"

"How about Fort Donelson?" our men shouted back.

A large number of our troops were panic-stricken,

and the stream of this class going to the river for the protection of the gunboats was increasing.

" Go and see if you can't persuade them to return to the front," the General said to Rowley; "and return to me when you have done that."

" Where shall I find you ?" inquired Rowley.

" Probably at head-quarters. If you don't, come to the front, *wherever you hear the heaviest firing.*"

All this time the Union forces were falling back, and the rebel army was advancing with yells and murderous cannonading. Nelson had not arrived with his command, nor Wallace, though it was nearly two o'clock in the afternoon. Soon, however, the arrival of Buell was announced, with the advance line of his re-enforcements.

"What preparations have you made for retreating?" inquired Buell.

"Why," answered Grant, "I have n't despaired of whipping them yet."

" Of course ; but in case of defeat ?"

" Well, we could make a bridge across the river with these boats, and protect it with artillery. But if we do have to retreat there won't be many men left to cross."

The Union army expressed their joy over the arrival of re-enforcements by cheer on cheer; and they were now re-assured for the conflict. An hour later, the enemy were greatly demoralized by the fall of their able General, Johnston. A piece of a shell struck him on the thigh, cutting a terrible gash.

" Are you hurt ?" inquired one of his aids.

" Yes ; I fear, mortally."

And in a moment he fell from his horse, and soon died in the arms of his friend.

The death of Johnston sent dismay through the rebel ranks. It disheartened them more than the arrival of Buell's re-enforcements; although they subsequently captured General Prentiss, with twenty-two hundred men.

Later in the day the enemy showed signs of exhaustion. In driving back our columns, too, they had come within range of the gunboats, whose deadly fire checked their ardor. General Grant smiled for the first time since he left Savannah in the morning. He beheld a gleam of victory to his arms through the battle-smoke.

"It was at such a crisis as this, when the enemy faltered, at Fort Donelson, that I ordered General Smith to make a charge on the ranks in front of him, and won the victory," he said.

The shades of night were gathering, and the battle must close for the day. Just then, Carson, one of General Grant's scouts, came up and reported to him. As he was turning away, a shot knocked off his head, bespattering General Grant with his blood.

Beauregard had promised his soldiers that they should sleep in the "Yankees' camp" on that Sunday night, and they did.

Grant was very busy on that night. He held a council of war, and said to his officers, —

"It is always of great advantage to be the attacking party. We must fire the first gun to-morrow morning."

There were officers and men who wondered that

Grant did not order a retreat on that Sunday night. Some of them thought it was foolhardy to engage in another battle the next day with their victors. But Grant had decided for battle, and that settled the matter.

During the whole day General Grant suffered much pain in his injured leg; and yet he kept in the saddle all day, always being "where the heaviest firing was heard." In the evening, his aids lifted him upon his horse, and he rode to see every division commander, to urge prompt, resolute, and united action; for the Union army would fall upon the foe early on Monday morning. Returning about midnight, he lay down upon some hay, with a stump for a pillow, and was soon fast asleep.

He was up before daylight on Monday morning, giving orders. To his staff he said,—

"Ride along the line, and see that every division moves up to attack and press the enemy hard, the minute it is light enough."

The men were in excellent spirits; for the arrival of Nelson, Wallace, and Buell had about doubled the Northern army, and began the contest of Monday at dawn of day. The enemy was surprised,— as much surprised as Grant's army was on the previous morning. They could not hold their ground, but kept falling back, until, at one o'clock P. M., our army had recovered their camp. At that time, Beauregard made a bold and heroic stand near the Shiloh chapel. Two regiments sent to re-enforce a wavering Union brigade were hesitating in the face of the enemy's fire as Grant rode up. Seeing that the men were faltering, the General shouted to them, —

"Come on, boys!" and placing himself at their head, he led them valiantly up to the battle-line, where they charged grandly.

As Grant returned, Sherman shouted to his gunners, —

"Drop your shots right over there," pointing to rebels on a hill in the distance. The Parrott guns responded furiously, and the rebels retired in confusion. Grant, looking on, shouted, —

"That's the last of them. They will not make another stand."

General Grant saw that the day was already won. He rode over to General Thomas with a glad heart, and said, —

"General, those fellows are completely demoralized. Take your division and another, and pursue. We can cut them all to pieces and capture a great many."

"My men are completely used up," replied Thomas. "They marched all Saturday and Sunday, and have been fighting all day. If you say so, they shall march, of course ; but they are hardly able to move."

Very reluctantly Grant relinquished his intention of pursuing the enemy ; and that night Beauregard fled with his beaten army to his entrenchments at Corinth. The next morning General Beauregard sent the following communication to Grant : —

"At the close of the conflict yesterday, my forces being exhausted by the extraordinary length of the time during which they were engaged with yours on that and the preceding day, and it being apparent that you had received, and were still receiving, re-enforcements, *I felt it my duty to withdraw my troops from the immediate scene of the conflict."*

General Grant laughed when he read it aloud to his staff, and jocosely remarked, —

"I believe, I shall reply that no apologies are necessary." But his very courteous reply was, —

"The dead are already buried, otherwise I should be glad to extend this or any other courtesy consistent with duty and dictated by humanity."

The result of this conflict must have been a fearful disappointment to the Rebel General Beauregard. For he had staked his all upon it; he expected to win; he had completely exhausted the south-west in preparation for the battle. His chagrin was so great that he could not bear to telegraph the truth to Richmond, so he telegraphed thus:—

"We have gained a great and glorious victory, eight to ten thousand prisoners, and thirty-six pieces of cannon. Buell re-enforced Grant, and we retired to our intrenchments at Corinth, which we can hold. Loss heavy on both sides."

A "great and glorious victory," which forces the army into its intrenchments to escape annihilation, is not such a victory as aspiring generals usually covet. But, while the rebel authorities at Richmond were rejoicing over the lying telegram of Beauregard, the real facts turned joy into sadness. Over twelve thousand Union soldiers were lost; and though Beauregard reported his loss at ten thousand, Grant believed it was double that number. It was a singular battle, too. Both armies were victors once, and both were defeated. On the first day, the Union army was driven back three miles, with heavy loss and virtual defeat. On the second day, the rebel army was driven back five miles, with heavy loss and *actual* defeat.

The South never recovered from the consequences of this battle. It gave New Orleans to the Union, and opened the river to Memphis. It proved as exhilarating to the North as it was depressing to the South. President Lincoln appointed a national Thanksgiving Day, and the people throughout the North assembled in their churches on that day, to thank the Lord for the victory at Shiloh, and the harbinger it was of the final triumph. The fame of General Grant was immensely increased by it, so that, in the estimation of loyal men, he stood head and shoulders above all other generals.

But the old hatred of contractors, and the miserable jealousy of conceited and aspiring officers, revived the old stories about insubordination, drunkenness, and inactivity, and they had their run once more. Grant minded little about them, except he wrote to his father, " I will go on and do my duty to the very best of my ability, and do all I can to bring this war to a speedy close. I am not an aspirant for anything at the close of the war. . . . One thing I am well assured of, I have the confidence of every man in my command."

The letter was published, and Grant saw it, whereupon he telegraphed that no more letters of his should go into print.

General Grant issued the following congratulatory order to his troops:—

"The General commanding congratulates the troops who so gallantly maintained their position; repulsed and routed a numerically superior force of the enemy, composed of the flower of the Southern army, commanded by their ablest generals, and fought by them with all the desperation of despair. In numbers engaged, no such contest ever took place on this continent. In importance of result, but few such have taken place in the history of the world."

General Grant would have moved immediately upon the rebel works at Corinth, while Beauregard's force was so demoralized, but General Halleck opposed the measure. Besides, General Halleck wanted to show the country what wonderful military genius he, himself, possessed; and, at the same time, gratify his jealousy of Grant. So he kept the army waiting some weeks, until he collected *one hundred and twenty thousand soldiers*, twice as many as Beauregard had. Then, instead of storming the works at Corinth, in Grant style, he crawled along up towards them, as if afraid of getting hurt, always taking good care to keep his own person at a respectable distance from "the heaviest firing."

But we stop here to record two or three facts about Grant. The war-correspondent of the *New York Tribune*, A. D. Richardson, messed at Grant's headquarters after the battle of Shiloh, and he wrote of him,—

"Our tent was always near the General's. Each evening he reclined on the logs, or stood before the camp-fire, smoking and talking of the Mexican war, or of Shiloh ; or sat for hours in the tent beside us, while we played whist or 'twenty-one,' offering an occasional suggestion about the game, *but never touching a card or a glass of liquor.*"

The correspondent never heard him allude, but once, to the base stories which reckless contractors and rival officers circulated about him, or to Halleck's unjust and cruel treatment of him. Once he said, —

"After we have all done our best, to have such a torrent of obloquy and falsehood poured among my own troops is too much. I am not going to lay off my shoulder-straps until the close of the war, but I should like to go to New Mexico, or some other remote place, and have a small command out of the reach of the newspapers."

One evening he remarked : "After the war is over — and I wish it might be over soon — I want to go back to Galena and live. I am saving money from my pay now, and shall be able to educate my children."

Halleck marched his army but fifteen miles in six weeks, he was so fearful of falling into some trap. Grant kept saying, —

"Every rebel will escape, and carry away all his property."

Generals Sherman and McPherson agreed with Grant, that the way to accomplish anything was to hurry at once to Corinth, and carry the works by storm. They agreed with him on another measure, also, viz : that an advance on *our right* was the way to drive the enemy. Halleck maintained that an advance on *our left* was the military way of doing it. One day Grant returned from Halleck's under excitement, which he had never exhibited before. His chief-of-staff, noticing that his lip quivered with emotion, said, —

"What now?"

"You know what we have always talked about," replied Grant, "that the way to attack Corinth was on the right?"

"Yes, by this road, I know."

"Well, I suggested it to Halleck, and he treated it with contempt. He pooh-poohed it, and gave me to understand that when he wanted my advice he would let me know."

When Halleck approached Corinth, after accomplishing the wearisome march of fifteen miles in six weeks, most of his officers were disgusted that he did not push right into the city. Grant said, —

"If I were in command, I would push in, and win or lose. I may be rash, but I would not wait here always. Corinth was conquered at Shiloh."

Thus Halleck exposed his incompetency until the twenty-ninth day of May, when his timidity reached its climax. On that day, there was a tremendous explosion in the town. Grant and the other generals knew at once that the rebels had fled, and were blowing up their works. But Halleck said, evidently scared out of his wits, —

"The enemy will attack us in force to-morrow morning," and he issued an order to that effect, and in the morning he actually drew up his army in battle-array to receive the shock. While he was doing this, most of the rebel army was miles away, running for dear life, and the explosion was the signal of the completion of one of the most thorough and deliberate evacuations on record. Halleck ordered General Logan to advance and intrench, which he did, laughing "in his sleeve" all the while, and his men were using shovels when a squad of Union cavalry had entered the city, and were scouring the forsaken streets. The enemy had been carrying away their property for several weeks. Halleck had given them abundant opportunity to escape, and they had improved it, leaving scarcely a knapsack as a memento of their occupation. An army of seventy thousand men escaped from the foe, whose advance line was within two hundred yards of him, and the conceited General did not know it!

General Logan said to another officer, " My men shall never dig another ditch for Halleck, unless it is to bury *him* in."

In July, General Halleck succeeded General McClellan as commander-in-chief of the great Union army, and removed to Washington. A prominent Union officer remarked, —

" It is the first time I ever knew an officer promoted for his blunders."

" It is done to take him out of the way, that we may do something," responded another.

Commodore Foote said, " If we could have had our way, we would have destroyed the rebellion in the West within a few months."

In justice to General Halleck it should be said

that he made a concession to General Grant, after he found that Corinth was evacuated.

" After all, General Grant," he said, "*you* fought the battle of Corinth at Pittsburg Landing."

And yet, he offered to turn over his command to another, who indignantly declined it. Then he telegraphed to the war department, to inquire whether the Government would appoint his successor, or he should turn the department over to the next in command. The Government replied, —

" The officer next in command will succeed you," and so General Grant had an opportunity to reduce the fortress at Vicksburg. But every loyal reader will agree with the writer, that Halleck's treatment of Grant was prompted by his conceit and jealousy.

General Grant turned his attention to Vicksburg at once. But first it was necessary that he should drive out or destroy the rebel forces, which might follow and annoy him there. The city of Memphis was already in his hands, having been captured by the gunboats, and he removed his head-quarters to Jackson, Mississippi, leaving General Rosecrans in command at Corinth. And here General Grant gave striking proof of his military genius.

He was satisfied that the rebel General Price designed to attack Corinth, and that certain movements in another direction were feints. He laid his plans accordingly. He would attack Price at Iuka, which would be the signal for Van Dorn to move on Corinth.

A force, under his Generals, Hurlburt and Ord, was sent where they could cut Van Dorn's army t•

pieces on his retreat. His plan assumed that he should whip Price, and Rosecrans would whip Van Dorn, — all of which transpired according to his programme. He never planned for defeat; and here was one of the secrets of his success.

General Grant was now ready to move on Vicksburg. We add, however, that when the enemy evacuated Corinth, the young colonel of the Second Michigan Cavalry made a dash upon the rear of five thousand rebel horse, and followed them twenty miles, capturing many prisoners, although his own troops numbered but two thousand. Subsequently General Grant sought him out, and recommended him for a brigadier to the war department. The young hero was Phil Sheridan.

Sometime after the battle of Corinth, General Grant was riding past a dwelling with his staff, when the report of a gun was heard in the house, and a mother and daughter came rushing out, followed by a Union soldier, who had attempted to violate their persons, and fired his gun to scare them. Leaping from his horse, the General seized the miscreant's gun, and with one blow over his head with the breech, he laid him prostrate.

"I guess you have killed him, General," remarked Rawlins, on looking at the fellow.

"If I have, it has only served him right," replied Grant.

He was only stunned, however. In a short time he recovered, and was put under arrest.

XIV.

ON TO VICKSBURG.

ENERAL GRANT brought his army under the strictest discipline. By order he limited the baggage of each soldier, his own with all the rest. His baggage was so light that a soldier jocosely remarked, —

"The General's baggage consists of a pipe and tooth-brush."

He entirely stopped depredations by making the soldiers responsible for all property taken, and subtracting the same from their pay-roll. By such rigid regulations his one hundred and thirty thousand men were disciplined into one of the best armies ever known.

Grant's first movement toward the capture of Vicksburg was a master stroke. In a speech at St. Louis, General Sherman said, —

"Grant moved direct on Pemberton, commander of Vicksburg, while I moved from Memphis, and a smaller force, under General Washburne, struck directly for Grenada; and the first thing Pemberton knew, the depot of his supplies was almost in the grasp of a small cavalry force, and he fell back in confusion, and gave us the Tallahatchie without a battle. The credit of this plan, which was as brilliantly conceived as executed, belongs to Grant."

General Sherman was sent with his command by water, in advance of Grant, who was to unite and co-operate with him in the attack on Vicksburg. But the disaster to Union arms at Holly Springs, in consequence of the inefficiency of Murphy, the commander of the post, delayed General Grant, sadly interfering with his plans. Sherman reached Vicksburg, and made two assaults upon the works, in which he was repulsed. But the movement disclosed the great strength of the works.

Vicksburg is located on a bluff, or hill, on the east side of the Mississippi, opposite a remarkable bend in the river. It has sometimes been called a "city of a hundred hills," because there are so many hills within and without it. The enemy, appreciating the importance of keeping possession of the Mississippi, had spent time and money lavishly in fortifying it. Every conceivable means of defense was adopted. Eight miles of batteries swept the river, so that Gen. John C. Pemberton, the commander, had reason to say,—

"No gunboat can pass without my consent."

He considered the place absolutely impregnable. He had not the least fear that any force the U. S. Government could send against it, could reduce the works. He felt perfectly secure. Nor were there wanting Union officers and civilians who regarded the proposed assault upon Vicksburg extremely unwise. But General Grant entertained the Western view of the case, that opening the Mississippi, from

St. Louis to the Gulf, would be substantially the end
of the Rebellion. And this conviction alone was
enough to enlist all the powers of his being in the
momentous enterprise.

Of his one hundred and thirty thousand troops, he
took fifty thousand on the expedition against Vicksburg, locating the remainder where they could render
him essential aid, and, at the same time, be of the
most service to the country. Destroying railroad
communications in the region he was leaving, so as
to cripple the enemy as much as possible, he took up
his line of march. His army encamped at Young's
Point, opposite Vicksburg. There Sherman joined
him with his command. Now the *modus operandi* of
capturing Vicksburg was thoroughly discussed. It
was the toughest problem to solve which the clearheaded General had ever undertaken. Pemberton
had sixty thousand men in the fort, and more than
that number were ready to come to his assistance.
He had all the ordnance he wanted, of every sort and
kind. The Union army could not pass down the
river, for the eight miles of water-batteries would
send every Union soldier into eternity before half
the distance was accomplished. The prospect of
capturing the stronghold was not encouraging.

Sherman's experience in his repulse, together with
his own observation now, convinced Grant that there
was only one way of capturing the place, and that
was to attack it in the rear; but how to get into the
rear, — that was the question. His army could not be
conveyed down the river on transports, for the waterbatteries would sink them on the way; nor could

they march down the banks of the river to a suitable place for crossing, because an impassable swamp, too extensive for corduroy roads, prevented. The swamp spread out into the country for twenty miles or more, so that to march around it would take his army from the base of supplies, a measure that would violate all military rules. Nevertheless, General Grant soon solved the difficult problem in his own mind — the gunboats could run the gauntlet of the rebel batteries on some dark night, and the army could march around the impassable swamp. But none of his officers believed it, except Rawlins and McPherson, and therefore he yielded to the trial of other expedients.

There was great complaint at this time against Sherman, because he failed in his assault upon the works at Vicksburg.

"The complaint is unjust and cruel," said Grant to a friend.

"Was not Sherman to blame?"

"Of course not; not in the least," was Grant's prompt reply.

"He was badly defeated."

"True; but that was not his fault, nor mine; it was one of the inevitable accidents of war."

It was proposed to cut a canal across the narrow peninsula, made by the bend of the river at Vicksburg. Grant acquiesced, though with little faith. If the canal was successful, and the river was turned from its ancient course, Vicksburg would be an inland city, six miles away; Grant's army could then pass below without danger. But the canal proved a failure; the Mississippi refused to change its old habits, and pursued the even tenor of its way. No one could explain it, but the aged river refused to budge an inch from its old channel. Another canal from Lake Providence to the Mississippi failed; so it was with the " Yazoo Pass," " Steele's Bayou," and " Milliken's Bend " projects—all failed. After wasting weeks of precious time, Grant becoming more and more impatient all the while, the army and the country grew disheartened; but Grant was more determined than ever.

" There is only one way to do it," he said with so much emphasis, that Rawlins knew what it meant.

He called his generals together, one night, for conference.

" What next?" he inquired. No response.

He proceeded to give his opinion as to the practicability of marching his army around the swamp, and the gunboats running by the batteries. And then he asked the opinion of each officer separately. Rawlins and McPherson only favored the enterprise.

" It is taking the army away from the base of supplies," said one.

" The enemy once between our army and supplies, and we are beaten," remarked another.

" The sacrifice of life will be too great; the country will not support us in it," said a third. And so on. Every officer but two opposed the plan.

" Nevertheless," said Grant, after having listened to each one, " it must be done. It is the only alter native left to us. Unless we do this, we can do nothing. Therefore we will do this I assume the whole responsibility. We will move as soon as possible."

This was the greatest risk that Grant ever assumed; and if his plan had failed, he would have been set aside forever from military life.

The conference closed about midnight, when General Sherman went over to the tent of Gen. John M. Thayer, from whom the author received this account of the affair, and peering in, —

"Are you awake, Thayer?" he said.

"Yes, what now?" replied General Thayer, arousing from a dreamy sleep.

"General Grant has decided to march the army around the swamp, and to steam the gunboats past the batteries. It is not a plan I could recommend; but he has settled it, and we must co-operate with him, and do the best we can."

"All right," answered General Thayer, whose confidence in General Grant's judgment was unfaltering

Taking the risk forced General Grant to take another. He knew that a telegram to General Halleck announcing his intentions, would bring back a veto of the plan at once, because it would be marching the army directly into the enemy's country, away from the base of supplies. So he ordered that no steamer should be allowed to pass up the river to Cairo for six days. By the expiration of this time he would be where it would make no difference whether Halleck should telegraph him to abandon the project or not. He made no provision for defeat. He counted upon success. A friend called at his office, to whom he said, —

"The problem is a difficult one, but I shall certainly solve it. Vicksburg can be taken. I shall give my days and nights to it, and shall surely take it."

A newspaper correspondent at that time gave such an accurate description of Grant, that we quote it here: —

"Grant is more approachable and liable to interruption than a merchant would allow himself to be in his store. Citizens come in, introduce themselves, and say, as I heard one man, — 'I have no business with you, General, but just wanted to have a little talk with you, because folks at home will ask me if I did.' He is one of the most engaging men I ever saw — quiet, gentle, extremely, even uncomfortably modest; but confiding, and of an exceedingly kind disposition. He gives the impression of a man of strong will and capacity underlying these feminine traits."

General Thayer, to whom we have just referred, has kindly furnished us with the following letter concerning his first impressions of Grant. And he confirms the testimony of a lady of the Christian Commission, whom we shall soon quote, by saying, that, during the two and a half years he was with him, he never saw him play cards, or take a drop of intoxicating liquors, or heard him utter a profane word.

"GRAND ISLAND, NEB., April 27, 1885.

"REV. WM. M. THAYER, Franklin, Mass.

"*Dear Sir*, — In reply to your inquiries in regard to my impressions of General Grant when my acquaintance with him began, I take pleasure in stating, that on arrival at

St. Louis with my regiment, the First Nebraska, in August, 1861, and reporting to General Fremont, then commanding the Western Department, he informed me that the Confederate General Hardee was moving up towards Pilot Knob, at the end of the Iron Mountain Railroad, eighty miles south of St. Louis, with the purpose of its capture. He also stated that General Grant was in command there with a small force, which he, Fremont, was increasing as fast as troops arrived, and he desired me to proceed by rail that night with my regiment to re-enforce him. Arriving at Pilot Knob at daylight, the next morning, I found the General in a small farm house n the outskirts of the town. Entering the room pointed out to me as his head-quarters, I found him seated at a little pine table, standing on one side of the room, engaged in writing. I gave him my name, and that of the regiment, stating I had been directed to report to him for service. He received me very pleasantly, and said, 'Please be seated a few minutes while I finish this communication.' I had never heard of Grant till a few days previously, and all that I had learned of him was, that he was a graduate of West Point, and was a lieutenant in the Mexican War. Expecting soon to be engaged with the enemy, I was very glad of the opportunity to become acquainted with our commander, and to take observations of him. His continuing his writing was very favorable for that purpose. There was no appearance o' show or of rank about the establishment; one orderly at the door of the house, and some troops in camp near by, were all that indicated anything like a military condition of things. The General was dressed in a suit of armyflannel, dark-blue, his coat and army-blouse with no sign of rank upon it. Having so good an opportunity to observe him, I made good use of it. His appearance, his features, the expression of his face, indicated to me that he was a man of marked will-force, of great self-determination, and of fixedness of purpose, and of great firmness. Something about him impressed me with the idea that he would adopt his plans only after mature deliberation, and then, having once fixed upon them, there would be no letting up on his part till his object was accomplished. His expression, his firm-set mouth, his whole face and bearing, indicated the possession of these qualities. While sitting there, thus observing him, he made such an impression upon me, that the thought passed through my mind, ' Who knows but there sits the man who is to come out of this war its great central figure — the great leader of our armies?'

"I could see far enough ahead to know that, no matter how many great commanders the war might develop, there must, in all probability, arise some one who would overtop all others by his military genius and his great achievements.

"After he had finished his writing, there was some conversation which still further impressed me with the possession, on his part, of remarkably good, practical, common-sense, self-reliance, and self-poise. Serving under him for over two years, I had many opportunities for observing that my first impressions in regard to him were fully correct, only in a far greater degree. His bearing and appearance were always modest and retiring utterly devoid of anything like vanity and ostentation He was a man of unflinching courage, both moral and physical. When convinced of the right, no power on earth could move him. Always regardful of the rights of others; always anxious to give full credit to others instead of to himself; never seeming to harbor resentments towards those who he thought had wronged him; it seemed as if his whole purpose was to do his duty to his country, and to all mankind. If I were asked to name a man who combined within himself all the qualities of a true and noble manhood, and who was also among the great commanders of the world, I should, without hesitation, name Gen. U. S. Grant.

"Very truly yours,
"JOHN M. THAYER."

The lady of the Christian Commission, whom we promised to quote, wrote:—

"At a celebration on the 22d of February, while all around were drinking toasts in sparkling champagne, I saw Grant push aside a glass of wine, and, taking up a glass of Mississippi water, with the remark, 'This suits the matter in hand,' drink to the toast, 'God gave us Lincoln and Liberty; let us fight for both.'

. . . "On board the head-quarters boat at Milliken's Bend, a lively gathering of officers and ladies had assembled. Cards and music were the order of the evening. Grant sat in the ladies' cabin, leaning upon a table covered with innumerable maps and routes to Vicksburg, wholly absorbed in contemplation of the great work before him. He paid no attention to what was going on around, neither did any one dare to interrupt him. For hours he sat thus, until the loved and lamented McPherson stepped up to him with a glass of liquor in his hand, and said, 'General, this won't do, you are injuring yourself; join with us in a few toasts, and throw this burden off your mind.' Looking up and smiling, he replied, 'Mac, you know your whiskey won't help me to think.'"

General Sherman was so much opposed to Grant's plan, of marching around the swamp, that he said to him,—

"Of course I shall give the movement my heartiest support; but I feel it to be my duty to protest in writing."

"Very well," replied the General, "send along your protest."

Sherman sent a letter to Rawlins, Grant's Chief-of-Staff, which closed with these very courteous words, —

"I make these suggestions with the request that General Grant simply read them, and give them, as I know he will, a share of his thoughts. I would prefer that he should not answer, but merely give them as much or as little weight as they deserve. . . . Whatever plan of action he may adopt, will receive from me the same zealous co-operation and energetic support as though conceived by me."

General Grant read the letter, smiled, slipped it into his pocket, and marched his army away from its base of supplies. Several months afterwards, he came across the letter, when hauling over some old papers, and passing it to Sherman, remarked, —

"By the way, Sherman, here is something that will interest you."

General Grant was confirmed in his opinion, that the gunboats could run past the batteries at Vicksburg without being destroyed, by conversation with rivermen. They were an uncultivated class. Such a man as Halleck would not expect to learn anything from this class; but Grant would. They were practical men, and their business entitled them to speak on this subject. One of them said, —

"The *Queen of the West* run past the batteries

with little damage, and these gunboats certainly can."

This was a small wooden ram that steamed past the batteries before Grant appeared upon the scene.

Before the memorable night on which the gunboats run past the batteries, General Grant saw that it would prove a great damage to Vicksburg to cut the railroad east of Jackson, Miss., as that was the chief source of supply to the rebel garrison. He wrote to General Hurlburt, —

"It seems to me that Grierson, with about five hundred picked men, might succeed in cutting his way south, and cut the railroad east of Jackson, Miss. This undertaking would be a hazardous one, but it would pay well if carried out."

Colonel Grierson undertook the raid, and achieved one of the most brilliant triumphs of the war. He rode six hundred miles, tore up fifty miles of railroad, broke down all the telegraph-wires he could find, destroyed bridges, and three thousand stands of arms, captured five hundred prisoners, and spread consternation among the rebels. His loss was only three killed and seven wounded.

General McClernand was posted off with the advance, the Eleventh Army Corps, around the swamp to New Carthage. General Grant remained to see the gunboats steam down the river, which occurred on the night of April 16th, — a very dark night. The plan was for the transports, loaded with army-stores, to glide down the river under the protection of the gunboats. It was an undertaking so perilous that General Grant thought it not best to order the crews to go, but to call for volunteers. So eager were the soldiers to take the risk, that twice as many offered their services as were needed. When the required number was obtained, others began to offer premiums to their comrades for their places on the gunboats and transports — ten, twenty, and even one hundred dollars.

At the appointed hour the craft glided out of their places of concealment, and silently stole down the river.

Commodore Porter's flag-ship led the fleet, the *Benton*, and the enemy, on the alert, discovered it about midnight, and at once the thunder of artillery made night hideous. The enemy set fire to buildings, and lighted, also, a great mass of combustible rubbish collected for the purpose, until the river for miles was ablaze with light. The barges and transports, clinging to the shore, pushed on as rapidly as possible. Again and again they were hit by shot and shell; but no great damage was done, except setting the *Henry Clay* on fire by a bursting shell, and sending her down the river a burning mass. Her crew, escaped in their yawls. On, on the fleet sped, our gunboats responding to the enemy's terrific fire, and before daylight, the entire fleet, except the *Henry Clay*, were received at New Carthage with yells of delight by McClernand's command, who had reached that place. General Grant was the happiest man on the continent then, or he ought to have been; for his enterprise was successful beyond his most sanguine expectations. One man only was killed, and but three wounded on the gunboats; and no one was hit or hurt on the transports. General Grant immediately gave a furlough of forty days to all the men engaged in running the batteries, with transportation to and from home.

In a few days six more steamers towed twelve barges loaded with supplies, on a dark night, past the batteries, with the loss of only one steamer and four barges.

On the night of the 16th, when the burning wreck of the *Henry Clay* floated down in sight of McClernand's command, anxiously awaiting the result, a rich secessionist, jubilant over the scene, said to General McClernand, —

"Where now are your gunboats? The batteries of Vicksburg have sunk them all."

When, an hour later, the remainder of the fleet appeared, the provoking Yankee nettled the rich old fellow by retorting, —

"Where now are our gunboats? Has Vicksburg destroyed them?"

This seccessionist owned one of the finest homesteads in the whole South. His costly residence, surrounded by green lawns and wide savannas of corn and cotton, stood near by. And he was so disappointed and maddened by the Union success, that he belched forth, —

"My house shall never shelter these Yankee miscreants."

He actually applied the torch to his beautiful home, and burned it to the ground.

General Grant transported his troops across the river to Grand Gulf, where he fought a battle and took possession of the place. Learning from an old negro of a better road at Bruinsburg to the rear of Vicksburg, he pushed on, and landed his force there.

Three newspaper correspondents attempted to pass the rebel batteries on a barge loaded with hay and provisions. They were Richard T. Colburn, of the *New York World*, and A. D. Richardson and J. Ross Browne, of the *New York Tribune*. A shell struck the boat and exploded, setting the hay on fire, and killing or burning all except those who leaped into the water and floated on bales of hay until the enemy's boats picked them up. Sixteen of the thirty-two on board were picked up by the rebels. The three correspondents were imprisoned; but Colburn was soon released because he served a Democratic paper that sympathized with the South; but Richardson and Browne endured two years imprisonment in seven different rebel prisons.

General Grant realized that he must move with celerity, that General Johnston might not have time to join Pemberton at Vicksburg. In the lightest trim possible, he and his army took up their line of march. Mr. Washburne, of Galena, who was on a visit to Grant to witness the capture of Vicksburg, said, —

"Grant took with him neither a horse, nor an orderly, nor a camp-chest, nor an overcoat, nor a blanket, nor even a clean shirt. His entire baggage for six days was a tooth-brush. He fared liked the commonest soldier in his command, partaking of his rations and sleeping on the ground, with no covering but the canopy of heaven."

On his way to the rear of Vicksburg, Grant fought

battles at Port Gibson, Raymond, Champion Hills,
Jackson, and the Big Black, taking possession of all
the places. In twenty days he marched two hundred
miles, and fought six battles, in which he captured
six thousand of the enemy, with ninety guns, killing
and wounding many more; drove Johnston's army
out of Jackson, so that he could not join Pemberton,
who had marched his army from Vicksburg to Edward's Station, half-way to Jackson; cut Pemberton's
communications, and forced him to retire, without
being re-enforced, to his entrenchments at Vicksburg.
He supported his army, also, from the country through
which he marched. His loss in killed, wounded, and
missing was but four thousand.

During this time, the authorities at Washington,
including President Lincoln, were extremely anxious.
They thought General Grant's plan of getting into
the rear of Vicksburg was not good generalship, and
anticipated that a terrible disaster would overtake
his command. He had scarcely reached the rear of
Vicksburg, when, as Gen. J. M. Thayer, an eye-witness, informs us, an officer came dashing up with an
order from General Halleck. Grant opened the envelope, and read the order aloud, which was that he
should turn back and proceed to Port Hudson to reenforce General Banks. Putting the message in his
pocket, he said to his fellow-officers standing by, —

"I am not in a situation to obey that order now."

Very fortunate for the country that he concealed
his purpose from General Halleck; for if the latter
had had his own way, the fall of Vicksburg never
would have thrilled the nation with delight.

Several incidents that occurred during the rapid and victorious march, are so charged with General Grant's characteristics, that we stop to rehearse them.

When he left Grand Gulf General Grant remarked, "I think we can reduce Jackson and re-open communication with the fleet above Vicksburg in about five days"; and they were just five days about it — an example of his promptness.

At the South Fork the retreating rebels had destroyed the bridge.

"This bridge must be rebuilt at once," said Grant to McClernand.

"I have ordered it done," answered the latter.

Four or five hours afterwards General Grant rode down to the river, expecting the bridge was completed, but found that it was not even begun.

"How is this, General?" he said, sharply, to General McClernand.

"My men are too much worn out," was the cool answer he received.

General Grant reined up his steed, and galloped off to tell Rawlins and Wilson to build the bridge in the shortest time possible. In three hours the bridge, one hundred and twenty feet long, was completed. Grant was happy, for that was promptness.

The General had just passed a wretched cabin, when a woman ran out swinging her bonnet.

"Go back and see what she wants," Grant said to one of his staff.

"We came here from Cairo just before the war," she told the officer. "We are Union people, but my husband was impressed into the rebel service, and lost his health, and he has been confined to his bed more than a year, and we are very poor. I only wanted to welcome the Union army, and so I swung my bonnet."

"Leave a guard at that house," ordered Grant, on receiving this report, and rode on. Suddenly he stopped again, and ordered, —

"Send back a surgeon to that sick man, with instructions to report his condition to me."

The order was obeyed. The General rode forward, but stopped again to give a third order : —

"Have the commissary leave rations at that house, that the woman and her husband may not suffer."

This tender care was just what the sick man needed, and in a short time Grant was pleased to give them transportation to Cairo. One would think that, with the mighty pressure of duties at that juncture, increased by the consciousness of running a campaign, which the War Department would not approve, if they knew it, and of marching away from his base of supplies in the enemy's country, the General would have been too much absorbed to stop to aid an unknown couple. But his humanity was equal to his valor.

A young rebel officer was captured, and brought to General Grant. He claimed to be a member of General Bowen's staff, and he was a dashing fellow. He rode a fine horse, with costly saddle and trappings.

"General Grant," he said, "this horse and saddle do not belong to the Confederate Government, but are my private property, presented by my father. I should be glad if I might retain them."

"Well," replied Grant, "I have three or four horses, which are also my private property, running about somewhere in the Confederacy. I will make an exchange with you. We'll keep yours, and when you find one of mine, just take it in his place."

Grave and thoughtful as the General usually was, there was a vein of humor in his soul, which sometimes created comedy, where tragedy was natural.

When General Grant was at the Big Black, he was between two wings of the rebel army. Pemberton was on his left, with fifty thousand men, and on his right, Johnston was collecting an unknown number. The latter must be conquered before he could attack the former, or his rear would be imperiled. Without hesitating a moment, he decided again to march away from his base of supplies at Grand Gulf, fall upon Johnston's army and crush it, and then take Pemberton in hand. Another instance of his readiness to assume risks!

His son, Fred, thirteen years of age, was with him in this campaign, riding a spirited charger beside his father. He rode ahead of the General and his staff into the city of Jackson, after the rebels were driven out. The presence of the lad became a source of interest to the staff-officers, because it drew out so much of the father from the great General.

After occupying Jackson, General Grant sent on details to destroy railroads, army-stores, manufactories, machine-shops, and whatever was aiding the rebel army. A manufacturer, who had a mill full of duck rushed to Grant, begging to have his factory saved

" For whom do you make duck?" inquired Grant

"My customers are many and widely scattered," replied the mill-owner, evasively.

"Wilson," called Grant, "did you examine that duck?"

"I did."

"What mark is there on it?"

"It bears the stamp of C. S. A." (Confederate States of America), Wilson replied.

"Then, sir, your factory must burn with the rest," said Grant forcibly, turning to the proprietor. He was putting down the rebellion, and duck must be put down, because it was a factor of the rebellion.

When General Grant entered Jackson, he drove directly to the hotel where General Johnston had his head-quarters before the evacuation. On leaving, he directed Rawlins to settle the bill with Confederate money.

"How much is our bill?"

"Ninety dollars."

The officer handed the amount to the proprietor in Confederate money.

"If I had known that you were going to pay in that money I should have charged you more," the proprietor said.

"Oh, well, charge what you please; we propose to pay you with this money."

"It will be two hundred dollars, then."

The bill was paid; and it was not dear living at all for the Government, General Grant thought; for he captured a large quantity of Confederate money at Fort Gibson.

"It will help to put down the rebellion, to pay

them in their own coin," remarked the General, humorously. He was equal to any emergency,— so cool, so observing, so fearless, and yet so wise!

A member of his staff said of him :—

"If you could see the General as he sits just over beyond me, with his wife and two children, looking more like a chaplain than a general, with that quiet air so impossible to describe, you would not ask me if he drinks. He rarely ever uses intoxicating liquors. He is more moderate in his habits and desires, and more pure and spotless in his private character, than almost any man I ever knew. He is more brave, has more power to command, and more ability to plan, than any man I ever served under; cool to excess when others lose nerve, always hopeful, always undisturbed, never failing to accomplish what he undertakes." . . .

Major Penniman wrote of him :—

"I have seen him in the familiarity and seclusion of camp-life, and I know perfectly well what his personal habits are. He messes with his staff as he would with his own family. No intoxicating liquors are on the table at dinner or at any other time. It is not his habit to use them, nor does he encourage it in others. No man of all the hundreds of thousands he has commanded ever heard General Grant use profane language. One of his highest meeds of praise consists in the fact, that, through all his commands to his present elevated post, he has had no jealousies, bickerings, or quarrels among his officers. He has the rare faculty of selecting the right man for the right place.

XV.

SIEGE OF VICKSBURG.

HAVING fought his way to the rear of Vicksburg, General Grant invested the city and its defences with his army, drawn up in a semi-circle, extending eight miles. He had no more doubt of capturing the city than he had of his own existence. Neither had General Sherman, now; for, on his way from Grand Gulf, he said to General Grant, —

"Until this moment I never thought that your expedition would be a success. I never could see the end clearly; but *this* is a campaign, — this is a success if we never take the town."

At first, General Grant thought to carry the works by storm. On the nineteenth day of May he ordered a general assault; and it was made in splendid style. The soldiers faced the "leaden rain and iron hail," and succeeded in capturing two or three outer works and quite a number of prisoners; but they were forced to withdraw. On the 22d of May another assault was ordered, — more deadly than the first. Union and rebel soldiers, in places, grappled in a hand-to-hand fight; but the works proved too strong for flesh and blood to carry by assault. Grant determined to carry it by siege, and at once set his army at work. A rebel woman, who came within the Union lines, asked Grant, tauntingly,—

"When do you expect to take Vicksburg?"

"I can't tell exactly," he replied, in a pleasant way; "but I shall stay until I do, if it takes thirty years."

Siege-work commenced with signal earnestness; and soon twelve miles of trenches were dug, and two hundred guns were in position. Then he set his men to work to mine Fort Hill,—one of the most important of the rebel works. The mine was partially successful. Fifteen hundred pounds of powder were exploded in it, destroying a portion of the fort. General Grant soon became satisfied, however, that exhaustion of food and powder only could reduce the stronghold.

It was not long before the rebel army and the inhabitants of the city were reduced to one meal per day. The bombardment of the city was terrible,— beyond description,—and the inhabitants dug caves in the earth for protection from shot and shell. Many dwellings were literally riddled to pieces The siege lasted forty-six days; and during that time, the storm of shot and shell was almost incessant, night and day. One-half of the Union army worked with the spade, while the other half cannonaded the fortress, and picked off rebels with their rifles. Probably no place ever had such a continuous fire concentrated upon it for so long a time. There was scarcely a building in the city that was not damaged more or less. After the war, a Vicksburg woman published a book, in which she said,—

"Caves were the fashion, — the rage, — over besieged Vicksburg. Negroes who understood their business hired themselves out to dig them at from thirty to fifty dollars, according to the size. Many persons, considering different localities unsafe, would sell them to others who had been less fortunate or less provident; and so great was the demand for cave-workmen, that a new branch of industry sprang up and became popular.

"So constantly dropped the shells around the city, that the inhabitants all made preparations to live undergound during the siege. . . . Our dining, breakfasting, and supper hours were quite irregular. When the shells were falling fast, and servants came in for safety, our meals waited for completion for some time; again they would fall slowly, with the lapse of many minutes between, and out would start the cooks to their work."

In the course of three or four weeks the enemy found their provisions short, and their ammunition, too. Soldiers and citizens alike were forced to omit one meal, and afterwards, two meals a day; for some time they lived on one meal per day. The last week before Pemberton's surrender, mule-meat was freely used.

General Grant had satisfactory knowledge of the want and suffering in the city. He had his own way of getting necessary information; sometimes it was a very ingenious way. At one time, while he was in charge of the Department of Tennessee, he wanted to send a spy into the enemy's lines near by, to acquire needful information. So he picked his

man, and made a great commotion over him by
charging him with being a rebel, and drumming him
out of the army. The enemy, of course, received
him gladly, wondering that the "Yankees" had not
shot him; and, within two or three days, he was
back again with the coveted information for Grant.
General Grant knew that Pemberton's surrender was
only a question of time. When flour was worth a
thousand dollars per barrel, and meat two dollars and
fifty cents a pound—as they were in Vicksburg, in
Confederate money—starvation or surrender were
not distant.

The advance ditches of the two armies were so
near each other that conversation between Confederate and Union pickets was common. The following was reported:—

"What are you fellows doing out there, any way?"
asked a rebel picket.

"Guarding thirty thousand of you prisoners," answered the Union picket, "and making you board
yourselves."

"Why don't you come and take Vicksburg, if you
are going to do it?"

"Oh, we are in no hurry at all. General Grant
has not transportation yet to send you up North."

"We have a lot of your blasted old flags in here.'

"Glad of it; you can make shirts of them; they'll
look vastly better than that old butternut!"

"Will you trade some coffee for corn-meal?"

"Yes, to oblige *you;* we've meal enough; but you
may throw it over here."

General Grant ordered the ground to be prepared

for a new battery in front of Logan's division, where the workmen were much exposed to the enemy's sharpshooters. The bullets came so thick and fast as to interrupt the work. The soldiers, with their spades, were less brave than they were with guns. General Grant, whose eye was on the alert, took in the situation, and he coolly took a seat upon a pile of rails close by, and went to whittling a stick and giving orders, as if the firing were a thousand miles away. The bullets fell around him as thick and fast as they did about the workmen, but he paid no attention to them. His example re-assured the exposed soldiers, their fear vanished, and there was no more dodging or disposition to run.

As early as the twenty-seventh day of May, Grant captured a letter from Pemberton to Johnston, which read, —

"I have fifteen thousand men and rations for thirty days — one meal a day. Come to my aid with an army of thirty thousand men. If you cannot do this within ten days, you had better retreat. Ammunition is almost exhausted, especially percussion caps."

On the fourteenth day of June, Johnston wrote to Pemberton, —

"By fighting the enemy simultaneously at the same points of his line, you may be extricated; *our joint forces cannot raise the siege of Vicksburg.*"

On the 19th of June, Pemberton wrote back, —

"My men have been thirty-four days and nights in the trenches without relief, and the enemy within conversation distance. We are living on very reduced rations, and, as you know, are entirely isolated. *What aid am I to expect from you?"*

On the twenty-eighth day of June, General Grant reported that his lines were about two hundred and thirty rods nearer the city than his original works were. No doubt that Pemberton took this factor into his account.

General Johnston had collected another force of twenty-five or thirty thousand men, and established his head-quarters again at Jackson. Grant had reason to believe that an attack upon his rear was contemplated. So he determined upon another and still more vigorous attack upon the enemy's works on the fourth day of July, as a fitting time for patriotism to do its best.

But on the morning of July 3d, a white flag was discovered floating above the Confederate works. Firing ceased immediately; and soon General Bowen was seen approaching the Union lines. He was met and blindfolded; then led to General Grant, to whom he delivered the following communication from General Pemberton: —

"HEAD-QUARTERS, VICKSBURG, July 3, 1863.

"MAJOR-GENERAL GRANT, commanding United States forces.

"*General,* — I have the honor to propose to you an armistic of — hours, with a view to arranging terms for the capitulation of Vicksburg. To this end, if agreeable to you, I will appoint three commissioners, to meet a like number to be named by yourself, at such place and hour as you may find convenient. I make this proposition to save the further effusion of blood, which must otherwise be shed to a frightful extent, feeling myself fully able to maintain my position for a yet indefinite period. The communication will be handed you, under a flag of truce, by Maj.-Gen. John S. Bowen.

"Very respectfully, your obedient servant,
"J. C. PEMBERTON.'

General Grant replied as follows:—

"HEAD-QUARTERS DEPARTMENT OF TENNESSEE,
"IN THE FIELD, NEAR VICKSBURG, July 3, 1863.
"LIEUT. GEN. J. C. PEMBERTON, commanding Confederate forces, etc.

"*General*,—Your note of this date, is just received, proposing an armistice for several hours, for the purpose of arranging terms of capitulation through commissioners to be appointed, etc. The useless effusion of blood you propose stopping by this course, can be ended at any time you may choose, by the unconditional surrender of the city and garrison. Men who have shown so much endurance and courage as those now in Vicksburg, will always challenge the respect of an adversary, and, I can assure you, will be treated with all the respect due prisioners of war. I do not favor the proposition of appointing commissioners to arrange the terms of capitulation, because I have no terms other than those indicated above.

"I am, General, very respectfully,
"Your obedient servant,
"U. S. GRANT,
"*Major-General*.'

At three o'clock, P. M., Generals Grant, Logan, Rawlins, McPherson, Smith, and Ord rode out of the trenches to a large oak tree, where they dismounted and sat down upon the grass. Ten minutes thereafter, General Pemberton, accompanied by General Bowen and one of his staff-officers, appeared. General Grant, who was with Pemberton and Bowen in the Mexican war, arose and shook hands with them both. General Bowen introduced the other Union officers to his chief. Pemberton proceeded to business at once.

"I have come, General Grant," he said, "to see if I can arrange terms for the capitulation of Vicksburg. What do you demand?"

"All the terms I have are stated in my letter of this morning," replied General Grant.

"If that is so," retorted Pemberton, putting on airs, "the conference may terminate, and hostilities be resumed."

"Very well," said Grant, "My army was never in a better condition to prosecute the siege."

General Bowen urged that a conference should be had.

"Suppose we do talk the matter over," continued Grant in a spirit of accommodation.

He and Pemberton went a short distance from the other officers, and conferred together. Fifteen minutes later Grant called up McPherson and Smith, and Pemberton called Bowen, and these three stepped aside for consultation. The terms of capitulation were finally agreed upon, when Grant said,—

"I will go home and write out the terms agreed upon. General, you can have rations for your men if you desire."

"Oh, no, we will use our own; we have plenty," Pemberton replied, telling a falsehood. If he had known that his communication to Johnston about "one meal a day" had fallen into Grant's hands, he would have known how to explain the smile that played over Grant's face, when he claimed a "plenty."

Just then the Union gunboats in the river opened a terrible fire upon Vicksburg. Grant sprang to his feet and said, —

"This is a mistake. I will send to Admiral Porter and have the firing stopped."

"Never mind," answered Pemberton; "let it go on. It won't hurt anybody; the gunboats never hurt anybody!"

Another falsehood. The cave-life of the people of Vicksburg was quite well understood in the Union ranks at that time.

The two commanders separated, and an hour later Grant sent the following communication to Pemberton: —

"HEAD-QUARTERS DEPARTMENT OF TENNESSEE,
"NEAR VICKSBURG, July 3, 1863.

"LIEUT-GEN. J. C. PEMBERTON, commanding Confederate forces, Vicksburg, Miss.

"*General,* — In conformity with agreement this afternoon, I will submit the following proposition for the surrender of the city of Vicksburg, public stores, etc. On your accepting the terms proposed, I will march in one division as a guard, and take possession at eight A. M., tomorrow. As soon as rolls can be made out and paroles signed by officers and men, you will be allowed to march out of our lines, the officers taking with them their sidearms and clothing, and the field, staff, and cavalry officers one horse each. The rank and file will be allowed all their clothing, but no other property.

"If these conditions are accepted, any amount of rations you may deem necessary can be taken from the stores you now have, and also the necessary cooking utensils for preparing them. Thirty wagons also, counting two two-horse or mule teams as one, will be allowed to transport such articles as can not be carried along. The same conditions will be allowed to all sick and wounded officers and soldiers, as fast as they become able to travel. The paroles for these latter must be signed, however, whilst officers are present, authorized to sign the roll of prisoners.

"I am, General, very respectfully,
"Your obedient servant,
"U. S. GRANT,
"*Major-General.*"

As soon as General Grant had forwarded this letter to Pemberton, he ordered General Sherman to march immediately upon Johnston's army at Jackson, and crush it, while the rebel general was considering what to do next. Johnston was taken wholly by surprise, though he made a bold stand. But Sherman's command swept all opposition before it, and drove the rebel force out of Jackson with heavy loss. Sherman captured eight hundred prisoners and thirty guns. This was the second time Grant had captured Jackson, and now Johnston was in as pitiable condition as Pemberton, and they might have held an experience meeting to the advantage of both, had circumstances favored their coming together.

Later in the day, Pemberton replied to Grant's last proposal: —

"HEAD-QUARTERS, VICKSBURG, July, 3, 1863.
MAJOR-GENERAL GRANT, commanding United States forces

"*General*, — I have the honor to acknowledge the receipt of your communication of this date, proposing terms of capitulation for this garrison and post. In the main, your terms are accepted ; but in justice both to the honor and spirit of my troops, manifested in the defense of Vicksburg, I have to submit the following amendments, which, if acceded to by you, will perfect the agreement between us. At ten o'clock, A. M., to-morrow I propose to evacuate the works in and around Vicksburg, and to surrender the city and garrison under my command by marching out with my colors and arms, stacking them in front of my present lines, after which you will take possession; officers to retain their side-arms and personal property, and the rights and property of citizens to be respected.

" I am, General, yours very respectfully,

"J. C. PEMBERTON,
" *Lieutenant-General.*"

About sunrise, July 4th, Grant sent his last communication : —

"HEAD-QUARTERS DEPARTMENT OF TENNESSEE,
"BEFORE VICKSBURG, July 4, 1863.
' LIEUTENANT-GENERAL PEMBERTON, commanding forces in Vicks burg.

" *General,* — I have the honor to acknowledge the receipt of your communication of 3d July. The amendment proposed by you can not be acceded to in full. It w ll be necessary to furnish every officer and man with a parole signed by himself, which, with the completion of the roll of prisoners, will necessarily take some time. Again, I can make no stipulations with regard to the treatment of citizens and their private property. While I do not propose to cause them any undue annoyance or loss, I can not consent to leave myself under any restraint by stipulations. The property which officers will be allowed to take with them will be as stated in my proposition of last evening — that is, officers will be allowed their private baggage and side-arms, and mounted officers one horse each. If you mean by your proposition for each brigade to march to the front of the lines now occupied by it, and stack arms at ten o'clock, A. M., and then return to the inside and there remain prisoners until properly paroled, I will make no objection to it. Should no notification be received of your acceptance of my terms by nine o'clock, A. M., I shall regard them as having been rejected, and shall act accordingly. Should these terms be accepted, white flags should be displayed along your lines to prevent such of my troops as may not have been notified from firing upon your men.

"I am, General, very respectfully,

"Your obedient servant,

"U. S. GRANT,

"*Major-General, U. S. A.*"

That was a great day for our country — the 4th of July, 1863. At ten o'clock A. M., Pemberton's exhausted, hungry, ragged army marched out of their entrenchments, and stacked their arms. Over two hours were occupied in this ceremony of surrender, and not an order was given, nor a word spoken. The silence of humiliation on one side, and the silence of sympathy on the other, ruled the hour.

Then the Union army marched into the city and took possession. General Logan's division occupied the post of honor, and raised the old flag over the court-house. Now the silence was broken; and the "boys in blue," who had refrained from all acts of exultation over the "boys in gray," broke forth in song with their favorite chorus, —

"Yes, we'll rally round the flag, boys, we'll rally once again.
    Shouting the battle-cry of freedom;
We'll rally from the hill-side, we'll gather from the plain,
    Shouting the battle-cry of freedom."

It was such a moment as comes to no man but once in a life-time; and there are very few to whom it comes even once. The scene was indescribable The participators only will ever know what it was.

And now occurred an incident illustrative of one of General Grant's strong characteristics. He rode away to call upon the vanquished general — Pemberton — accompanied by his staff. Pemberton was sitting upon the porch of his head-quarters with several of his officers. Neither he nor one of his officers offered General Grant a seat. He took one after the lapse of ten or fifteen minutes, which was vacated by some one who preferred to stand. Being thirsty, Grant asked for water, when Pemberton pointed to the back side of the house, as much as to say, Go and help yourself. Grant went for the water, and found, on his return, his chair occupied. He remained standing during the remainder of the interview.

After leaving the group of distinguished rebels, General Grant's staff expressed their indignation in strong language ; but Grant himself laughed heartily, and said, —

"Well, if Pemberton can stand it, in the circumstances, I can."

One city newspaper had been published through the siege, although the last two weeks its size was reduced to a foot square, on account of the scarcity of paper. Some Union soldiers, printers by trade, were curious enough to examine the printing office, where they found the following paragraph in type, ready to go into the paper : —

"ON DIT. — That the great Ulysses — the Yankee Generalissimo, surnamed Grant — has expressed his intention of dining in Vicksburg on Saturday next, and celebrating the Fourth of July by a grand dinner, and so forth. When asked if he would invite General Jo Johnston to join, he said, 'No! for fear there would be a row at the table.' Ulysses must get into the city before he dines in it. The way to cook a rabbit is, 'first catch the rabbit.'"

The printer-soldiers set to work and issued the paper, with the above paragraph, adding another as follows : —

"The rabbit is caught and cooked. The Yankee Generalissimo, surnamed Grant, did take his dinner in Vicksburg on the glorious Fourth of July, without inviting Gen. Jo Johnston, whom he is to whip again soon."

General Grant's receipts on that Independence Day are worthy of mention, viz : Fifteen generals, thirty-one thousand six hundred soldiers, and one hundred and seventy-two cannon, which some have claimed to be the largest capture at one time ever known in history. He had captured ten thousand four hundred and fifty-nine rebels since the 1st of May, making the sum total forty-two thousand and fifty-nine.

The surrender of Vicksburg filled the North with joy, and the South with dismay. Grant was now "the greatest general on earth." All the reports of the past derogatory to his private or public character were swept out of existence. Nobody would believe that such stories were true of the conqueror of Vicksburg. Eulogistic resolutions from legislatures, conventions, Sunday-schools, and Christian conferences; splendid swords, gold-headed canes. fine horses, university degrees, and other testimo nials of gratitude and love, were showered upon him.

Ordinary men would have been ruined by this sudden and lavish ovation, from Maine to California; but Grant's head was not turned in the least. It kept level as ever, although every paper he read, and every man he met, had only praise for him. He was forced to hear praise, see praise, and eat praise. He had it for breakfast, dinner, and supper. It was cooked in all sorts of ways, and came upon his table in all sorts of dishes. Great men praised him, and little men praised him. Even General Halleck praised him, — one of the most remarkable facts of the war. Halleck wrote to him: —

"In boldness of plan, rapidity of execution, and brilliancy of routes, these operations will compare most favorably with those of Napoleon about Ulm. You and your army have well deserved the gratitude of your country; and it will be the boast of your children, that their fathers were the heroic army which re-opened the Mississippi River."

President Lincoln, whom General Grant resembled in several of the noblest traits of his character, wrote a letter to him, in which his own characteristic magnanimity loomed up grandly, in his purpose to praise the conqueror for his country · —

"EXECUTIVE MANSION, WASHINGTON, July 16, 1863.
"TO MAJOR-GENERAL GRANT.

"*My Dear General*, — I do not remember that you and I ever met personally. I write this now as a grateful acknowledgment for the almost inestimable service you have done the country. I wish to say a word further. When you first reached the vicinity of Vicksburg, I thought you should do what you finally did — march the troops across the neck, run the batteries with the transports, and thus go below; and I never had any faith, except a general hope that you knew better than I, that the Yazoo Pass expedition and the like could succeed. When you got below and took Port Gibson, Grand Gulf, and vicinity, I thought you should go down the river and join General Banks; and when you turned northward east of the Big Black, I feared it was a mistake. I now wish to make the personal acknowledgment *that you were right and I was wrong.* Yours very truly,

"A. LINCOLN."

And yet, Grant's MODESTY never surrendered. It was a tremendous bombardment it received from big and little guns, artillery, infantry, and cavalry; but its flag continued to float over his entrenched manhood, more beautiful, even, than the star-spangled banner which he bore in triumph. It was never trailed in the dust, never abandoned in the field, and never lowered at the call of fame.

General Grant sent Rawlins to Washington immediately upon the fall of Vicksburg, with his report. Rawlins found that the steamers on the Mississippi River were charging soldiers going home on furloughs enormous prices. He reported the facts to General Grant, who issued an order at once, requir ing the steamboat companies to carry soldiers at Government prices. Soon after, word was brought to Grant that the *Hope*, about leaving Vicksburg for Cairo, was charging officers and men from ten to twenty-five dollars each to Cairo. At once, the General wrote an order, requiring the captain to refund to every officer the excess above seven dollars paid, and to every enlisted man the excess above five dollars, and he sent a file of soldiers to enforce the order.

"I will teach these steamboat-men," he said, "that soldiers who have periled their lives to open the Mississippi for their benefit must not be imposed upon."

Grant could never excuse extortion, nor advantage taken of the Government; hence, he opposed speculators, who asked for permits to buy cotton and other merchandise. One day a gentleman handed him a recommendation, signed by several members of Congress and prominent Northern politicians. Grant ran his eye over the document, and said, —

"This is for a permit to buy cotton, is it not?"

"Yes."

"Well, you can take it, and leave these head-quarters at once. If I find you here again I will have you arrested. Men of your class are doing more to corrupt this army than all other kinds of rascality put together."

General Grant said to one speculator, "I have not yet found one honest man following the army as a trader."

It was the last of August now, and the presidential election would occur in November. Northern

States made provision for their soldiers to vote in the field. An inquiry on the subject was sent to him from Iowa, and he replied, —

"Your letter, asking if citizens of the State of Iowa will be allowed to visit this army and distribute tickets when the election is held for soldiers to vote, is just received. In reply I will state that loyal citizens of Northern States will be allowed to visit the troops from their States at any time. Electioneering, or any course calculated to arouse discordant feelings, will be prohibited. The volunteer soldiers of the army will be allowed to hold an election, if the law gives them the right to vote, and *no power shall prevent them from voting the ticket of their choice.*"

How General Grant, himself, would vote, we learn from what he wrote to General Logan, who was stumping the State of Illinois for the Union candidates: —

"I send you ten days' extension of leave, and will give you as many more as you require. I have read your speeches in Illinois, and feel that you are really doing more good there than you could possibly here, while your command is lying idle."

President Lincoln proposed to enlist a hundred thousand colored soldiers, and he wrote to General Grant about it.

"By all means do it. The colored people are thoroughly loyal, and colored men are more easily disciplined than white men. Put as many of them as possible under my command."

Senator Henry Wilson wrote a letter to Mr. Washburne about calling General Grant to the East, and

Mr. Washburne sent the letter to Grant. It called out a characteristic letter from Grant, in which his ruling virtue of modesty is conspicuous, and his views of slavery plainly stated. We extract the following : —

"I fully appreciate all Senator Wilson says. Had it not been for General Halleck and Dana, I think it altogether likely I would have been ordered to the Potomac. My going could do no possible good. They have there able officers who have been brought up with that army, and to import a commander to place over them certainly could produce no good.

"Whilst I would not positively disobey an order, I would have objected most vehemently to taking that command, or any other, except the one I have I can do more with this army than it would be possible for me to do with any other, without time to make the same acquaintance with others I have with this. I know that the soldiers of the Army of the Tennessee can be relied on to the fullest extent. I believe I know the exact capacity of every general in my command to command troops, and just where to place them to get from them their best services. *This is a matter of no small consequence.*

. . . "The people of the North need not quarrel over the institution of slavery. What Vice-president Stevens acknowledges as the corner-stone of the Confederacy is already knocked out. Slavery is already dead, and cannot be resurrected. It would take a standing army to maintain slavery in the South, if we were to make peace to-day, guaranteeing to the South all their former constitutional privileges

"I never was an Abolitionist — not even what could be called Anti-slavery — but I try to judge fairly and honestly; and it became patent to my mind early in the rebellion, that the North and South could never live in peace with each other except as one nation. *As anxious as I am to see peace, and that without slavery, re-established, I would not therefore be willing to see any settlement until this question is forever settled."*

Port Hudson was evacuated soon after the fall of Vicksburg, as Grant predicted. General Halleck thought that Grant should co-operate with Banks and reduce Port Hudson before Vicksburg was assaulted. Grant held that the fall of Vicksburg would necessitate the fall of Port Hudson, and he was right.

He visited New Orleans to confer with General Banks. While there, Banks ordered a grand review, and provided General Grant with the finest horse in the city for the occasion. A steam-whistle frightened the animal, and he ran against a carriage, and both horse and rider fell. This time Grant did not find himself at the top, as usual. The horse was top, and the result was that Grant was in bed twenty days, and then walked with crutches two months. It is the only instance we find of Grant falling from a horse, although he began to ride horseback at five years of age. This time the conqueror was almost conquered by a horse!

On his return to Vicksburg, his wife and children spent some time with him in that city — an episode in his military life, which he enjoyed as only a devoted husband and father can.

XVI.

GREATER THINGS YET.

THE "Father of Waters" rolling now, as President Lincoln said, "unvexed to the sea," greater things than ever were expected of General Grant. Lincoln's confidence in him was confirmed, and those croakers who had worried him for months because he adhered to Grant were silenced. Lincoln disclosed to the editor of *Forney's Chronicle* the trouble he had experienced, when the latter called, just as the news of the fall of Vicksburg reached the President.

"Mr. President, have you any news to give me to-night?" the editor inquired.

"Yes, great news; but you must hurry up, for I have company down stairs, and can't wait long. Grant has taken Vicksburg! Here are two dispatches, one from Rawlins, the other from Hurlburt. Don't stop to read them, but I'll copy the short one, while you copy the long one, as you can write faster than I."

"Mr. Lincoln, this must be most gratifying to you, after standing by Grant so steadfastly," suggested the editor.

"Yes, it is. No man will ever know how much trouble I have had to carry my point about him. The opposition from several of our best Republicans has been so bitter that I could hardly resist it."

"The newspapers assailed him outrageously," added the editor.

"True, but that was n't half the trouble. Why, after Shiloh, a Republican senator from Iowa denounced him to me as blood-thirsty, reckless of human life, and utterly unfit to lead troops; and because I would n't sit down and dismiss him at once, went out in a rage, slamming the door after him. Even within the last two days, senators have demanded his immediate removal."

If President Lincoln had not possessed as much sound common sense, good judgment, self-reliance, and courageous decision as General Grant himself, the latter would never have had the opportunity to capture Vicksburg.

At this time, General Rosecrans was cooped up at Chattanooga with his army of sixty thousand men. The rebels had invested the place with eighty thousand troops, in order to starve him into surrender. He had fought the hard battle of Chickamauga, and was driven back to Chattanooga, within his entrenchments. His situation was critical. His army was subsisting on half-rations, and supplies could reach him only by one hard mountain-road. General Bragg was threatening General Burnside at Knoxville, whose situation was also precarious. General Grant was appointed to command all these forces, including the division of Thomas, the department extending a thousand miles, from Natchez on the Mississippi to Knoxville on the Tennessee. He was to lead the three armies of the West, numbering two hundred thousand men, and provide for them. In order to leave him untrammeled, he was clothed with the powers of a dictator, in part. His control of the "Grand Military Division of the Mississippi" was absolute, necessarily so. If Grant could not save the army of Rosecrans, and deliver the Union cause from great peril in the West, then no one could. This was the feeling of Lincoln and the country.

Grant, by telegram, directed General Thomas to supersede Rosecrans at once, and instructed him—

"To hold Chattanooga at all hazards."

Thomas, whom the soldiers named "Rock of Chickamauga," for his heroic deeds in the late battle, replied,—

"We will hold it till we starve."

On the 23d of October, at midnight, in a hard storm and dense darkness, General Grant reached Chattanooga, and proceeded at once to provide a way to feed the half-starved army. His orders flew like wind in every direction. In five days he brought order out of confusion, had possession of Lookout Valley, with ample food for man and beast pouring into the city; and what was better still, inspired the disheartened army with the hope and enthusiasm of his own soul.

The enemy commanded three important elevations,—Lookout Mountain, Raccoon Mountain, and Missionary Ridge; and here heavy batteries were planted and protected by earth-works. The first elevation was two thousand four hundred feet above the river, the second nearly as high, and the third four hundred feet. To human view it was impossible for Grant, with any number of heroic men, to scale those heights and capture the batteries or drive the foe. Jefferson Davis, the Confederate President, visited Lookout Mountain, and looking down upon the Union forces in pent-up Chattanooga, said, —

"I have them now in the trap I have set for them."

Nevertheless, General Grant resolved to possess the heights. Can't was not in his dictionary. He was still suffering from his injury at New Orleans; and, when he took possession of Lookout Valley, and was obliged to dismount in some hard places, his soldiers had to carry him in their arms. But his presence was absolutely necessary to the successful execution of his plans.

Grant could not assault the aforewarned strongholds until Sherman, who was marching across the country from Memphis with his command — a distance of four hundred miles — arrived. Neither could he send re-enforcements to Burnside until Sherman's arrival. He could make feints — he had a tact for that. He telegraphed Sherman at Florence, —

"The enemy have moved a great part of their force from this front towards Burnside. I have to make an immediate move from here towards their lines of communication, to bring them back if possible. I am anxious to see your old corps he e at the earliest moment."

It became so evident that General Bragg was about to attack Burnside, that Grant resolved to make an assault upon the enemy's works before the arrival of Sherman. He sent the following order to General Thomas, —

"The news is of such a nature, that it becomes an imperative duty for your force to draw the attention of the enemy from Burnside. I deem the best movement to attack to be an attack on the north end of Missionary Ridge with all the force you can bring to bear against it; and, when that is carried, to threaten and attack even the enemy's line of communication between Dalton and Cleveland. Rations should be ready to issue — a sufficiency to last four days — the moment Missionary Ridge is in our possession; rations to be carried in haversacks.

"When there are not horses to move the artillery, mules must be taken from the teams, or horses from ambulances, or, if necessary, officers dismounted and their horses taken; immediate preparations should be made to carry these directions into execution. The movement should not be made a moment later than to-morrow morning."

But so many horses had perished that Grant was obliged to delay the attack until Sherman arrived. The interim was used to complete arrangements for a pontoon bridge five miles above Chattanooga, for the purpose of conveying a portion of Sherman's command across the Tennessee, to operate in the rear of Missionary Ridge.

On the arrival of General Sherman, Grant moved upon Orchard Knoll, and carried it in fifteen minutes; driving the enemy pell-mell out of their works.

Lookout Mountain was fought, and the enemy driven from it. When the reader considers that this mountain was two thousand and four hundred feet above the river, covered with forest trees, and broken by abrupt rocky cliffs, he will understand what bravery and efficiency the Union soldiers must have possessed to carry it by storm. In the face of an appalling fire, they climbed the rugged sides of the mountain, fighting their way up, up, up, until the terrified rebel soldiers broke and ran. General Hooker fought this "battle above the clouds," though the programme was Grant's. The enemy fled to Missionary Ridge, where another battle was fought the next day, and the Ridge captured. Sherman moved upon the Ridge from the north, and Hooker from the south. Then Thomas pushed forward his whole force from the centre, to carry the Ridge by storm. Grant's programme contemplated that, at this juncture, Bragg would send a column to meet Sherman's assault; and he did, much to Grant's satisfaction, who had taken his position on Orchard Knoll, where he could watch the progress of the fight. Thomas' army, in four columns, was concealed by the knoll, awaiting the call of Grant. The moment the latter saw a column of Bragg's army going to repel Sherman, he shouted, —

"Now, boys, onward!"

Six rousing guns gave the signal to charge, and

Grant himself cheered lustily as Thomas' four columns, led by Johnson, Sheridan, Wood, and Baird, started off upon the double-quick. Not a word was spoken, nor a gun fired; but, with glistening bayonets fixed, they rushed upon the first line of rifle-pits, capturing them in three minutes, with a thousand prisoners; then chasing the rebel fugitives, — many of whom threw down their arms, and fled in dismay,— to the second line of rifle-pits higher up. Thirty pieces of artillery, and regiments of musketry, poured a deadly fire upon our brave troops as they clambered up the hill, cutting down five men in succession, who bore the same Union colors; but the rank and file wavered not, but swept on, on, up, up, capturing the second line of pits, and more prisoners still, amid the wildest cheers that were ever raised in the name of freedom. On the summit was still another line of rifle-pits, where sharp-shooters swarmed, and gunners hurled shot and shell in showers. But, with unbroken columns, the brave patriots pressed on in the face of death, with shouts of triumph which wellnigh drowned the roar of the artillery, and poured into the rebel works upon the crest — a living torrent of victorious men. The movement was executed so speedily, and with such resistless power, that flesh and blood could not resist the charge. And still the battle raged upon the summit. The enemy fought with desperation; sixty cannons belched fire every minute; conquerors and conquered grappling in deadly contest; the cheers of the living mingling with the cries and groans of the dying in horrible confusion, until whole regiments threw down their arms and fled for safety; the Union soldiers turning the rebel batteries, which they had faced, upon the fugitives, to accelerate their flight. The day was won; the Union flag was raised. General Grant appeared upon the scene, which was the signal for a fresh round of cheers, which were heard with delight in Chattanooga. Seven thousand prisoners were taken, ten thousand stands of arms, and fifty-two pieces of artillery; and the battle-ground was literally covered with the rebel slain.

General Grant's telegram to General Halleck at the close of that terrible day was like all his reports, — *modest* to a fault :—

"Although the battle lasted from early dawn till dark this evening, I believe I am not premature in announcing a complete victory over Bragg. Lookout Mountain-top, all the rifle-pits in Chattanooga Valley, and Missionary Ridge entire, have been carried, and are now held by us. I have no idea of finding Bragg here to-morrow."

Early the next morning General Grant in person conducted a vigorous pursuit of the enemy. All along the way he found proof that the rebel army was terribly demoralized and broken; for broken wagons, abandoned guns, scattered fire-arms, cartridge-boxes, maimed and exhausted men, strewed the roads. Whole regiments, finding themselves closely pursued, threw down their arms and ran like sheep in every direction, or gave themselves up as willing captives. The overthrow of the enemy was complete. The rank and file of the Southern army saw how wickedly their leaders had deceived them.

Jefferson Davis said in a speech at Memphis in 1861:—

"You need not fear to cast off your allegiance to the General Government. There will be no war. The Yankees will never fight. One Southern man can, at any time, whip five Northern men,—if he can only run fast enough to catch them."

And now the flower of his army was routed, and were fleeing in consternation from the Yankees who had not courage enough to fight! The Southern Confederacy was broken; and destruction and desolation were taking the place of thrift and progress.

An amusing incident occurred when Longstreet discovered the Union forces on the hills above Lookout Valley, showing how the comic will sometimes mingle with the tragic in war. The Confederate general saw at once that the siege of Chattanooga must be raised if Grant's men were not driven from that position. So, in the darkness of night, he attacked them, and a severe battle was fought. In the engagement, a large number of mules became frightened, broke from their wagons, and ran furiously towards the enemy, who supposed, in the darkness, that it was a cavalry-charge; and they became panic-stricken and fled. A soldier-poet produced the following parody the next day:—

> "Mules to the right of them,
> Mules to the left of them,
> Mules in front of them,
>   Pawed, brayed, and thundered.
>
> Breaking their own confines,
> Breaking through Longstreet's lines,

> Into the Georgia troops,
> Stormed the two hundred.
>
> Wild all their eyes did glare,
> Whisked all their tails in the air,
> Scattering the 'Chivalry' there,
> All the world wondered."

As soon as the pursuit of the enemy was relinquished, General Grant sent Sherman with his command to relieve Burnside. Longstreet had invested Knoxville with his army, expecting to starve out Burnside; but the brave general did not starve easily. Before Sherman reached Knoxville, Longstreet made a vigorous assault upon Burnside's works, and a severe battle was fought. Longstreet was repulsed with heavy loss. Hearing that the Union army had captured the rebel strongholds at Chattanooga, and that re-enforcements were on the way to Burnside, he very wisely raised the siege, and ran away.

How thoroughly the rebel commanders trusted in their works at Chattanooga, the following fact shows: A woman residing on the plateau of Missionary Ridge told one of our Union generals, that Bragg had not the least idea that the whole Union army could capture Lookout Mountain or Missionary Ridge.

"Just before you all came up here," she said, "I asked him, 'What are you going to do with me, general?' and he answered, 'Lord! madam, the Yankees will never dare to come up here!' And it was not more than fifteen minutes before you were all around here."

The author of the Military History of General Grant says of this memorable battle:—

"Few battles have ever been won so strictly according to the plan laid down. Grant's instructions in advance would almost serve as a history of the contest. Hooker was to draw attention to the right, to seize and hold Lookout Mountain; while Sherman, attacking Missionary Ridge on the extreme left, was still further to distract the enemy; and then, when re-enforcements and attention should be drawn to both the rebel flanks, the centre was to be assaulted by the main body of Grant's force, under Thomas. Everything happened exactly as had been foreseen.

"Each event proceeded regularly according to the calculation. Each subordinate carried out his part exactly as he had been ordered. Each army, brought from a distance, came upon the spot intended, crossed a river or climbed a mountain at the precise moment; and even the unexpected emergencies of the fight contributed to the result, as if anticipated and arranged. In this respect Chattanooga was one of the most notable battles ever fought."

Again the loyal States were made wild with enthusiasm over Grant's victories, and no eulogy of the chief was considered extravagant. President Lincoln appointed another day of National Thanksgiving for the Chattanooga victory, and both pulpit and press exalted the genius and bravery of Grant. Other generals had a forte in creating Fast Days; but General Grant's forte lay in another direction—that of Thanksgiving.

Congress assembled just after this last great victory, and adopted the following resolution:—

"That the thanks of Congress be, and they hereby are, presented to Maj.-Gen. Ulysses S. Grant, and through him to the officers and soldiers who have fought under his command during this rebellion, for the gallantry and good conduct in the battles in which they have been engaged; and that the President of the United States be requested to cause a gold medal to be struck, with suitable emblems, devices, and inscriptions, to be presented to Major-General Grant."

The medal was designed by Leutze. On one side was a profile likeness of Grant, surrounded by a laurel-wreath. His name and victories were inscribed upon it, and all surrounded by a galaxy of stars. On the reverse was the figure of Fame, sitting on the American Eagle, in her right-hand a trumpet, in her left a scroll bearing the names of Corinth, Vicksburg, Mississippi River, and Chattanooga on her head a helmet; front of the eagle the emblematical shield of the United States; beneath, the pine and palm entertwined; and over all, " Proclaim Liberty through the Land."

President Lincoln sent to him the following:—

"Understanding that your lodgement at Chattanooga and at Knoxville is now secure, I wish to tender you, and all under your command, my more than thanks, my profoundest gratitude, for the skill, courage, and perseverance with which you and they, over so great difficulties, have effected that important cb ject. God bless you all!"

On the 10th of December, General Grant issued the following congratulatory order to his troops, in which he ascribes all the glory to them, as if their illustrious commander were of no account whatever: —

"The General commanding takes the opportunity of returning his sincere thanks and congratulations to the brave armies of the Cumberland, the Ohio, and the Tennessee, and their comrades from the Potomac, for the recent splendid and decisive successes achieved over the enemy. In a short time you have recovered from him the control of the Tennessee River, from Bridgeport to Knoxville. You dislodged him from his great stronghold upon Lookout Mountain; drove him from Chattanooga Valley; wrested from his determined grasp the possession of Missionary Ridge; repelled, with heavy loss to him, his repeated assaults upon Knoxville; forced him to raise the siege there, driving him, at all points utterly routed and discomfited, beyond the limits of the State.

"By your noble heroism and determined courage, you have most effectually defeated the plans of the enemy for regaining possession of the States of Kentucky and Tennessee. You have secured positions from which no rebellious power can drive or dislodge you. For all this the General commanding thanks you collectively and individually. The loyal people of the United States thank and bless you. Their hopes and prayers against this unholy rebellion are with you daily; their faith in you will not be in vain; their hopes will not be blasted; their prayers to Almighty God will be answered. You will yet go to other fields of strife; and with the invincible bravery, and unflinching loyalty to justice and right, which have characterized you in the past, you will prove that no enemy can withstand you, and that no defenses, however **formidable,** can check your onward **march."**

XVII.

THE ROLL OF HONOR.

GENERAL GRANT wasted no time after the Chattanooga victory.
"The enemy must not be allowed to rest or concentrate," he said. "The war will be brought to an end only by the destruction of the Confederate army."

He wrote to General Halleck,—

"I am now collecting as large a cavalry force as can be spared, at Savannah, Tenn., to cross the Tennessee River, and co-operate with the cavalry from Hurlburt's command, in clearing out entirely the forces now collecting in West Tennessee under Forrest. It is the design that the cavalry, after finishing the work they first start upon, shall push south through East Mississippi, and destroy the Mobile Road as far south as they can. Sherman goes to Memphis and Vicksburg in person, and will have Grenada visited, and such other points on the Mississippi Central Railroad as may require it. I want the State of Mississippi so visited that large armies cannot traverse there this winter."

His three armies were distributed as follows:—

General Thomas was at Chattanooga, watching the movements of Bragg; General Schofield was at

Knoxville, looking after Longstreet; and General Sherman went on a raid into the interior of Mississippi — all parts of one plan by Grant's fertile brain. Sherman's raid was magnificent in its results, furnishing additional proof of his chief's remarkable knowledge of the situation, enabling him to strike blows at the right time and in the right place. Sherman marched four hundred miles; drove the rebels out of Mississippi; destroyed all the railroads; supported his army upon stores which he captured, and brought back four hundred prisoners, five thousand negroes, a thousand white refugees, and three thousand animals. His loss was twenty-one killed, and one hundred and forty-nine wounded and missing.

Grant must know his armies, their condition, needs, and spirit, even to the outposts; so he determined upon a tour of inspection, though it was cold winter weather. He visited Nashville and Knoxville, infusing not a little of his own enthusiasm into his soldiers; and from the latter place traveled on horseback to Louisville, by the way of the Cumberland Gap, because he desired to know the exact condition of the roads. The weather was bitter cold in the mountains, and the exposure and peril great. The officers who accompanied him described their sufferings as intense; yet the General did not appear to mind so slight an inconvenience, so absorbed was he in conquering the rebellion.

At Lexington thousands of people assembled to see the hero of Vicksburg and Chattanooga. They crowded into the city from the surrounding country to do him honor.

"A speech! a speech! a speech!"
The call for a speech from the conqueror was general and earnest. They would not take *no* for an answer. Finally, General Coombs of his staff mounted a chair and said, —

"General Grant has told me, in confidence, that he never made a speech, knows nothing about speech-making, and has no disposition to learn."

He was summoned to St. Louis to see one of his children who was seriously ill. The citizens grew wild over him. Thousands gathered about the hotel to get sight of him. They ran after him on the streets, and cheered until they were hoarse. Finally, they invited him to a public dinner. He replied: —

"Your highly complimentary invitation to meet old acquaintances, and make new ones, at a dinner to be given by citizens of St. Louis, is just received. I will state that I have only visited St. Louis on this occasion to see a sick child. Finding, however, that he has passed the crisis of his disease, and is pronounced out of danger by his physicians, I accept the invitation. My stay in this city will be short, — probably not beyond the first proximo. On to-morrow I shall be engaged. Any other day of my stay here, and any place selected by the citizens of St. Louis, it will be agreeable for me to meet them.

"I have the honor to be,

"Very respectfully, your obedient servant,

"U. S. GRANT."

A large number sat down to the dinner. When the toast was given, "Our distinguished guest, Major

General Grant," the band played "Hail to the Chief," and General Grant arose with less self-possession than he ever maintained in the direst battle, and said, —

"Gentlemen, in response, it will be impossible for me to do more than to thank you."

In the evening he was serenaded, and an immense crowd gathered around and near the hotel. They wanted to see the General whose fame had gone out through all the land; and, of course, they clamored for a speech. That would bring him out upon the balcony His appearance upon the balcony, with hat in hand, was the signal for one of the craziest demonstrations of delight the city ever witnessed. As soon as the cheering ceased, the General said, —

"Gentlemen, I thank you for this honor. I cannot make a speech. It is something I have never done and never intend to do; and I beg you will excuse me."

The General's statement was not quite correct. He had forgotten the little speech he made for a Methodist minister in his boyhood, — "You'd scarce expect one of my age," etc.; with that exception, his statement was literally true.

"A speech! a speech!"

The call was louder than ever for a speech. The multitude would not be put off.

"Tell them that you can fight for them, but cannot talk for them," suggested a friend. "Do tell them that."

"No; I must get some one else to tell them that."

Then, leaning over the railing, the General spoke,—

"Gentlemen, making speeches is not my business. I never did it in my life and never will. I thank you, however, for your attendance here," then bowed and retired.

While these things were going on as here narrated, the leading men of the country, in Washington, were trying to arrange suitable honors for the conquering General. Congress, by special act, revived the rank of lieutenant-general, which a grateful country created for Washington; since which time, no one but General Scott had shared the honor. It was done that the President might appoint General Grant to fill the high position.

Mr. Lincoln remarked, after having signed the bill,—

"I have never seen Grant. Before I appoint him to the command of the armies, I want to learn all about him. Who of his friends knows him best?"

"Russell Jones, United States Marshal for Illinois," answered Mr. Washburne. "You know him well; and he knows Grant thoroughly."

So Mr. Jones, who was in Washington at the time, was summoned to the White House.

"What do you know about Grant, Mr. Jones?" inquired the President.

"I know he is a great general, whose modesty is equal to his bravery; and a thoroughly honest man."

The conversation continued for some time, the President asking many questions, until he had no more questions to ask.

"Now, Mr. President," continued Jones, "perhaps you would like to know whether Grant is going to be a candidate for the presidency?"

"Yes; I confess to a little curiosity on that point."

"Well, I have just received a reply from him to my questions on the subject. It is a private letter; but I see no impropriety in showing it to you, and it will be more satisfactory than anything I can tell you."

The President read the letter, in which Grant said that "he had not the least wish for the high office; and that even if he had an ambition in that direction, he would not permit his name to be used, because he himself was in favor of Abraham Lincoln above all men, and under all circumstances."

President Lincoln laughed as he returned the letter to Jones, remarking, —

"I wanted to know; for when this presidential grub once gets to gnawing at a man, nobody can tell how far in it has got. It is generally a good deal deeper than he himself supposes."

It was the last of February, 1864, and people were discussing presidential candidates. General Grant was the favorite candidate of many; and he was consulted by several leading men about running for the office. Most of these letters he did not answer, because he was personally opposed to the candidacy of Ulysses S. Grant. One of these letters was written by a son of Senator Morris, who secured Grant's appointment to West Point, and this letter he answered. It is so characteristic, and so decidedly confirms all that we have said concerning

Grant's leading qualities, from boyhood to manhood, that we quote it entire : —

"Your letter of the 29th of December I did not see until two days ago. I receive many such, but do not answer. Yours, however, is written in such a kindly spirit, and as you ask for an answer confidentially, I will not withhold it.

"Allow me to say, however, that I am not a politician, never was, and I hope never to be, and could not write a political letter. My only desire is to serve the Country in her present trials. To do this efficiently it is necessary to have the confidence of the army and of the people. I know no way to better secure this end than by a faithful performance of my duties.

"So long as I hold my present position, I do not believe I have the right to criticise the policy or orders of those above me, or to give utterance to views of my own, except to the authorities at Washington, and the general-in-chief of the army. In this respect I know I have proven myself a good soldier.

"In your letter you say that I have it in my power to be the next President. This is the last thing in the world I desire. I would regard such a consummation, as highly unfortunate for myself, if not for the Country. Through Providence I have attained to more than I ever hoped, and, with the position I now hold in the regular army, if allowed to retain it, will be more than satisfied.

' I certainly shall never state a sentiment, or the expression of a thought, with the view to being a candidate for office. I scarcely know the inducement that could be held out to me to accept office, and unhesitatingly say that I infinitely prefer my present position to **that of any civil office within the gift of the people.**

"This is a private letter to you, and not intended for others to see, or read, because I want to avoid being heard from by the public except through my acts, in the performance of my legitimate duties."

On the third day of March, General Grant was summoned to Washington by the Secretary of War He received, also, a communication from General Halleck, as follows: —

"The Secretary of War directs me to say that your commission as lieutenant-general is signed, and will be delivered to you on your arrival at the War Department. I sincerely congratulate you on this recognition of your distinguished and meritorious services."

Before leaving for Washington, he penned a familiar and noble letter to General Sherman, to whom he was attached as to a brother. The letter is so charged with Grant, that we want our readers to study it carefully: —

"*Dear Sherman*, — The bill reviving the grade of lieutenant-general has become a law, my name has been sent to the Senate for the place. I now receive orders to report to Washington immediately in person, which indicates a confirmation, or a likelihood of confirmation. I start in the morning to comply with the order.

"Whilst I have been eminently successful in this war. in at least gaining the confidence of the public, no one feels more than I how much of this success is due to the energy, skill, and the harmonious putting forth of that energy and skill, of those whom it has been my good fortune to have occupying subordinate positions under me.

"There are many officers to whom these remarks are

applicable to a greater or less degree, proportionate to their ability as soldiers; but what I want is, to express my thanks to you and McPherson, as the men to whom, above all others, I feel indebted for whatever I have had of success.

" How far your advice and assistance have been of help to me, you know. How far your execution of whatever has been given you to do entitles you to the reward I am receiving, you cannot know as well as I.

"I feel all the gratitude this letter would express, giving it the most flattering construction. The word *you*, I use in the plural, intending it for McPherson also. I would write to him, and will some day; but, starting in the morning, I do not know that I will find time just now.

" Your friend,

"U. S. GRANT."

Grant's letter to Sherman could be excelled in its magnanimity and real friendship only by Sherman's reply to Grant, which ought to be read with it; because together the communications show how the great natures of two illustrious men trusted each other: —

" Dear General, — I have your more than kind and characteristic letter of the 4th inst. I will send a copy to General McPherson at once.

" You do yourself injustice, and us too much honor, in assigning to us too large a share of the merits which have led to your high advancement. I know you approve the friendship I have ever proffered to you, and will permit me to continue, as heretofore, to manifest it on all proper occasions.

" You are now Washington's legitimate successor, and occupy a position of almost dangerous elevation; but if you can continue, as heretofore, to be yourself, — simple, honest, and unpretending, — you will enjoy through life the respect and love of friends, and the homage of millions of human beings who will award you a large share in securing to them and their descendants a government of law and stability.

" I repeat, you do General McPherson and myself too much honor. At Belmont, you manifested your traits, neither of us being near. At Donelson, also, you illustrated your whole character. I was not near, and General McPherson was in too subordinate a capacity to influence you.

" Until you had won Donelson, I confess I was almost cowed by the terrible array of anarchical elements that presented themselves at every point; but that admitted a ray of light I have followed since. I believe you are as brave, patriotic, and just, as the great prototype, Washington; as unselfish, kind-hearted, and honest as a man should be; but the chief characteristic is the simple faith in success you have always manifested, which I can liken to nothing else than the faith a Christian has in the Savior.

" This faith gave you the victory at Shiloh and at Vicksburg. Also, when you have completed your best preparations, you go into battle without hesitation, as at Chattanooga, — no doubts, no reserves ; and, I tell you, it was this which made us act with confidence.

" My only point of doubt was in your knowledge of grand strategy, and of books of science and of history; but I confess your common-sense seems to have supplied all these.

" Now, as to the future. Don't stay in Washington. Come West; take to yourself the whole Mississippi Valley. Let us make it dead sure ; and, I tell you, the Atlantic slopes and Pacific shores will follow its destiny as surely as the limbs of a tree live or die with the main trunk. We have done much, but still much remains. Time, and time's influence, are with us. We could almost afford to sit still, and let these influences work.

"Here lies the seat of the coming empire; and from the West, when our task is done, we will make short work of Charleston and Richmond and the impoverished coast of the Atlantic. Your sincere friend,

"W. T. SHERMAN."

The telegraph had told the whole country that Grant was summoned to Washington. As a result, his journey thither was that of a mighty conqueror, without any planning of his, and very much to his annoyance. At every railroad station where the train stopped, crowds of people gathered, with bands and banners; and "Hail to the Chief" was played, and cheers for the hero of Donelson, Vicksburg, Corinth, and Chattanooga, repeated, until the modest General was surfeited.

On reaching Washington he went quietly to Willard's Hotel, and sat down unobserved at the dining-table. A gentleman at the table knew him; and he immediately arose, and said, —

"Ladies and gentlemen, we are honored at this table by the presence of Gen. Ulysses S. Grant."

The announcement was electric. Every guest rose as by instinct, and men and women joined in the ovation to the world-renowned General. The men sent up cheer after cheer, and women waved their white handkerchiefs, like flags of truce, to the utter surprise of the warrior.

In the evening he attended the President's levee at the White House. The crowd rushed in to see aim. The mansion was crammed. Hundreds could not gain admittance. The enthusiasm was unbounded. The President himself joined in the cheers and every other demonstration in Grant's honor, with the liveliest interest. Lincoln and Grant were alike in their unselfish, humble, and patriotic spirit. As he retired from the levee or that night, he remarked to a friend, —

"I hope to get away from Washington as soon as possible, for I am tired of the show-business already. This is the hottest campaign I ever fought."

He was more at home on the battle-field than he was in Washington. His whole soul was absorbed in conquering the Rebellion, for which he asked no reward.

On March 9th, the President presented him with his commission as lieutenant-general. The ceremony took place in the Executive Chamber. The Cabinet were present, and many invited guests. President Lincoln thus spoke : —

"General Grant: The Nation's approbation of what you have already done, and its reliance on you for what remains to do in the existing great struggle, is now presented, with this commission constituting you *Lieutenant-General* of the Army of the United States. With this high honor devolves on you a corresponding responsibility. As the country here intrusts you, so under God it will sustain you. I scarcely need add, that with what I here speak for the Nation goes my own hearty personal concurrence."

General Grant replied : —

"Mr. President: I accept this commission with gratitude for the high honor conferred. With the aid of the noble armies, who have fought on so many fields for our common country, it will be my earnest endeavor not to disappoint your expectations. I feel the full weight of the responsibility now devolving upon me. I know that, if it is properly met, it will be due to these armies, and, above all, to the favor of that Providence which leads both nations and men."

While the General was in Washington, prominent ladies desired to have a ball in his honor. There was to be a grand review of the Army of the Potomac; and they proposed that it should be on the evening of that day. A committee of ladies waited upon him, to secure his consent thereto; but he dashed several pailfuls of very cold water on the scheme, by saying, —

"Ladies: I am not a cynic, and enjoy rational pleasure as well as any one else; but I would ask you, in all candor and gentleness, if this is a time for music and dancing and feasting among officers in the army? Is our country in a condition to call for such things at present? Do army balls inspire our troops with courage in the field? Do they soothe our sick and wounded in the hospitals?"

Mrs. Lincoln gave a grand military dinner in honor of General Grant. Twelve other prominent generals were invited. But Grant was in a hurry to return to the West, and he so stated to Mrs. Lincoln, whereupon she pressed her claim as a woman only can.

"I trust that you will excuse me, in the circumstances," he urged. "My presence is needed now in the field."

"I do not see how we *can* excuse you," pleaded Mr. Lincoln. "It would be Hamlet with the Prince left out."

"I appreciate fully the honor Mrs. Lincoln would do me, but time is precious; and — really — Mr. President, *I have had enough of the show business.*"

Doubtless he spoke the truth in the last sentence. This lavish bestowal of public admiration upon him was not at all congenial. It was a terrific charge upon his modesty. He had to flee.

Mrs. Lincoln gave her grand military dinner, but General Grant was not there — he was on his way to the "Grand Military Department of Mississippi." The society of twelve generals, in conference, to destroy the Confederate army, he coveted; but their society in feasting and pleasure, he did not seek.

He reached Cincinnati on Sunday morning, where he was to spend the day with his parents. His father sent his carriage to the station for him; but before the carriage returned, he was surprised to see the Lieutenant-General coming into the house with his carpet-bag in his hand. The driver looked for a great man with epaulettes and gold braid; but discovered no such one in the crowd alighting from the cars. The General wore no badge of honor and his overcoat was plain army-blue.

When he reached Nashville, he found an order from the War Department, appointing him to the command of all the armies of the United States, with head-quarters in the field ; superceding General Halleck, who treated him rudely in the early part of the war. Halleck was to remain in Washington as his chief-of-staff ; Sherman to succeed him in command of the Military Division of Mississippi ; and McPherson to take Sherman's place as commander of the Department of Tennessee.

General Grant was obliged to retrace his steps to Washington as soon as possible ; and that was in half the time ordinary generals would have required for so important a change. He took with him his wife and children, and Rawlins, Rowley, Duff, Bowers, Leet, Parker, and Badeau, of his staff. His arrival in Washington, as commander of all the armies of the United States, was hailed with universal joy ; for it augured to loyal hearts the speedy overthrow of the "Southern Confederacy."

XVIII.

ON TO RICHMOND.

WHEN General Grant assumed command of all the armies of the United States, with head-quarters at Culpepper Court House, the skein of military affairs was very much tangled. General Halleck could not pick out the snarl. Things were discouragingly mixed. True, some victories had been achieved in the East; but, on the whole, little progress had been made. Grant was expected to remove the tangle. "The two men were as opposite in their ideas of how the war should be carried on as they were in how a battle should be fought. One was for cutting off the tail first, and then the claws, and so work by regular, safe approaches up to the head; the other, for a close and deadly interlock, in which the life of one or the other should go out before it should unloose. One wished to carry on the war by operating with different armies in separate points; the other, for concentrating them all on one vital point. Like Napoleon, Grant had no idea of winter-quarters, or the proper season for carrying on a campaign. When once his blows began to fall, he proposed they should never cease falling until the object was ground to powder.'

"Lincoln is right," said Grant. "'Keep pegging away' is his motto. To hammer continuously against the armed force of the enemy until, by the mere attrition of the lesser with the larger body, the former shall be worn out, — is the way to do it."

Grant was often like Lincoln in his illustrations, — homely, but pat. To the inquiry, "What is the trouble?" he answered, —

"The armies in the East and West acted independently and without concert, like a balky team, no two ever pulling together; enabling the enemy to use to great advantage his interior lines of communication for transporting troops from East to West, re-enforcing the army most vigorously pressed; and to furlough large numbers during seasons of inactivity on our part, to go to their homes and do the work of providing for the support of their armies; so that it was a question whether our numerical strength and resources were not more than balanced by these disadvantages, and the enemy's superior position."

Grant knew how to manage a "balky team," and no team was long "balky" under his control; and this homely view of the situation enabled him to draw the reins just right on the fiery steed of war. Halleck was a book-general, made to order at West Point, and sent out to wage war according to rules taught in the text-books for generations. Grant ignored books, and took a plain, common-sense view of things, and acted accordingly, rule or no rule. A way of fighting which seemed practical, and therefore promising, to him he adopted, though it upset all the military text-books, and defied the whole curriculum of West Point. This fact explains a remark of Sherman:—

"General Grant is not a man of remarkable learning; but he is one of the bravest I ever saw. I do not say he is a hero—I do not believe in heroes; but I know he is a gentleman and good man."

And just here we might record Grant's opinion of Sherman, since it has so much horse in it, and is, withal, so pat:—

"I always find it the best way to turn Sherman out like a young colt, and let him kick up his heels. I have great confidence that he will come in all right in due time."

Grant's sharp observation learned more from a *horse*, to help him in crushing the Rebellion, than some of the generals acquired at West Point! Thirty years before, he found that the best way to do with a balky colt was to sell him; and, on the same principle, he got rid of McClernand in the Vicksburg campaign, and other balky officers, at different times, later in the war.

Grant always shouldered great responsibilities; and he seemed to carry a great one with the same ease that he carried a small one. He drove a pair of horses at eight years of age, as we have seen; at ten, loaded logs which usually required five men to load; at twelve, went to Louisville to transact legal business for his father; bought and sold horses as men buy and sell them ; and so, bearing heavy burdens of care from boyhood upward, Providence disciplined him to shoulder the greatest responsibility in 1864 that any one man ever bore. At the outbreak of the war, he doubted whether he could lead a regiment; but now he was the commander of nearly a million men; his field of operations extending from the Potomac to the Rio Grande, — FIVE THOUSAND MILES, — including, also, a naval force of SIX HUNDRED vessels of war, on the rivers and along the coast for two thousand five hundred miles; while FOUR THOUSAND CANNON waited for his command to belch their thunders. What a mountain of care! What an empire of war to control! What mighty power! Going back to his remarkable childhood, the way in which the Lord led him on and up to this imperial charge, is both clear and marvellous.

General Grant soon brought order out of confusion, and had his great army well in hand, to fall upon the foe. Richmond, Atlanta, and Mobile must be captured, and movements against them at once inaugurated. Their fall would be the fall of the Rebellion. Such was General Grant's view of the situation. His plan was for General Banks to operate against Mobile; General Sherman against Atlanta; while he himself would move on Richmond. These were parts of one stupendous whole.

Circumstances, however, interfered with the operations of Banks against Mobile, so that the whole army was hurled against Richmond and Atlanta.

Some ladies in Washington asked Mrs. Grant, at this time, what she thought of her husband's prospects in this new and more difficult field of action.

"Mr. Grant has succeeded thus far," she replied,

"wherever the Government has placed him; and he will do the best he can."

"Do you think he will capture Richmond?"

"Yes, before he gets through. *Mr. Grant always was a very obstinate man.*"

Another example of General Grant's magnanimity we must record here. He asked to have Rawlins, his chief-of-staff, made brigadier-general; and some senators thought it could not be done legally, because he had never led a command on the field. This objection drew out the following, addressed to Senator Wilson: —

"General Rawlins has served with me from the beginning of the Rebellion. I know he has most richly earned his present position. He comes the nearest being indispensable to me of any officer in the service. But if his confirmation is dependent on his commanding troops, he shall command troops at once. There is no department commander, near where he has served, that would not most gladly give him the very largest and most responsible command his rank would entitle him to. . . . If he fails to be confirmed, besides the loss it will be to the service and to me personally, I shall feel that, by keeping with me a valuable officer, because he made himself valuable, I have worked him an injury."

The fourth day of May was fixed as the time for Grant's great army to start for Richmond. Sheridan led the advance, followed by four thousand covered wagons, and column after column of well-trained troops, under floating banners, farther than the eye could see; moving forward out of sight to make room for other hosts marching with glittering bayonets to strains of martial music that filled the air from a hundred bands.

The army crossed the Rapidan at two fords, six miles apart, and lay down for rest at night in the edge of a vast wilderness. The next morning the "Battle of the Wilderness" opened. It was a fearfully bloody contest in the woods, where neither artillery nor cavalry was of any service. An eyewitness wrote, —

"Manœuvering here had been out of the question, and only Indian tactics told. The troops could only receive direction by a point of the compass; for not only were the lines of battle entirely hidden from the sight of the commander, but no officer could see ten files on each side of him. Artillery was wholly ruled out of use, the massive concentration of three hundred guns stood silent. Cavalry was still more useless. But in that horrid thicket there lurked two hundred thousand men, and through it lurid fires played; and, though no array of battle could be seen, there came out of it the crackle and roll of musketry, like the noisy boiling of some hell-caldron, that told the dread story of death."

It was an unexpected battle to Grant, in an unexpected place, at an unexpected time; but he held his own with great slaughter.

Longstreet arrived during the night to re-enforce Lee; and early the next morning, the two armies, without waiting for breakfast, fell upon each other again. Grant drove back the rebel force, many of whom retreated upon the run, until Longstreet's fresh troops came up to share the brunt of battle. Now the retreating columns stopped, and again the battle raged in a perfect storm of fire. Grant's troops were driven back a mile; but just then Burnside arrived with his thirty thousand soldiers, and the conflict continued, fierce, bloody, and hideous. At the close of the day, Grant's army held the position they did in the morning, Soldiers did not stop for rations during the day, and both sides were completely exhausted. At night the enemy took refuge within his entrenchments.

Both armies rested on the next day; and, at night, Grant silently marched away for Spottsylvania, for the purpose of getting between the enemy and Richmond. But Lee learned of the movement, and took up his march for Spottsylvania, also; a hard battle followed, and the Union advance was repulsed. The day after, Grant started Sheridan off on a raid to break Lee's communications with Richmond, and moved again upon the enemy's works with renewed energy. Through the whole day the battle raged with great fury; five times the Union General Hancock was driven back, and five times he rallied and pushed back the enemy, capturing four thousand prisoners and thirty guns. But the enemy was still safe within the works.

Grant said to a journalist, —

"It has been my experience that, though the Southerners fight desperately at first, yet when we hang on for a day or two, we whip them awfully."

We have said that Grant did not expect a battle

in the wilderness on Thursday. An orderly came dashing up and said, —

"Warren has met the enemy."

Grant scarcely believed it.

"Then the rebels have left a division here to fool us while they concentrate toward the North Anna," suggested General Meade, commander of the Army of the Potomac.

Just then a dispatch arrived from Sheridan, —

"The enemy mean to fight us here."

"Very well," answered Grant; "let him be attacked vigorously wherever he appears."

When night had put an end to hostilities, Grant ordered, —

"Move upon the enemy at four o'clock in the morning. It is of great importance that *we* should begin the battle."

At Spottsylvania, Grant lost one of his best generals — Sedgwick. He was leading his corps in the face of sharp-shooters when he saw some of his men dodge the bullets. Laughingly he said, —

"Pooh, men, don't duck; they couldn't hit an elephant at that distance."

The words were scarcely uttered when a bullet pierced his brain, and he fell dead instantly.

Rumors reached Washington, after the fight at Spottsylvania, that Grant was in full retreat. Fugitives from the army poured into Washington, several hundreds of them, and four runaway Union colonels were taken in irons to the War Department. There was great consternation in the city. Lincoln and Stanton were exceedingly anxious, and they started off Dana, Assistant Secretary of War, to the front, at midnight, by special train. But they called him back from Alexandria, by telegram.

"We are afraid to have you go to-night. The langer of your capture is too great," said Mr Lincoln.

"Then I will go home to bed; good-night."

"Are you afraid to make the journey?" inquired the President.

"Oh, no; I have a good escort, and two of Sedgwick's officers, who know every ford of the Rapidan and every foot of the country."

"Then," added Mr. Lincoln to Stanton, "I guess we'd better let him go."

He did go, and found Grant and Meade safe and hopeful on Saturday noon, making their dinner of sandwiches.

Cadwallader, correspondant of the *New York Herald*, accompanied Grant's army; and he started from Spottsylvania for Washington with a bag full of letters for head-quarters and dispatches of his own. He was captured by guerillas at midnight; but in the morning a small force of Union soldiers were encountered, and, in the skirmish, Cadwallader gave the sergeant who had him in charge, a horse, saddle, and bridle, and two hundred dollars, to look in the opposite direction while he escaped.

The country was so agitated by false rumors about Grant, after the Spottsylvania affair, that President Lincoln issued the following :—

"*To the Friends of Union and Liberty*,—Enough is known of the army operations within the last five days to claim our special gratitude to God. While what remains undone demands our most sincere prayers to, and reliance upon, Him without whom all human effort is vain, I recommend that all patriots, at their homes, in their places of public worship, and wherever they may be, unite in common thanksgiving and prayer to Almighty God."

The bloodiest battle was on the 10th of May. Nearly three hundred thousand soldiers and five hundred guns, on both sides, engaged in mortal combat, and over ten thousand men fell on each side. The Union army made decided gain on this day. In answer to the inquiry, "How does it look, General?" Grant said, —

"We are going through; there is no doubt about it."

Mr. Washburne, of Galena, Grant's old friend, had accompanied him to Spottsylvania, and was going to return to Washington on the morning after the battle.

"What word have you to send to Stanton, General Grant?" he asked.

"None, I think; except that we are fighting away, here."

"Hadn't you better send Stanton just a scratch of the pen?"

"Perhaps so," Grant answered; and stepping into his tent he dashed off the following without stopping a moment for reflection, and handed it to Washburne without even reading it over: —

"We have now ended the sixth day of very hard fighting. The result, to this time, is much in our favor. Our losses have been heavy, as well as those of the enemy. I think the loss of the enemy must be greater. We have taken over five thousand prisoners in battle, while he has taken from us but few, except stragglers. *I propose to fight it out on this line, if it takes all summer.*"

This hasty message not only reassured the War Department, but the whole country. It was full of Grant — the veritable Grant who carried Donelson and Vicksburg. The closing sentence, published in every part of the land, became a motto on loyal lips. Through the papers it was spread throughout the army, and became an inspiration to the troops. It was like Grant. It added to his fame.

F. B. Carpenter, the artist, who painted "Signing the Proclamation," asked Mr. Lincoln about this time, —

"How does Grant impress you as a leading General?"

"The great thing about him is," replied Mr. Lincoln, "cool persistency of purpose. He is not easily excited, and he has the grip of a bull-dog. *When he once gets his teeth in, nothing can shake him off.*"

Another long and fearful battle was fought on the 12th, and our army captured thirty stands of colors, and over three thousand prisoners, among them Generals Johnson and Stewart. General Hancock was well acquainted with both of them in the old army, and he stepped up and courteously shook hands with Johnson, who said, with tears in his eyes, —

"I wish death had overtaken me rather than this disaster."

Turning to Stewart, Hancock said, —

"And how are you, Stewart?"

"Sir, I am General Stewart, of the Confederate army," answered the captive, "and, under present circumstances, I decline to take your hand."

"Under any other circumstances, General, I should not have offered it."

Hancock wrote briefly to Grant, —

"I have finished up Johnson, and am now going into Early."

And by a sudden, bold movement, he captured Early's rifle-pits.

The battle-ground of the 12th of May was literally covered with the dead. One tree, eighteen inches in diameter, was cut entirely off by bullets. Grant lost eight thousand men; but he drove the enemy. He was doing this now every time. He forwarded the following dispatch to Washington:

"The eighth day of battle closes, leaving between three and four thousand prisoners in our hands for the day's work, including two general officers. The enemy are obstinate, and seem to have found the last ditch."

So far Grant's plan to capture Richmond was working well on the whole. It was said that he formed this plan when he was before Vicksburg. An officer asked him, —

"Do you think Richmond can be taken?"

"With ease," General Grant replied.

"By the Peninsula?"

"No; if I had charge of the matter, I should want two large armies, one to move directly on Lee's, and the other to land at City Point and cut communications to the southward. Lee would be then compelled to fall back, and the army from the north could press, and, if possible, defeat him. If he would open up communications again with the Cotton States, he must fight the army south of the James; and, to do this, he must cross his whole force, otherwise he would be defeated in detail. If he did so cross, the northern army could take Richmond. If he did not, that from the south could move up to the heights south of the James, and shell and destroy the city."

When Grant was near Spottsylvania, and the anxiety of the country was great, a stranger called at his tent and found him in conversation with a staff-officer.

"General," said the stranger, "if you flank Lee, and get between him and Richmond, will you not uncover Washington, and leave it exposed to the enemy?"

"Yes, I reckon so," was the General's quiet answer, with a significant twinkle in the eye.

"Do you not think, General," continued the stranger, "that Lee can detach sufficient force to re-enforce Beauregard at Richmond, and overwhelm Butler?"

"I have not a doubt of it."

"And is there not danger that Johnston may come up and re enforce Lee, so that the latter will swing round and cut off your communications, and seize your supplies?"

"Very likely," Grant replied, without showing the east concern.

The stranger must have been as much puzzled with the General as his neighbors were with his boyhood. Evidently the stranger intended to suggest to Grant what he supposed the latter had never thought of before; but not a point was suggested which Grant had not thoroughly canvassed and provided for. While the disasters suggested by the stranger were possible, Grant had no fear that they would occur, because a part of his programme was to prevent them.

On the twenty-fifth day of May, Sheridan returned from his raid, having rendered Grant essential service in tearing up railways, capturing supply-trains, and harassing the enemy. He defeated a large cavalry-force within six miles of Richmond, and mortally wounded the famous rebel cavalry-leader, J. E. B. Stuart. He pursued the rebels he routed into their defences at Richmond, capturing a section of artillery and a hundred prisoners.

General Grant moved forward, multiplying flanking movements, his arms becoming more and more victorious. He fought a long and hotly contested battle at Cold Harbor, driving his foe, and marched on to Petersburg to unite with General Butler in capturing that city. Thus far his losses had been heavy, but he had inflicted lasting injury upon the enemy, and taken thirteen thousand prisoners. He had conducted his marching and flanking movements with great skill. During much of the time he supplied more than a hundred thousand soldiers over roads so narrow that one wagon could not pass another, yet his men never suffered for food, nor did he lose a single wagon.

XIX.

FALL OF THE CONFEDERACY.

ENERAL GRANT telegraphed to Halleck, on his way to Petersburg: —
"Our forces will commence crossing the James to-day. The enemy shows no signs of yet having brought troops to the south side of Richmond. I will have Petersburg secured, if possible, before they get there in much force. Our movement from Cold Harbor to the James River has been made with great celerity, and, so far, without loss or accident."

Abraham Lincoln replied with his own hand: —
"I have just received your dispatch of one P. M. yesterday. *I begin to see it.* You will succeed. God bless you all!"

Of course Grant would succeed. He always did; if not by one plan, then by another. After he invested Petersburg, and Lee had entered the city with a hundred thousand troops to defend it, Grant said to one of his staff, —

"I shall capture Richmond, and Lee knows it."

General Grant reached Petersburg, and, on the fifteenth day of June, the bombardment of the city began. He meant to carry the works by assault before Lee could reach the place with his hundred thousand men. Three successive days he charged upon the defences, with some success, but was unable to hold the advance he made. They were three days of awful battle and carnage. One who saw it, says,—

"Could one have looked down from a balloon upon the scene presented, a very extraordinary spectacle would have met the eye. Three hundred thousand men, in organized masses, were spread over a space about fifteen miles in breadth and nearly forty in length. They were marching in all directions, in apparently inexplicable confusion. The heads of antagonistic columns were continually meeting in deadly fight. Batteries were thundering from hilltops; squadrons of cavalry were sweeping the plains; shot and shell shrieked through the air; long lines of infantry rushed, like ocean surges, in the impetuous charge; clouds of smoke were rising in all directions Piercing the tumult of musketry and artillery, wild battle-cries blended with shrieks of agony and death-groans. Such a scene cannot be described. No mortal mind can conceive it."

At the close of the three days' fight, General Grant was satisfied that Petersburg could be carried only by siege. Lee had arrived with his great army, rendering further assaults upon the defenses more discouraging. In these circumstances, he addressed himself earnestly to the capture of Petersburg and Richmond by siege. It was a heavy job on his hands, as he well knew ; and it turned out to be heavier than he supposed.

To add to the tremendous burden laid upon him,

many Northern people were dissatisfied, including influential, loyal men. Some Senators and Representatives in Congress grew impatient; and, because Grant did not march directly into Richmond, they complained, and attacked him in the rear. This army in his rear tested Grant's patience more than the army in front. Yet, he kept his temper, and even turned aside to silence the guns that were belching away at his back. He wrote:—

"The enemy do not propose to fight in future, except behind strong intrenchments. To capture these strongholds is a work of time, or else involves terrible destruction of human life. The enemy is now concentrated in two great armies, both besieged, and neither daring to risk a battle outside of their fortifications. The South has no more men to put into the army,—their last man has been recruited. Rebel soldiers are deserting by thousands, and other thousands are dying of disease or wounds, or being captured; and this heavy loss can never be replaced. I can see the end of the Rebellion!"

Many anxious hearts were cheered by these hopeful words, and many were not. Many continued to find fault, depreciate Grant's generalship, and Lincoln's statesmanship, and, in other ways, to hinder the Union cause—for which acts they ought to have been ashamed of themselves to this day. Again Grant wrote a letter of encouragement and hope, to quiet these Northern enemies, who were too cowardly to oppose the war openly. He said,—

"If the Rebellion is not perfectly and thoroughly crushed, it will be the fault, and through the weakness, of the people of the North. Be of good cheer, and rest assured that all will come right."

But neither his sword nor pen, nor both together, could satisfy the class whose hearts were secretly disloyal to the Government under which they lived. Nevertheless, he fought on, like the patriot that he was, determined to save the country or die in the trenches.

Lee scraped together all the soldiers he could muster outside of Petersburg and Richmond, and sent Early with them to invade the North and threaten Washington, hoping thereby to force Grant to raise the siege at Petersburg, and rush to the rescue of the North. The raid into Maryland and Pennsylvania did create a panic in the loyal States; but Grant did not budge an inch. He understood the game perfectly, and laughed to think what a signal failure it would be. The enemy cut a few railways, burned a few houses, and captured a quantity of horses, cattle, hogs, sheep, and clothing, of which they were in perishing need; and that was all. The Union General was not to be fooled by such tactics.

In July Mr. Washburne received the following communication from General Scott:—

"I heard, a short time ago, that some one had informed Lieutenant-General Grant that I had spoken slightly of him as an officer. As it is probable that your frank may enable this letter to reach him, I beg leave to say, through you, that I have never uttered an unkind word about him.

"The inquiry has frequently been addressed to

me, 'Do you know General Grant?' I have answered that he made the campaign of Mexico with me, and was considered by me, and I suppose by all his brothers in commission, a good officer, and one who attained special distinction at Molino del Rey. Of his more recent services, I have uniformly spoken in terms of the highest admiration; and added that, in my opinion, he had richly earned his present rank. I hope he may speedily put down the Rebellion."

A few months later, General Grant was in New York city, and called upon General Scott, whose autobiography had just been issued from the press Scott presented a copy to Grant, first writing on the fly-leaf, —

"From the oldest to the ablest General in the world.

"WINFIELD SCOTT."

In July a great sorrow overtook Grant. His very dear friend, General McPherson, who was with General Sherman, on his "grand march to the sea," was killed in battle. When Grant received the sad intelligence., he remarked, —

"The country has lost one of its best soldiers, and," bursting into tears, "I have lost my best friend."

A short time thereafter, General Grant received the following touching letter, dated at Clyde, Ohio : —

"I hope you will pardon me for troubling you with the perusal of these few lines from the trembling hand of the aged grandmother of our beloved Gen. James B. McPherson, who fell in battle. When it was announced at his funeral, from the public prints, that when General Grant neard of his death he went into his tent and wept like a child, my heart went out in thanks to you for the interest you manifested in him while he was with you.

"I have watched his progress from infancy up. In childhood he was obedient and kind; in manhood interesting, noble, and persevering, looking to the wants of others. Since he entered the war, others can appreciate his worth better than I can.

"When it was announced to us by telegraph that our loved one had fallen, our hearts were almost rent asunder; but when we heard the commander-in-chief could weep with us too, we felt, sir, that you have been as a father to him; and this whole Nation is mourning his early death. I wish to inform you that his remains were conducted by a kind guard to the very parlor where he spent a cheerful evening in 1861, with his widowed mother, two brothers, only sister, and his aged grandma, who is now trying to write. In the morning he took his leave at six o'clock, little dreaming he should fall by a ball from the enemy.

"His funeral services were attended in his mother's orchard, where his youthful feet had often pressed the soil to gather fruit, and his remains are resting in the silent grave, scarce half a mile from the place of his birth. His grave is on an eminence but a few rods from where the funeral services were attended, and near the grave of his father. The grave, no doubt, will be marked, so that passers-by will often pause to drop a tear over the dear departed.

"And now, dear friend, a few lines from you would be gratefully received by the afflicted friends. I pray that the God of battles may be with you, and go forth with

your armies till the Rebellion shall cease, the Union be restored, and the old flag wave over our entire land.
"With much respect,
"I remain your friend,
"LYDIA SLOCUM,
"Aged eighty-seven years and four months."

General Grant replied, —

"*Dear Madam*, — Your very welcome letter of the third instant has reached me. I am glad to know the relatives of the lamented Major-General McPherson are aware of the more than friendship existing between him and myself. A Nation grieves at the loss of one so dear to our Nation's cause. It is a selfish grief, because the Nation had more to expect from him than from almost any one living. I join in this selfish grief, and add the grief of personal love for the departed. He formed for some time one of my military family. I knew him well, and to know him was but to love him.

"It may be some consolation to you, his aged grandmother, to know that every officer and every soldier who served under your grandson felt the highest reverence for his patriotism, his zeal, his great, almost unequaled ability, his amiability, and all the manly virtues that can adorn a commander. Your bereavement is great, but can not exceed mine. U. S. GRANT."

This affecting correspondence is valuable as a key to a side of Grant's character, which the severities of war are likely to conceal. He was a devoted, loving friend, because he was a true man. Like David and Jonathan, Grant and McPherson were united by mutual confidence and love, and when the latter fell, the tears of the former were honest

The General was accustomed to stroll about his camps and defences, often at midnight, to see that everything was rightly conducted ; and in one of these strolls, he approached a commissary warehouse guarded by negroes.

"You must throw away that cigar, sir," exclaimed one of the sentries.

"Why so ? " replied Grant.

"My instructions are, not to let any man pass my beat who is smoking. If you want to go by you must throw away that cigar."

"That is right," said Grant, throwing away the cigar. "Always stick to your instructions." And he passed on without disclosing his identity to the faithful sentinel.

During the autumn of 1864 and the beginning of 1865, startling events occurred. While Grant was doing nothing more before Richmond than recruiting and disciplining his army for the spring campaign, and looking out for his defenses, he was accomplishing much elsewhere through his ablest generals, strictly obeying his orders. Sheridan cleared the valley of the Shenandoah, and relieved Washington, Pennsylvania, and Maryland of all fear ; Sherman captured Atlanta, and Thomas crushed the command of Hood before Nashville.

Sherman, having completed his triumphant march to the sea, was ordered to report before Richmond with his victorious army, and join Grant in his final blow at the Rebellion. So Sherman left the seacoast upon another conquering march ; but to the North now. Grant spent much time and thought in arranging a final campaign, in which his whole army might engage directly or indirectly. 'He had no more doubt that this last great struggle for the possession of Richmond would be successful than he had of his own existence. He knew that the rebel army was ragged, hungry, and dispirited; that over seventy thousand deserters had left it since October, 1864; and that a large number of rebel soldiers in the ranks did not want to fight another day.

"The Confederacy is on its last legs," he wrote to Lincoln.

Another has said of that time and situation: —

"Grant had his mighty team well in hand now, and the western teamster was handling it with consummate skill. He had winnowed out the inefficient and impracticable and unfit commanders, so that he knew it would prove no '*balky team*,' but pull together, and with a power that nothing could withstand."

Just then Grant received the following brief but cheering communication from President Lincoln: —

"If there be anything wanting which is within my power to give, do not fail to let me know it. And now, with a brave army and a just cause, may God sustain you."

The final gigantic movement would begin on the twenty-ninth day of March. The closing paragraph of Grant's last order was, —

"By these instructions a large part of the armies operating against Richmond is left behind. The enemy, knowing this, may, as an only chance, strip their lines to the merest skeleton, in the hope of ad vantage not being taken of it, whilst they hurl everything against the moving column, and return. It can not be impressed too strongly upon commanders of troops left in the trenches not to allow this to occur without taking advantage of it. The very fact of the enemy coming out to attack, if he does so, might be regarded as almost conclusive evidence of such a weakening of his lines. *I would have it particularly enjoined upon corps commanders that, in case of an attack from the enemy, those not attacked are not to wait for orders from the commanding officer of the army to which they belong, but that they will move promptly, and notify the commander of their action. I would also enjoin the same action on the part of division commanders, when other parts of their corps are engaged. In like manner, I would urge the importance of following up a repulse of the enemy."*

This order breathes the spirit of one who is confident of accomplishing his object. His expectation of the downfall of Richmond is seen in every line of the order. Let his programme be carried out, and the Confederacy tumbles to pieces.

President Lincoln was on the ground by General Grant's invitation, to witness the final collapse of the Southern cause.

The enemy contested every foot of ground, and fought with desperation; but Grant's army was flushed with victory, and no opposition could block their way. They swept on and on, narrowing the investing circle on the 29th, capturing many prisoners, and wounding and killing many more. Again, on the 30th and 31st, repeating the victories of the previous day at great cost of life; until, at four o'clock, on Sunday morning, April 2d, Lee's line of communication south of Petersburg was broken, thousands of his soldiers were captured, and a large force cut off from the main army. Grant said to Sherman, on the 28th: —

"I will compel Lee to weaken his line and afford opportunity for attack, *or* to come out and fight."

He did both; and the result was the complete destruction of Lee's right, against which the Union army had been beating in vain for ten months.

Grant telegraphed to Bowers, at City Point, —

"The whole captures since the army started out gunning will not amount to less than twelve thousand men, and probably fifty pieces of artillery. . . . If the President will come out on the nine A. M. train to Patrick Station, I will send a horse and an escort to meet him. It would afford me much pleasure to meet the President in person at the station; but I know he will excuse me for not doing so, when my services are so liable to be needed at any moment."

Lincoln replied: —

"Allow me to tender to you, and all with you, the Nation's grateful thanks for this additional and magnificent success. At your kind suggestion, I think I will meet you to-morrow."

The inhabitants of Richmond did not learn before meeting, on that Sunday, what disaster had befallen them; not even Jefferson Davis. The church bells, as usual, called the people together, or the few who

had a heart to respond, and among them the rebe
President.

The Sentinel said, on Saturday: —
"We are very hopeful of the campaign which i
opening; and trust that we are to reap a large ac
vantage from the operations evidently near at hanc
We have only to resolve *that we never will surrende**
and it will be impossible that we shall ever b
taken."

Service had scarcely commenced when a mes
senger entered the church, with a dispatch for Davi
from Lee. He opened and read what made hir
deadly pale.

"The enemy has broken my lines in three places
Richmond must be evacuated to-night."

Davis went out of the church as calmly as h'
could, so as not to spread consternation, and th'
services continued. He walked rapidly to his house
where he wrote orders to remove coin from th'
banks to Danville, and to carry thither, or burn
the archives of the Confederacy. He planned fo:
his own escape, also.

By the time services in the churches were con
cluded, news of the disaster was spreading like wild
fire through the streets. The greatest excitemen'
immediately prevailed throughout the city. Men
women, and children ran through the streets half
crazed. They knew not what to do. Every sorl
of a vehicle was soon in extravagant demand. Ten
twenty, fifty, and even a hundred, and a thousanc
dollars for conveyance to a place of safety. "Army
wagons, loaded with boxes and trunks, drove fu

riously towards the Danville depot; pale women and ragged children streamed after, going they knew not whither; excited men filled the air with blasphemies, while the more desperate surged up around the commissary depots, awaiting the signal for pillage. There was no order—no attempt on the part of any one to enforce it."

To add to the consternation, the rebel General Ewell ordered the iron-clads in the river to be blown up, the deafening explosion of which reminded the terrified citizens of the last judgment. The desperate class broke open the warehouses, and helped themselves to goods. Whiskey was free as water; and men and women drank themselves into an incontrollable mob, staggering through the streets, robbing houses, pillaging stores, and making day hideous. Ewell set fire to the shipping in the river and the Government warehouses, thus kindling a fire which consumed a thousand houses in the heart of the city; and would have consumed more, but for the timely arrival of Union soldiers, who threw down their arms, manned the engines, and extinguished the fire.

When the Battle of the Wilderness was in progress, a staff-officer said to Ewell,—

"Grant will retreat."

Ewell, who knew Grant well, replied,—

"He will not retreat. Grant is not a *retreating* man."

His words were confirmed. No retreating-general could ever have captured Richmond.

At eight o'clock in the evening Jefferson Davis

and his Cabinet fled to Danville by rail. The Southern Confederacy had bursted like a bubble. Its President was a fugitive — his fortunes ruined forever. A more complete wreck of a political organization never defaced the world. Its builders had to run to escape its falling walls.

Colored Union soldiers were the first to enter the city; and they were jubilant. They marched singing through the streets: —

> "John Brown's body lies a mouldering in the grave,
> But his soul is marching on."

On Monday President Lincoln visited Richmond; walked through the streets without escort, sat in the head-quarters of Jefferson Davis, passed through Libby Prison, and everywhere beheld the evidence of a defeated army. The negroes crowded about him, and laughed and cried, as they implored the blessing of God upon him.

General Grant had other work on his hands. Lee's army was in full retreat towards Danville, to unite with Johnston's army for further fight. Grant resolved to interfere with that arrangement, and he started in hot pursuit. "Burke's Station, where Lee proposed to strike the Danville Railroad, was fifty miles from Richmond; and both armies put forth almost superhuman energies to reach it first. If Lee did, his escape from immediate surrender was almost assured; if Grant did, he was lost. The troops, on one side, goaded on by desperation, on the other, urged by the prospect of a speedy, crowning victory, pressed on night and day towards this goal. Grant reached it first; and Lee, with a sinking heart, saw his last hope cut off. It was true, he might reach Lynchburg and escape to the mountains, and thus avoid the mortification of a surrender; but even this poor consolation was denied him. "For Sheridan was after him there."

On the fifth day of April, Grant wrote to Sherman: —

"Sheridan is up with Lee, and reports all that is left — horse, foot, and dragoon — at twenty thousand men, much demoralized. We hope to reduce this number one half. I shall push on to Burkesville and if a stand is made at Danville, will, in a very few days, go there. If you can do so, push on from where you are, and let us see if we cannot finish the job with Lee's and Johnston's armies.

Lee struck for Lynchburg, and the next night encamped near there. While holding council of war with his generals, to decide what to do, Sheridan's cannon boomed in his front, proclaiming that the way of Lee's army in that direction was blocked. The rebel general, with his shattered army, was caught. Two days before, General Grant had sent the following to Lee: —

"*General*, — The result of the last week must convince you of the hopelessness of further resistance on the part of the Army of Northern Virginia in this struggle. I feel that it is so, and regard it as my duty to shift from myself the responsibility of any further effusion of blood, by asking of you the surrender of that portion of the Confederate States Army known as the Army of Northern Virginia."

Lee replied by saying that he did not think he was under the necessity of surrendering; but yet inquired for Grant's conditions.

But on the 9th, when the booming of Sheridan's cannon was heard in the front, he sent General Gordon to cut his way through the Union forces, saying to a staff-officer, —

"If that fails, further resistance will be vain."

It did fail; and on the receipt of the news, Lee said to Longstreet, —

General Longstreet, I leave you in charge. I am going to hold a conference with General Grant."

On the day previous, Lee wrote to Grant as follows : —

"*General,*— I received, at a late hour, your note of to-day. In mine of yesterday I did not intend to propose the surrender of the Army of Northern Virginia, but to ask the terms of your proposition. To be frank, I do not think the emergency has arisen to call for the surrender of this army; but as the restoration of peace should be the sole object of all, I desired to know whether your proposals would lead to that end. I can not, therefore, meet you with a view to surrender the Army of Northern Virginia; but as far as your proposal may affect the Confederate States forces under my command, and tend to the restoration of peace, I should be pleased to meet you at ten A. M. to-morrow, on the old stage-road to Richmond, between the picket-lines of the two armies."

Grant did not receive it until early the next morning, April 9th. He immediately replied, —

"*General,* — Your note of yesterday is received. I have no authority to treat on the subject of peace; the meeting proposed for ten A. M. to-day could lead to no good. I will state, however, General, that I am equally anxious for peace with yourself, and the whole North entertains the same feeling. The terms upon which peace can be had are well understood. By the South laying down their arms they will hasten that most desirable event, save thousands of human lives, and hundreds of millions of property not yet destroyed. Seriously hoping that all our difficulties may be settled without the loss of another life, I subscribe myself, etc."

Two hours after Grant's letter was sent, an orderly dashed up on his foaming steed, and delivered a dispatch to him; it was a reply from Lee. Grant read it with a smile, and, passing it to Rawlins, said, —

"Here, General Rawlins, read this."

Rawlins read as follows: —

"9th APRIL, 1865.

"*General*, — I received your note of this morning on the picket-line, whither I had come to meet you, and ascertain definitely what terms were embraced in your proposal of yesterday, with reference to the surrender of this army. I now ask an interview, in accordance with the offer contained in your letter of yesterday, for that purpose.

"R. E. LEE,
"*General*.

"Lieut.-Gen. U. S. Grant."

"Well, how do you think that will do?" inquired General Grant.

"I think *that* will do," answered Rawlins.

Grant returned this answer, —

"*General*, — Yours of this date is but this moment (fifty minutes past eleven) received, in consequence of my having passed from the Richmond and Lynchburg to the Farmville and Richmond road. Am at this writing about four miles west of Wallace Church, and will push forward to the front for the purpose of meeting you. Notice sent to me on this road where you wish the interview to take place will meet me here."

So the way was open for Lee to confer with Grant when Gordon's last effort to escape failed. He repaired to Appomattox Court-house; and Sheridan, also, went thither. General Ord was there. Grant had not arrived; but he soon came galloping up, covered with mud.

"Sheridan, how are you?" he said.
"First-rate, thank you; how are you?"
"Is General Lee here?"
"Yes."

And soon the two generals were conferring together, not under an apple-tree, according to the song, —

> "If you ask what State he hails from,
>   Our sole reply shall be —
> He comes from Appomattox
>   And its famous apple-tree,"

But under a kind of thorn-tree. After a few moments in conversation, Lee and Grant mounted their horses, accompanied by the members of their staff present, to ride to the village near by; Maj. Wilmer McLean met them, and invited the party to his house, a brick mansion containing eight rooms; and his invitation was accepted.

It is a notable fact, that this Mr. McLean lived near Manassas, at the outbreak of the war, and the battle of Bull Run was fought near his house, so that he was forced to leave it; and he removed to Appomattox Court-house. The house he left was riddled to pieces by deadly missiles; and his house at Appomattox was used by the generals and their aides, at the close of the war, for signing the terms of surrender, embraced in the following document: —

"APPOMATTOX COURT-HOUSE, "VA., April 9, 1865.

" *General*,— In accordance with the substance of my letter to you of the 8th instant, I propose to receive the surrender of the Army of Northern Virginia on the following terms, to wit: Rolls of all the officers and men to be made in duplicate, one copy to be given to an officer to be designated by me, the other to be retained by such officer or officers as you may designate. The officers to give their individual paroles not to take up arms against the Government of the United States until properly exchanged; and each company or regimental commander sign a like parole for the men of their commands. The arms, artillery, and public property to be parked and stacked, and turned over to the officers appointed by me to receive them. This will not embrace the side-arms of the officers, nor their private horses or baggage. This done, each officer and man will be allowed to return to his home, not to be disturbed by United States authority so long as they observe their paroles and the laws in force where they may reside. "U. S. GRANT,
" *Lieutenant-General*.
"Gen. R. E. Lee."

After the signatures were attached, Lee remarked, —

"I forgot one thing, General. Many of the artillery and cavalry horses in my army belong to the men who have them in charge. But it is too late to speak of that now."

Grant (interrupting). — "I will instruct my paroling officers that all the enlisted men of your cavalry and artillery who own horses are to retain them, just as the officers do theirs. They will need them for their spring plowing and other farm work."

Lee (with great earnestness). — "General, there is nothing you could have done to accomplish more good, either for them or for the Government."

After hesitating a moment, Lee added, —

"I would like also to have my soldiers furnished with a parole to protect them from Confederate conscription officers."

"It shall be done," answered Grant.

Greater courtesy and magnanimity was never shown by a conqueror to the conquered. Northern criticism of Grant's lenient policy were numerous and sharp; but time has vindicated it.

Three days after the aforesaid document was signed, the ceremony of surrender occurred at Appomattox Court-house. In order to avoid all parade, and to gratify his own feelings of true sympathy for the conquered general, Grant did not appear on the scene. General Chamberlain, of Maine, was delegated to receive the sword of Lee, with instructions to return it to him in recognition of a brave and able officer. When the Southern soldiers marched out to lay down their arms, and battered colors, hundreds of them did it with streaming eyes, while Union soldiers looked on in silence, not a word or act of exultation appearing throughout the lines. On the day of the surrender, General Grant ordered twenty thousand rations to be distributed to the Confederate army, who were hungry and exhausted.

On the next morning, General Grant's rebel cousin, of Virginia, was brought in to him, a cousin he had not seen since boyhood.

Grant. — "Are you one of Aunt Rachel's sons?"

Prisoner. — "Yes; Charley."

Grant. — "What are you doing here?"

Prisoner. — "I have been fighting in Lee's army."

Grant. — "Bad business, Charley. What do you want to do now?"

Prisoner. — "*I want to go home!*"

Grant. — "Have you got a horse?"

Prisoner. — "No; mine was killed under me, day before yesterday."

Grant. — "Have you got any money?"

Prisoner. — "No."

"Well, here are fifty dollars, and you will be furnished with a horse and pass. That is the best I can do for you."

Union and rebel officers and men mingled together freely. A Confederate officer said, —

"You astonish us with your generosity."

Another said, "I loved the cause, but we are fairly beaten; now the stars and stripes are my flag, and I will be as true to it as you."

General Gordon remarked, "This is bitterly humiliating to me; but I console myself by thinking that the whole country rejoices that the war is over."

XX.

THE NATION'S GRATITUDE.

HE fall of Richmond on April 2d, set all the bells of the North ringing, cannons firing, and people shouting. Excepting some of the large cities, the news of its capture did not reach the prople generally until early Monday morning, when it was hailed with almost frantic demonstrations of joy. Business was suspended, mills stopped, legislatures adjourned; nobody could work with a will; they wanted to rejoice. They knew that the fall of Richmond was the end of the Rebellion. The enemy might evade capture for a time, and fight more, but the end was near. The bottom had dropped out of the Confederacy, and no miracle could put it back. There was reason for general rejoicing.

But the climax of joy was not attained until Lee surrendered to Grant, just one week later. The country had witnessed no such demonstration of joy since Cornwallis surrendered at Yorktown, bringing to a close the eight years' war of the American Revolution. We shall make no attempt to describe the scene throughout the loyal States; nor to measure the gratitude to General Grant which was manifested in every public gathering. The names of Lincoln and Grant were on every loyal lip; and no gift, or praise, or honor, was too great for these remarkable benefactors.

The surrender of Johnston to Sherman soon followed, and then every other scattered fragment of the Confederate army; and war ceased throughout the land.

On the morning of April 13th, Grant arrived at Washington. In the evening there was an illumination of the public buildings never before equalled in that city. Unbounded enthusiasm possessed the crowds of people in the street. President Lincoln, ordering his carriage, requested General Grant to drive out with Mrs. Lincoln to witness the display. His appearance on the street was the signal for renewed expressions of delight. Round after round of cheers rent the air, and spread wildly from street to street. The heart of the victorious chief must have swelled with an honest pride, though friends could discover no change in his demeanor. The same quiet, thoughtful, unpretentious appearance characterized him in the hour of victory as in that of battle.

There was a meeting of the Cabinet on the 14th, to consider the grave questions which peace at once raised. General Grant was present by special request. It was just four years on that day since the flag of Sumter was assailed. Plans for the early restoration of the South were discussed, in which General Grant participated with more than ordinary interest.

President Lincoln was very much exhausted by continued application to business, night and day, and

Mr. Colfax and other friends had secured his promise to attend the theatre that night, thinking it would prove a much needed relaxation. General Grant was invited to join them, but he had planned to accom pany Mrs. Grant to Burlington, N. J., where their children were attending school, and he begged to be excused. On that night President Lincoln was assassinated in Ford's Theatre; and an attempt was made upon the life of Secretary Seward in his room. As learned thereafter, General Grant was included in the conspiracy of the assassins; and had he remained in Washington on that night it is probable that he would have fallen with Mr. Lincoln. It was remembered afterwards that J. Wilkes Booth, the assassin, galloped for some distance beside the carriage in which Mr. and Mrs. Grant rode to the station, looking in to discover who was there. That watchful Providence which had shielded him through four years of peril on the battle-field, guarded and guided him now that secret enemies sought his life. His work was not all done. Providence had other labor for him to perform; and the Nation wanted he should do it.

General Grant reached Philadelphia at midnight, on the 14th, and had crossed the city in a carriage to the railway ferry, when a telegram from Stanton, announcing the terrible tragedy, reached him. He accompanied his wife to Burlington, where he ordered a special train, and immediately returned to Washington.

Perhaps if Lincoln had not been assassinated, the loyal people of the country would have readily acquiesced in Grant's terms of surrender to Lee. But the baseness of that act, approved if not instigated by Southern leaders, arrayed multitudes of them against Grant's lenient policy. They demanded severity and retaliation. Forgetting the eminent services of Grant in saving the country, in their sorrow and madness they denounced him in terms that were unjustifiable and cruel. But whatever else may be said about those terms, they certainly proved General Grant to be one of the most humane soldiers ever known, incapable of exultation over a fallen foe, and merciful even to his worst enemies. If true magnanimity and generous sympathy on the part of a victor ever excelled this, we know not on what page of history to find it recorded. One who knew the General's motives well said, —

"Grant had given his very liberal terms at Appomattox partly from policy. He knew that if Lee declined them his troops could not be kept together after learning their nature; and that if he accepted, Johnston's army also, learning their generosity, would grow clamorous for peace.

"He had given them partly from feeling. Like all our soldiers, he realized how fearfully the South had been punished; and if the rebels were now willing to lay down their arms, obey the laws, and not oppress Union white men or Union black men at the South, he thought it unworthy of a great people to degrade or humiliate them. He wanted no more bloodshed, no vengeance, no requiring that men who had staked all should be glad that they had lost all, or manifest any sudden affection for their conquerors. The national authority restored; those who had helped to restore it fully protected from their late foes; and he was willing to leave the rest to the softening influences of time."

On the sixteenth day of April, our Government paroled and liberated all prisoners of war, numbering *sixty-three thousand*. The aggregate number of the enemy surrendered in all the rebel commands, was only about one hundred thousand, although on the rolls there were one hundred and seventy-five thousand. The rolls of the Union military force, on the first day of May, showed ONE MILLION FIVE HUNDRED AND SIXTEEN MEN. Over EIGHT HUNDRED THOUSAND soldiers were mustered out in six months. The fact is without a parallel in history.

On the twenty-second and twenty-third days of May, a grand review of the Union army, on their way home from the battle-fields of the South, occurred in Washington. Such a military review was never before known in the world, so imposing, so extensive, so captivating, with uniforms, banners, caparisoned steeds, and martial music. The whole city was arrayed in bunting and flags. Beautifully decorated mottoes appeared by the hundred. "HONOR TO THE BRAVE!" "WELCOME, SOLDIERS!" "VICKSBURG!" "SHILOH!" "WILDERNESS!" On the Capitol was this inscription, —

"THE ONLY NATIONAL DEBT WE CAN NEVER PAY, IS THE DEBT WE OWE TO THE VICTORIOUS UNION SOLDIERS!"

The school-children of the city came out in force, with music and banners, and sung, "WHEN JOHNNY

COMES MARCHING HOME," and other favorite airs with loyal people.

Through two whole days, General Grant, President Johnson, and other high officials, stood to review the triumphant Union army, as regiment after regiment filed past the presidential mansion, in such a display of military glory as none of them ever witnessed before. It is probable that General Grant himself never had so exalted an idea of the grandeur of his army as that review afforded him.

On the second day of June, the Lieutenant-General issued his final congratulatory order to his vast army:

"*Soldiers of the Army of the United States:* — By your patriotic devotion to your country in the hour of danger and alarm, your magnificent fighting, bravery, and endurance, you have maintained the supremacy of the Union and the Constitution, overthrown all armed opposition to the enforcement of the laws, and of the proclamations forever abolishing slavery (the cause and pretext of the Rebellion), and opened the way to the rightful authorities to restore order, and inaugurate peace on a permanent and enduring basis on every foot of American soil.

"Your marches, sieges, and battles, in distance, duration, resolution, and brilliancy of results, dim the lustre of the world's past military achievements, and will be the patriot's precedent in defense of liberty and right in all time to come.

"In obedience to your country's call, you left your homes and families and volunteered in its defense. Victory has crowned your valor and secured the purpose of your patriotic hearts; and with the gratitude of your countrymen and the highest honors a great and free nation can accord, you will soon be permitted to return to your homes and families, conscious of having discharged the highest duty of American citizens.

"To achieve the glorious triumphs, and secure to yourselves, your fellow-countrymen, and posterity the blessings of free institutions, tens of thousands of your gallant comrades have fallen and sealed the priceless legacy with their lives. The graves of these a grateful Nation bedews with tears, honors their memories, and will ever cherish and support their stricken families."

This document is alike worthy of the head and heart of the General. No wonder that the soldiers loved him!

In June, General Grant was called to West Point; and, on his return, a grand reception was tendered him at the Fifth Avenue Hotel in New York. It was one of the most brilliant companies that ever assembled in the metropolis. Everything about it was on a grand scale. Among the decorations was the national flag made of tuberoses, jessamines, heliotropes, and camellias. It was a part of the "show-business" which eclipsed anything which General Grant had seen hitherto. He quailed before the costly compliments and honors more than he did before the grape and canister of Shiloh.

At the close of the war, the Lieutenant-General established his head-quarters at Washington, where, as head of the armies of the United States, his hands were as full of business as ever, only less bloody. The military department of the Government could not be abandoned, while the work of reconstruction was in its incipient stages.

In June, a great fair opened in Chicago to assist disabled soldiers and their families. General Grant was invited to be present, in order to draw the people. Mrs. Sherman invited him, also, to make a contribution to the fair. He responded cheerfully by contributing "Old Jack," the cream-colored horse which he rode the first eighteen months of the war. So "Old Jack" was shipped to Chicago, and was the centre of attraction until Grant himself arrived. The Lieutenant-General put the horse in the shade; and yet the "Great North-west" could not pay suitable tribute to the hero of Donelson without the aid of the horse.

When Grant alighted at the station in Chicago, he found a multitude which no man would think of numbering, crowded into that city to do him honor. The crowd extended from the station, not only as far as the eye could see, but through nearly all the streets of the city — a patriotic, happy, uproarious mass of humanity. And there, waiting at the station, was "Old Jack," with saddle and bridle on, to bear his master through the streets. The General was somewhat confused at first, for "Old Jack" was not to carry him now into a Shiloh battle, but into the "show-business"; and to this the conqueror of Lee demurred at first. But the Fair Committee insisted that it was a part of their well-considered programme, and he must ride faithful "Old Jack" once more before the beast was placed upon the retired list.

General Grant, being a very pliable man, notwithstanding his wife's assertion that he always was "*very obstinate*," yielded to their solicitations, and mounted the horse, without spur or whip, and jogged through the streets, amidst cheers that seemed to jar the skies, and the thunder of a hundred guns announcing, "THE CONQUERING HERO COMES!"

He had been drawn in "a coach and six," both white and black, and now he was forced to confess that the managers of the fair had selected the most appropriate mode of conveyance possible for the occasion. The people enjoyed his ride hugely, whether he did or not; and ten thousand people welcomed him to Union Hall. The band played "The Red, White, and Blue" as he entered, but the deafening applause of ten thousand voices drowned the music. General Hooker presided, and he introduced Genera Grant to the immense audience as the hero of the war. The General said, —

"Ladies and Gentlemen: As I never made a speech myself, I will ask Governor Yates to return the thanks which I should fail to express."

Governor Yates responded in one of his glowing speeches, that stirred every heart. Then General Sherman was called for, and he replied, —

"I am here to-day to listen; I am not going to make any speech whatever. Always ready, always willing, always proud to do anything the Lieutenant-General asked me to do, I know he never asked me to make a speech."

"No," quickly responded Grant, "I never asked a soldier to do what I could not do myself." Great applause followed.

With all his gravity, the General was quick-witted, and often entertained his friends by his dry humor. Since we began to write his life, we have met with the following incident, which is one of the best on record, — in the line of humor.

When Grant was in command in South-eastern Missouri, he led an expedition against a rebel force in North-east Arkansas, one hundred and ten miles distant. Much of the way was through a wilderness, and there were few settlers anywhere in that region. Lieutenant Wickfield of an Indiana Cavalry regiment, commanded the advance guard, consisting of eight mounted men. About noon of the second or third day out, Wickfield came across a cabin. He dismounted and entered with his men.

"Can you get us something to eat?" he inquired
The woman looked him over, and then asked, —
"Who are you?"
"I am Brigadier-General Grant."

She had heard of Grant, so she and other members of the family hastened to put on the table all there was in the cabin, of which the men partook heartily and thankfully. When they got through, there was only one pie left.

"What is to pay?" asked Wickfield.
"Nothing, sir; you are welcome."

They hurried forward, and one hour after Grant came up to the same cabin, and said to the woman who stood in the door, —

"Can you cook us a meal?"

"No, we can t; for General Grant has just been here, and eaten everything in the house except one pumpkin-pie."

"Well, that's bad," replied Grant, perceiving at once that Wickfield meant to play a joke. "What is your name?"

"Selvidge," answered the woman.

Flinging a half-dollar to her, Grant added, —

"Will you keep that pie till I send an officer for it."

"I will, certainly," she answered.

After selecting a camping-ground, towards night, Grant issued an order for a parade at half-past six, and requested officers to see that their men turned out.

"What can it mean?" said one.

"The enemy is near, no doubt," said another.

"Some important instructions," a third.

But when the men were formed in lines, the assistant adjutant-general rode in front, and read the following order: —

"HEAD-QUARTERS, ARMY IN THE FIELD.
"SPECIAL ORDER No. —.

"Lieutenant Wickfield, of the Indiana Cavalry, having on this day eaten everything in Mrs. Selvidge's house, at the crossing of the Trenton and Pocahontas and Black River and Cape Girardeau roads, except one pumpkin-pie, Lieutenant Wickfield is hereby ordered to return with an escort of one hundred cavalry and eat that pie also.

"U. S. GRANT,
"*Brigadier-General Commanding.*"

The parade was over, and every one was inquiring to know what it all meant. They learned very soon, however; and the camp was filled with merriment. The jocose Lieutenant collected his escort to return and eat the pie that night, and departed amidst peals of laughter; and he never heard the last of it. Nor did Grant ever know that his name was used thereafter by any party foraging for himself.

To return to the Chicago Fair. "Old Jack" brought a thousand dollars for the benefit of disabled soldiers. Nothing could have been more appropriate. The proceeds of the Fair were over *two hundred and fifty thousand dollars;* twice as much as it would have been if General Grant had not been there. The revolver which Jeff. Davis had in his hand when he was captured brought a large price. So did the eagle of the Eighth Wisconsin Infantry, which was carried all through the war; fifteen thousand dollars' worth of his photographs were sold. The following characteristic letter from President Lincoln to a lady in St. Louis, who wrote to him for his autograph, was a relic sold for a great price: —

"Fondly do we hope, fervently do we pray, that this mighty scourge of war may speedily pass away. Yet, if it should be God's will that it should continue until all the wealth piled up by the bondman's two hundred and fifty years of unrequited labor shall be sunk, and every drop of blood drawn by the lash shall be paid by another drawn by the sword, as was said three thousand years ago, so still it must be said, 'The judgments of the Lord are true and righteous altogether.'"

General Grant returned to Washington, to find delegations there to urge him to visit New England. The request was too urgent to be refused. In July he went to Saratoga, and from there to Massachusetts and Maine; making a brief tour through Canada, and returning to Galena, his old home.

In Boston the welcome extended to him was remarkable. People crowded into the city from every part of New England. Some came a hundred, and even two hundred, miles. The last yard of bunting was bought in the stores for the display, and thousands of flags fluttered from the tops of buildings and ships in the harbor. Everywhere throughout his tour, the effort to do him honor was the same.

When he reached Galena, one dense mass of human beings filled the town, and the enthusiasm was unbounded. Cannon boomed, bands played, banners waved, the people cheered; and he was conducted through an arch spanning a street, bearing the inscription, wrought in flowers: "GENERAL, THE SIDEWALK IS BUILT."

The citizens had presented him with a house costing sixteen thousand dollars, thoroughly furnished; and built a sidewalk from it to the station, a half mile away

Two hundred flags floated over the De Soto House; and a triumphal arch spanned the main street, having inscribed on one side:—

"*Welcome to Our Citizen.*"

"WELDON RAILROAD."   "FAIR OAKS."
"WILDERNESS."   "PETERSBURG."
"RICHMOND."   "FIVE FORKS."

On the other side:—

"*Hail to the Chief, who in Triumph Advances.*"

"BELMONT."   "LOOKOUT MOUNTAIN."
"DONELSON."   "CHATTANOOGA."
"SHILOH."   "VICKSBURG."
"CORINTH."   "APPOMATTOX COURT-HOUSE."

He was escorted past the old leather-store, where a magnificent arch was erected, under which stood thirty-six girls in white, each representing a State of the Union, and bearing the National colors. As Grant passed beneath the arch, the girls rained a shower of bouquets upon his head. Then Hon. E. B. Washburne delivered an address of welcome, to which Rev. J. H. Vincent replied for the General. At the close of the public demonstration, he was driven to his new house, where old friends and neighbors rejoiced to see him alight.

His duties made it necessary for him to dwell in Washington so long as he held the position of lieutenant-general. In due time he repaired thither, and important work accumulated upon his hands. The President and Cabinet never decided important questions relating to reconstruction without consulting him. His knowledge and judgment were constantly brought into requisition.

Congress enacted a bill reviving the grade of "General of the Army of the United States," which no American, but Washington, ever held. It was done specially to honor Grant, — with no design that any other American should ever share it, — and he was appointed to fill the office. When the bill was under discussion, Senator Yates of Illinois, who signed Grant's commission as colonel, said, —

"Lincoln wisely read the Nation's will in committing to him the command of all our armies, and particularly of the unlucky, but heroic, Army of the Potomac; which, baffled, but not beaten, had stood for long years like a wall of fire against the assaults of treason. And here, again, victory followed the invincible Grant; and in a series of battles more bloody than Waterloo, more brilliant than Austerlitz, he displayed the sterling qualities of the great commander. . . . It was the two-handed sword of Cœur de Lion against the flashing cimeter of the Paladin; it was the axe of the Norseman, thundering on the light shield of the Saxon, or the Celt."

XXI.

BETWEEN WAR AND THE WHITE HOUSE.

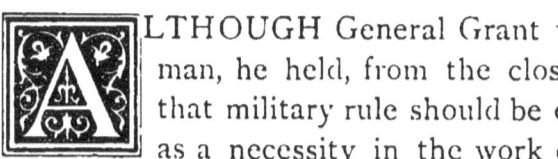LTHOUGH General Grant was a military man, he held, from the close of the war, that military rule should be employed only as a necessity in the work of reconstruction. It should be abandoned altogether, as soon as civil government could assert and maintain itself in the late rebellious States. For example: President Johnson's apparently disloyal course was attracting attention; and his policy towards Maryland, in respect to apprehended troubles in electing a Legislature, was declared, by leading Republicans, to be identical with the policy of Jefferson Davis. He proposed that General Grant should send United States troops into the State, to maintain order; but the General protested as follows:—

"The conviction is forced on my mind that no reason now exists for giving or promising the military aid of the Government to support the laws of Maryland. The tendency of giving such aid or promise would be to produce the very result intended to be averted. So far, there seems to be merely a very bitter contest for political ascendency in the State.

"Military interference would be interpreted as giving aid to one of the factions, no matter how pure the intentions, or how guarded and just the instructions. It is a contingency I hope never to see arise in this country, while I occupy the position of General-in-Chief of the army, to have to send troops into a State, *in full relations with the general Government*, on the eve of an election, to preserve peace. If insurrection does come, the law provides the method of calling out forces to suppress it. No such condition seems to exist now."

The President desired that he should go to Mexico, to represent the Government, for the purpose of preventing or adjusting difficulties there; but he declined, for fear that the military power would be used in his absence where it would serve to complicate affairs. General Sherman said to Grant, —

"You are right; don't you go. We need you here every moment."

And he went to the President and said, "Grant ought not to go to Mexico, — he is needed here; but I can go as well as not. My trunk is always packed."

Until Sherman thus expressed himself, President Johnson supposed that he would favor military intervention in Maryland; and Sherman would have filled Grant's place during his absence in Mexico. Hence, Johnson's anxiety to send him thither. But Grant remained at home, and Sherman went.

On the question of negro suffrage, he said, —

"I never could have believed that I should favor giving negroes the right to vote; but that seems to me the only solution of our difficulties."

A *necessity* commanded his support at once, whether in war or peace.

Leading Southerners, in the winter of 1866-7, opposed to giving the ballot to negroes, asked his advice, and he gave it plainly, thus:—

"Go to the Union Republicans in Congress, and to them alone. Have nothing whatever to do with Northerners who opposed the war; they will never again be intrusted with power. The more you consort with them, the more exacting the Republicans will be, and ought to be. When you get home, urge your people to accept negro suffrage. If you had promptly adopted the constitutional amendment abolishing slavery, or the one making negroes citizens, and guaranteeing the public debt, Congress would undoubtedly have admitted you ere this. Now it will add impartial suffrage. The sooner you accept that, the better for all concerned."

President Johnson was opposed to these views of General Grant; but the latter held the confidence of the loyal people to such an extent, that the former had not the courage to wage a direct war upon him.

The President came into collision with Secretary Stanton, and conferred with Grant about removing him; but the latter stoutly opposed the measure verbally, and subsequently opposed it even more strenuously by letter, because of "the great danger to the welfare of the country." At the same time, Johnson proposed to remove General Sheridan, which Grant opposed with all his might, saying, —

"He is universally and deservedly beloved by the

people who sustained this Government througn its trials, and feared by those who would still be its enemies. It fell to the lot of but few men to do as much against an armed enemy as General Sheridan did during the Rebellion; and it is within the scope of the ability of but few in this or any other country to do what he has."

And he closed his letter with the following plain, fearless opposition: —

"In conclusion, allow me to say, as a friend desiring peace and quiet, the welfare of the whole country, North and South, that it is, in my opinion, more than the loyal people of this country (I mean those who supported the Government during the great Rebellion) will quietly submit to, to see the very men of all others whom they have expressed confidence in, removed.

"I would not have taken the liberty of addressing the Executive of the United States thus but for the conversation on the subject alluded to in this letter, and from a sense of duty, feeling that I know I am right in this matter."

But the obstinate President, — made more obstinate, no doubt, by his intemperate habits, — did remove Secretary Stanton, when Congress was not in session; and he appointed General Grant in his place as Secretary of War. In the circumstances, probably, he did not dare to remove Stanton and put any one but Grant in his place. General Grant accepted the appointment solely because he feared that, if he did not accept, another man, in full sympathy with the President, would be appointed; and such a Secretary would come into immediate collision with Congress, and hinder the work of reconstruction.

The President, also, issued an order on the 17th of August, removing Sheridan, to which order General Grant protested in the following communication, which elicited the universal commendation of loyal people: —

"I am pleased to avail myself of your invitation to urge [Johnson accompanied his order with a request to Grant to make any suggestions] in the name of a patriotic people, who have sacrificed hundreds of thousands of loyal lives, and thousands of millions of treasure, to preserve the integrity and union of this country, that this order be not insisted on. It is unmistakably the expressed wish of the country, that General Sheridan should not be removed from his present command. This is a republic, where the will of the people is the law of the land. I beg that their voice may be heard.

"General Sheridan has performed his civil duties faithfully and intelligently. His removal will only be regarded as an effort to defeat the laws of Congress. It will be interpreted by the unreconstructed element in the South, — those who did all they could to break up this Government by arms, and now wish to be the only element consulted as to the method of restoring order, — as a triumph. It will embolden them to renewed opposition to the will of the loyal masses, believing that they have the Executive with them."

Attorney-General Stanberry, who was in full

sympathy with Johnson, gave his opinion that department commanders could not remove civil officers
who attempted to obstruct the laws of Congress.
Bul General Grant believed they could, and said that
"they are responsible for the faithful execution of
the reconstruction acts of Congress." After the
Attorney-General published his opinion, Grant telegraphed to Pope : —

"Enforce your own construction of the military
bill, until ordered to do otherwise. The opinion of
the Attorney-General has not been distributed to district commanders in language or manner entitling it
to the force of an order ; nor can I suppose that the
President intended it to have such force."

When Congress reassembled, the Senate refused
to sanction the removal of Stanton, whereupon
Grant resigned. His brief conduct of the business
of the War Department proved his eminent fit
ness for that position. Many leading Republicans
claimed that the office had never been administered
with so much ability. He stopped the employment
of mounted orderlies and of ambulances not absolutely
required ; selling the horses and vehicles. He required all proposals for supplies to be properly
advertised, and let to the lowest bidder, instead of
being given to some friend or favorite. He ordered
that soldiers on the frontier should gather the hay
and fuel necessary, instead of paying contractors a
great price for them, and that Government teams
should deliver them. He prohibited commanding
officers employing civilians as clerks, mechanics, or
laborers, or to do any work which the soldiers could

do; and he gave notice that any officer who disobeyed should have the expense incurred charged to his own personal account. In this way he reduced the current expenses of the department more than half a million a month; and, at the same time, sold stores and material in the quarter-master's department to the amount of many millions of dollars.

General Grant was firm, too, in his opinion that the National Government must not exhibit a spirit of exultation or retaliation in the final settlement of the difficulties. He had an eye to the future harmony of the North and South, as indispensable to the unity and prosperity of the Nation; and he believed that the largest magnanimity possible towards the conquered was absolutely necessary to this end. Hence, his magnanimous spirit in submitting terms of surrender to Lee, — terms which he ever vindicated with the soundest logic and the noblest sentiments.

He did not hesitate to come directly in collision with the President and Congress, in urging national magnanimity in the treatment of even traitors.

When it was proposed to arrest General Lee for treason, he protested against the measure as a violation of the terms of surrender which he accepted. He was called before the Judiciary Committee of Congress in July, and said, —

" . . . I frequently had to intercede for General Lee and other paroled officers, on the ground that their parole, so long as they obeyed the laws of the United States, protected them from arrest and trial. The President at that time occupied exactly

the reverse grounds, viz. : that they should be tried
and punished. He wanted to know when the time
would come that they should be punished. I told
him not so long as they obeyed the law and com
plied with the stipulation."

Eldridge. — " You looked on that in the nature of
a parole, and held that they could only be tried
when they violated that parole ? "

Grant. — " Yes, that is the view I took of the
question.'

Eldridge. — " Did you consider that that applied
to Jefferson Davis ? "

Grant. — " No, sir ; he did not take any parole.
. . . It applied to no person who was captured —
only to those who were paroled."

Eldridge. — " Did the President insist that General Lee should be tried for treason ? "

Grant. — " He contended for it. . . . I insisted
on it that General Lee would not have surrendered
his army, and given up all their arms, if he had supposed that after surrender he was going to be tried
for treason and hanged. I thought we got a very
good equivalent for the lives of a few leaders, in
getting all their arms and getting themselves under
control, bound by their oaths to obey the laws. . .

" I never claimed that the parole gave these prisoners any political rights whatever. I thought that
that was a matter entirely with Congress, over
which I had no control; that simply as General-in-Chief commanding the army, I had a right to stipulate for the surrender on terms which protected
their lives That is all I claim. The parole gave

them protection and exemption from punishment for an offense not in violation of the rules of civilized warfare, so long as their parole was kept."

That General Grant's lenient and magnanimous policy prevailed, was fortunate for the country. If his views and recommendations on certain other difficult questions had been adopted, instead of following the lead of partisan Congressmen, there is no question but that Government would have been the gainer.

After the surrender of Lee, the Union army began to salute Grant by firing cannon. He directed the firing to cease at once, saying, —

"It will wound the feelings of our prisoners, who have become our countrymen again."

A few months after the war closed, Grant was waited upon by a Congressional Committee, of which Charles Sumner was chairman, to propose that a picture of Lee's surrender should be painted, and placed in the rotunda of the Capitol. The General listened respectfully to their proposal, and replied, —

"So far as I am concerned, I can never consent to any picture being placed in the Capitol to commemorate a victory in which our own countrymen were the losers."

However much any of us may have differed from General Grant in his policy then, there are very few thoughtful citizens who do not approve of it now. Rebellion in the family can never be succeeded by peace, except by forgiving and forgetting; and it is equally true of the Nation. Like Abraham Lincoln, Grant was tender and kind, incapable of malice even towards his enemies, and altogether too great to be revengeful. In consequence, the North and the South are more rapidly becoming one people.

General Badeau has recently said, in *The Century*, —

"The men whom he conquered never forgot his magnanimity. A few months after Appomattox, he made a tour through the Southern States, and then entered Richmond for the first time. Had he been the savior instead of the captor of the town, he could hardly have been more cordially received. The Southerners felt indeed that he had been a savior to them. He had saved them from the rancor and revengeful spirit of many at the North. The terms he had granted them at Appomattox were unexampled for clemency; and when Andrew Johnson attempted to violate those terms, Grant declared he would resign his position in the army unless they were respected. At Richmond, Raleigh, Charleston, Savannah, the most important Southerners, civilians, and soldiers made it their duty to call upon him, to welcome him, to show him their gratitude.

"At Raleigh the State Legislature was in session, and he was invited to be present, and the body rose as he entered the Capitol which his armies had captured not six months before. Important Southerners soon addressed him, requesting him to become a candidate for the Presidency, assuring him of the unanimous desire of the South to see him at the head of the Government. Gen. Richard Taylor came to me on this errand, and urged that

Grant should allow himself to become the candidate of the Democrats."

General Grant made the tour through the South to which General Badeau refers above, in the winter of 1866-7. On his return he made a report, at the request of President Johnson, from which we extract the following:—

"I am satisfied that the mass of thinking men of the South accept the present situation of affairs in good faith. The questions which have hitherto divided the sentiments of the people of the two sections — slavery and State rights, or the right of a State to secede from the Union — they regard as having been settled forever by the highest tribunal — arms — that man can resort to. I was pleased to learn from the leading men whom I met, that they not only accepted the decision arrived at as final, but, now that the smoke of battle has cleared away, and time has been given for reflection, that this decision has been a fortunate one for the whole country, they receiving the like benefits from it with those who opposed them in the field and in the council. . . . .

"The Southern States are anxious to return to self-government within the Union as soon as possible; that while reconstructing they want and require protection from the Government; that they are in earnest in wishing to do what they think is required by the Government, not humiliating to them as citizens, and that if such a course was pointed out they would pursue it in good faith. It is to be regretted that there can not be a greater commingling at this time between the citizens of the two sections, and particularly with those intrusted with the law-making power."

In February, 1867, he visited New York again, where the leather-trade invited him to a costly banquet. He was presented with ONE HUNDRED THOUSAND DOLLARS from the citizens. The citizens of Philadelphia had previously given him *thirty thousand*.

On this trip he visited the rooms of the Union Relief Committee, and was there shown two hundred and seventy specimens of penmanship executed by soldiers who had lost their right arms. Grant remarked, —

"These boys write better with their left hands than I do with my right."

There was no part of his experience in New York city, at this time, which won his heart so much as the achievements of these "boys in blue" in penmanship, with their left hands.

We have called attention to a few of the complex tasks to which General Grant was called, between the close of the war and his occupancy of the White House. These facts confirm previous statements, that General Grant has never been understood and appreciated until actual work has proved his fitness for every position. In every office he has surprised his friends by his singular ability to perform whatever he undertook, readily, easily, speedily. Questions of statesmanship were no more difficult for his versatile talents to compass than questions of the camp and field. We have seen that he was alike at home in all.

The absence of petty jealousies, never indulging resentment or a personal pique, conceding to all their just deserts, whether friend or foe, happy in the successes of others, and always simple and unassuming in the highest position — these qualities made the General great as a military leader. Small men never rise above piques and jealousies; these are proof of weak minds.

History can furnish no parallel to the moral grandeur of that scene in Washington, when Mr. Blaine and other leaders proposed to fix matters so in Congress that Grant could return to his post of general-in-chief, after having served the country as President

"We will adopt a resolution in both Houses of Congress, giving you leave of absence for four years, so that you can resume your position at the close of your Presidency," said Mr. Blaine to Grant a short time before his inauguration.

General Grant was not favorably impressed by the proposition. Another added, —

"The rank of general-in-chief was created for you alone, and it is not just that you should sacrifice it by going up higher for four years to serve your country."

"It strikes me differently," replied Grant; "and I cannot consent to such an arrangement. I could not sleep at night if I felt that I was depriving Sherman and others of promotion which they have earned as fairly as I can be said to have earned mine."

He insisted that General Sherman should succeed him in the office, and he did.

We have said that history does not furnish a parallel to the above, in honest friendship and unselfish aims. But perhaps it is paralleled by another incident, illustrating the lofty spirit of patriotism and true friendship, which characterized both Grant and Sherman. General Grant had been for several months in front of Petersburg, apparently accomplishing nothing, while General Sherman had captured Atlanta, and completed his grand "march to the sea." Then arose a strong cry to promote Sherman to Grant's position as Lieutenant-General. Hearing of it, Sherman wrote to Grant, —

"I have written to John Sherman to stop it. I would rather have you in command than any one else. I should emphatically decline any commission calculated to bring us into rivalry."

General Grant replied, —

"No one would be more pleased at your advancement than I, and if you should be placed in my position, and I put subordinate, it would not change our relations in the least. I would make the same exertions to support you that you have done to support me, and I would do all in my power to make our cause win."

Two great souls striving to be equally magnanimous! Could anything be more beautiful and noble in public life, where jealousy, selfishness, and double-dealing appear to rule the hour, than such self-abnegation, where "each esteems the other better than himself?"

General Grant not only accorded to each officer his mede of praise, but he came promptly to his rescue when he was unjustly criticised. Thus, when critics were sharp on Sheridan, he said to the public, —

"The people don't understand Sheridan. Though he has all the popularity any man could desire, his capacity is not appreciated. The impression seems to be that he is only a brave, downright fighter. Really, he is a man of admirable judgment; capable of handling, under any circumstances, the largest army ever seen in the United States."

And he is reported as saying more recently, "Sheridan is the peer of any soldier living."

We shall close this chapter by quoting from the article of General Badeau his estimate of General Grant's character and ability in the field and forum: —

"At the close of the war, the man who had led the victorious armies was not forty-three years of age. He had not changed in any essential qualities from the captain in Mexico and merchant in Galena. Developed by experience, taught by circumstance, learning from all he saw, and even more from what he did, as few have ever been developed or taught, or have learned, — he, nevertheless, maintained the self-same personality through it all. The characteristics of the *man* were exactly those he manifested as a soldier — directness and steadiness of purpose, clearness and certainty of judgment, self-reliance, and immutable determination.

"No capture of places, or outflanking of armies, would have annihilated the Confederacy. It had to be stamped out; its armies and its resources had to be destroyed; its territory and its people conquered; its soldiers killed. Its own magnificent bravery, the spirit of its armies, the heroism of its population, rendered just such a course as Grant pursued indispensable. His greatness lay in the fact that he perceived the situation, and adapted his means to the end. His good fortune was, that his nature was fitted for just such emergencies.

"He who was capable of the combinations that stretched across a continent, who could direct the operations of a twelvemonth so that every movement was a part of the plan, and finally concentrate all his forces toward a single point, and consummate exactly what he set out to do, a year before, with a completeness unexampled then, and unsurpassed since in war, may laugh at the critics who pronounce him inept and blundering.

"There are many traits in Grant resembling those displayed by Moltke. All great soldiers, indeed, have much in common; but perhaps the parallel between these two is closer than any other in recent history. Both lived simply and almost unknown to their countrymen for many years. Both are plain in behavior, modest under unexampled success, undemonstrative in manner, simple in habits and tastes, unassuming and retiring, though thrust into the highest position. Neither ever sought advancement, but each earned it by his deeds. Both are admirable in the family, and attach friends warmly despite their reserved and dispassionate demeanor.

"Both have expressed in their public career the tremendous determination, the sustained energy, the persistency of purpose, which the world has recognized. Both have exhibited the power to hurl men in successive masses to certain danger, or even destruction, in order to gain the victory which they deemed essential to their country, as well as the ability to control different armies simultaneously on the widest theatres; moving them in apparently opposite directions only to concentrate them at last for a single aim. One general struck down an empire, and accomplished the capitulation of a sovereign; the other overthrew a rebellion greater than the world had ever seen before, and stamped out every vestige of resistance on a continent."

XXII.

AT THE TOP.

DANIEL WEBSTER'S reply to a young man who complained that all departments of business were crowded with aspirants for promotion, "ROOM ENOUGH AT THE TOP," may be true in one sense; but its application in the case before us is at least doubtful. There is room at the top of the Nation for only one man in four years. General Grant was the eighteenth man who had reached that high position in nearly one hundred years. There is room in the White House for only one man at a time. The largest encouragement that can be held out to aspiring men here is twenty-five chances in one hundred years. That is not a particularly wide opening. The way to the top is rather "straight and narrow," with only "here and there a traveler." Many there are who seek it, but "few there be that find it." General Grant was one of the few; and he found the "way" without seeking for it. The "way" came to him; he did not go to the "way." To numerous friends who proposed to assist him to step upon the top round of the ladder, he turned a deaf ear. There was no *plan* to raise him there which met his approval.

"General, we want you for President," said an

editor from Texas. "I am going to support you, and so are my people. What shall I say of your views when I get home?"

"Say nothing about them," was Grant's quick reply.

To a leading Republican who suggested to him, "The loyal people will not take NO for an answer," he said, "I do not want the office, and others do."

To the suggestion that the condition of the country required that a military man be President, he said,—

"All the military service necessary now in the administration of the Government I can render where I am, and more effectually, too; besides, in a republic like ours, there is a reasonable objection to making a President of a general."

If interested friends had not ceased to confer with him in respect to becoming a candidate for the presidency, he never would have been their nominee. It was not that the honor would not have been congenial to him; but it was too delicate a subject for his great modesty to discuss. He could always see reasons why some one else should be President instead of himself. Nevertheless, but one sentiment seemed to possess loyal hearts. The "War Governor" of Massachusetts, — John Albion Andrew, — expressed it, when he wrote to a personal friend:—

"The tendency of the hour is toward Grant, and that is best. It is not the ideal good. It is bad for the country that he must leave his present post — bad for him, the soldier, to try to endure the hard fate which awaits him in civil life. But it is apparently the best practical good the country can have; and Grant is so square and honest a man, that he is bound to be right in the main anywhere."

Andrew died very suddenly three days after he wrote as above.

A national Republican convention, in Chicago, May 19, 1868, nominated Grant unanimously for the presidency. Every State in the Union was represented in that convention; and the unanimity and enthusiasm of the delegations were remarkable. There were SIX HUNDRED AND FIFTY delegates present; and when, as usual, the roll of States was called to name a presidential candidate, General Grant was named by SIX HUNDRED AND FIFTY delegates! He carried every vote in the convention, which was without a parallel.

The result was hailed with great delight by members of the convention. The whole assembly sprang to their feet at the announcement of the vote, and a scene of the wildest enthusiasm followed. The band played, hats were tossed into the air, cheer after cheer arose, loud and long continued. Scarcely had the glad tumult ceased, when a curtain arose in the rear of the stage, exhibiting "a painting of two pedestals standing in front of the White House; one (bearing the figure of Grant) labeled, 'Republican nominee of the Chicago Convention, May 20, 1868'; the other, 'Democratic nominee, New York Convention, July 4, 1868.' Between the two stood the Goddess of Liberty, pointing with one hand to Grant, and with the other to the vacant pedestal. Overhead was the motto: MATCH HIM! At that moment a dove, painted in the national colors, was let loose, and flew back and forth; and the historic eagle of the Eighth Wisconsin added his screams to the tumult."

There was no such thing as mistaking the wishes of the people after this demonstration. That was a representative body of men, who understood the strong desire of their constituents to make the victorious leader of the American army President of the United States.

Ex-Governor Hawley, of Connecticut, was president of the convention; and, a few days after, officially notified General Grant of his nomination, to which the General replied:—

"*Mr. President, and Gentlemen of the National Union Convention,* — I will endeavor, in a very short time, to write you a letter accepting the trust you have imposed upon me. Expressing my gratitude for the confidence you have placed in me, I will now say but little orally, and that is to thank you for the unanimity with which you have selected me as a candidate for the presidential office. I can say, in addition, I looked on during the progress of the proceedings at Chicago with a great deal of interest, and am gratified with the harmony and unanimity which seem to have governed the deliberations of the convention. If chosen to fill the high office for which you have selected me, I will give to its duties the same energy, the same spirit, and the same will that I have given to the performance of all duties which have devolved upon me heretofore. Whether I shall be able to perform these duties to your entire satisfaction, time will determine. You have truly said, in the course of your address, that I shall have no policy of my own to enforce against the will of the people."

On the 29th he wrote to the Committee: —

"In formally accepting the nomination of the National Union Republican Convention of the 21st of May, inst. it seems proper that some statement of views beyond the mere acceptance of the nomination should be expressed.

"The proceedings of the convention were marked with wisdom, moderation, and patriotism, and I believe express the feelings of the great mass of those who sustained the country through its recent trials. I indorse the resolutions.

"If elected to the office of President of the United States, it will be my endeavor to administer all the laws in good faith, with economy, and with the view of giving peace, quiet, and protection everywhere. *In times like the present it is impossible, or at least eminently improper, to lay down a policy to be adhered to, right or wrong, through an administration of four years. New political issues, not foreseen, are constantly arising;* the views of the public on old ones are constantly changing, and a purely administrative officer should always be left free to execute the will of the people. I always have respected that will, and always shall.

"Peace and universal prosperity—its sequence—with economy of administration, will lighten the burden of taxation, while it constantly reduces the national debt. *Let us have peace!*"

These views exhibit the spirit with which General Grant entered upon his duties as President of the United States. "With malice towards none and charity for all," he became the Chief Executive. Though first in war, he planned and labored for "peace." Though conqueror of the South, he was its best friend. His leading purpose continued to be, to heal the breach between the North and

South, that the two sections of country might dwell together in unity. To this end he bent his energies, willing to bear the severest criticisms of leaders in his own party, if, by tolerant means, he could restore peace to the distracted Nation.

Here he found more than one army to meet and vanquish. The humbled South, the Democratic party of the North, and some leaders of his own party—all these were factors in the intricate problem of national affairs to be solved. "Grant wished all personal hatred and animosities laid aside—the past to be wiped out, and the welfare of the country — the whole country — the only object to be sought after. As President, he determined to treat his former enemies with the same magnanimity that he did as General in the field. He would not even listen to arguments for this or that measure that looked only to party success."

Of course it was a period of critical importance when Grant became President. Had all loyal citizens believed with him, the difficulties of the hour would have largely diminished. But there was much difference of opinion in respect to public policy, and these differences were sustained by an inexcusable amount of personal bitterness. To bring harmony out of the chaotic state of affairs existing, with hostilities waged in his own party, was well-nigh as difficult a campaign as Donelson or Shiloh. Only a self-reliant, independent, and honest President could carry himself successfully through such a conflict.

General Grant was inaugurated President March

4, 1869. His Cabinet were, Elihu B. Wash his old friend and townsman of Galena, Ill., fo ᴀ retary of State; Alexander T. Stewart, of New York, Secretary of Treasury; Jacob D. Cox, o Ohio, Secretary of the Interior; Adolph E. or of Pennsylvania, Secretary of the Navy; John Schofield, of Illinois, Secretary of War; John A. Creswell, of Maryland, Postmaster-General; Rockwell Hoar, of Massachusetts, Attorney-Gen eral. Schuyler Colfax was Vice-President.

It was found, however, that Mr. Stewart was disqualified for the position by an act of 1789, prohibiting a person engaged in trade and commerce being appointed to the office; and George S. Boutwell, of Massachusetts, received the appointment. Soon, also, Mr. Washburne was appointed Minister to France, and Hamilton Fish, of New York, became Secretary of State. Mr. Schofield also retired from the War Department, and John A. Rawlins, Grant' friend and neighbor of Galena, his true and tried staff-officer through the war, became Secretary of War. Rawlins died, however, in four months, and William W. Belknap, of Iowa, was appointed to fill his place. Mr. Borie resigned in June, and George M. Robeson, of New Jersey, took his place. Mr. Hoar resigned in July, 1870, and was succeeded by A. T. Akerman, of Georgia, who, in turn, resigned in December, 1871, and was succeeded by George H. Williams, of Oregon. Mr. Cox resigned in November, 1870, and Columbus Delano succeeded him.

The work of reconstructing the late rebellio States had been obstructed by the antagonism

President Johnson to Congress; but now both President Grant and Congress addressed themselves to the work with industry and determination. President Johnson, with whose dissolute habits and public career the loyal people had become disgusted, was no longer an obstacle to just and necessary legislation.

On his first message to Congress, President Grant recommended a return to specie payment as soon as possible, "for which no substitute can be devised." Also, civil service reform and a more humane and satisfactory Indian policy were recommended; these, in addition to the numerous questions connected with reconstruction. President Grant said, in his message, —

"On my assuming the responsible duties of Chief Magistrate of the United States, it was with the conviction that three things were essential to its peace, prosperity, and fullest development. First among these is strict integrity in fulfilling all our obligations. Second, to secure protection to the person and property of the citizen of the United States in each and every portion of our common country, wherever he may choose to move, without reference to original nationality, religion, color, or politics, demanding of him only obedience to the laws and proper respect for the rights of others. Third, union of all the States — with equal rights — indestructible by any constitutional means."

President Grant proceeded early to reform the management of Indian affairs, which had been conducted by the military arm of the Government.

His acquaintance with Indians on the frontier, as well as his correct knowledge of human nature, led him to repudiate the old method of dealing with the Indians. In his first message he said, —

"From my own experience upon the frontiers and in Indian countries, I do not hold either legislation or the conduct of the whites who come most in contact with the Indian, blameless for these hostilities The past, however, cannot be undone, and the question must be met as we now find it. I have attempted a new policy towards these wards of the Nation (they cannot be regarded in any other light than as wards), with fair results so far as tried, and which I hope will be attended ultimately with great success. The Society of Friends is well known as having succeeded in living in peace with the Indians in the early settlement of Pennsylvania, while their white neighbors of other sects, in other sections, were constantly embroiled. They are also known for their opposition to all strife, violence, and war, and are generally noted for their strict integrity and fair dealings. These considerations induced me to give the management of a few reservations of Indians to them, and to throw the burden of selection of agents upon the Society itself. The result has proven most satisfactory."

Here is the great warrior and fighter, so intent upon "peace" and "good will" among all men, that he selects agents who repudiate all war as wicked in the extreme, to govern and educate the most savage tribes of men! He stoutly maintained that the Church instead of the State should have the man agement of the Indians throughout the land. He submitted the matter, at one time, to the officers of the American Missionary Association, whose special field of labor was among the Freedmen of the South; and they decided to assume the responsibility, at least so far as a portion of the Indian tribes were concerned; and they appointed some of their most successful missionaries for Indian agents The plan proved successful.

President Grant's Indian policy introduced a new era of hope for the Indian in our country ; and from that time, the improvement of this class has been rapid, and that, too, with increased economy for the government, and fewer outbreaks in violence and war by the Indians. If Grant's administration were distinguished for nothing more than his new Indian policy, this alone would be sufficient to give it a foremost place in history.

The opposition to his Indian policy, civil-service reform, renewal of specie payment, and other measures in Congress, was decided, and sometimes even violent. A few leading Republicans of the country, like Charles Sumner and Horace Greeley, arrayed themselves against him, and bandied about severe criticisms, as unwise as they were partisan.

A formal petition from Santo Domingo was received by our Government, asking to be taken under its protection. President Grant had no particular interest in the matter, except that he believed the United States should have some foothold in the West Indies to promote commerce. First, he sent his own agents thither to investigate the state of affairs and report. Their report was favorable in every respect; whereupon the President submitted a treaty to the Senate. At the same time, for the purpose of furnishing all available information, he sent a commission, composed of public men in whom the country had entire confidence, to investigate further. B. F. Wade of Ohio, A. D. White of New York, and S. G. Howe of Massachusetts, constituted that commission — the best selection of men that could possibly have been made. Frederick Douglas was sent with them, also, that all sides of the question might be represented. This commission reported unanimously in favor of annexation; and nothing was left for the President but to recommend the measure. Charles Sumner opposed the project vehemently, to the surprise of some of his best friends. For he had advocated the payment of seventy-one million dollars for Alaska; and an equal sum for St. Thomas. Subsequent events proved conclusively that the defeat of the measure was unfortunate for the best interests of the country. To-day the wisdom of Grant is more conspicuous than that of Sumner in this affair.

He was bitterly assailed, also, for his acts in the line of civil-service reform. That he *should* sometimes make a mistake in the appointment of thousands of men to office, is not strange. Even some good men cannot withstand the temptations of a political life, and break down morally after their appointment. But that Grant intentionally appointed a bad man to any place of trust, no man believes to-day. But he was persistently opposed by members of Congress. This body was so slow to adopt his recommendations upon civil-service reform, that he said, in his fourth message, "In three successive messages to Congress, I have called attention to civil-service reform." The difference between Grant and most of his opponents in Congress, was that he was thoroughly honest, ever deciding for what he thought was right and for the highest good of the country, while most of his Republican opponents had an eye to the loaves and fishes of political promotion, either for themselves or their party.

His Indian policy, too, stirred up a nest of fault-finders, though the most thoughtful and honest people regarded it as singularly humane and wise. It was not altogether strange that there should be difference of opinion in the settlement of this and other important questions; but the degree of bitterness manifested by a class of opponents was very good evidence that personal animosity, selfish interest or a partisan spirit, was the real source of the opposition.

The Governor of Louisiana called upon President Grant for United States troops, to assist him in preserving order. The President responded by sending troops, as the Constitution required that he should do. Some of Grant's opponents held that the election of Governor was fraudulent, which was true, no doubt; but that was a question for Congress to investigate, and not the President. The duty of the latter was plain — to respond to the demand of the Governor of Louisiana for troops. But this was made the occasion of renewed attacks upon the President by a class of politicians who were determined not to be satisfied with his administration. Some of them had been aspirants for the presidency, and were sorely disappointed that he had beaten them in the race. Others were aspirants for other positions, which they failed to secure, much to their chagrin and mortification. In his appointments, Grant disappointed many prominent Republicans, because he selected men who had not figured largely in politics, but were men of integrity and ability in their vocations. The President believed that, in this way, he would secure a better class of public servants, than by the usual plan of selecting men who had worked hard for the party. Besides, this plan alone would enable him to carry out his ideas of civil-service reform far more successfully than the other.

When the Electoral Commission were transacting their important business, the President removed United States troops nearer Washington, which raised a great hue and cry among his enemies. The opponents of the measure, who were the strong friends of Tilden, threatened violence in Washington. The authorities of that city and many of its leading citizens, together with influential members of Congress, believed that there was imminent danger of mobocratic rule, and earnestly besought the President to provide for the emergency. To provide thus against a possible rebellion could do no hurt, though the troops might not be needed. The President adopted the measure in the interest of good order; and the result vindicated his wisdom

Without speaking of other measures which caused the opposition of President Grant's enemies, those considered show that his civil administration was well-nigh as stormy as his military life. It was a political Shiloh, for which only a man of steel, like himself, was qualified. The heaviest guns never caused him to quail; and he stood by his colors like one who was expected to defend them or die. His triumphant election to a second term of office proved that the great majority of the loyal people endorsed his administration.

Hon. J. A. J. Creswell, who was five years in President Grant's Cabinet, as Postmaster-General, has just spoken as follows: —

"General Grant's great characteristic was his sublime and unflinching courage. It was of that kind that no impression could be made upon it by opposition. He discharged his duties always without selfishness; never stopping to consider how an action would affect him personally. He wanted to know what was just, what was right. I remember an instance of this kind at the time we had a postal treaty with Japan, which gave us almost entire control of the Japanese postal service. When their relations grew more intimate with us and with other nations, they desired to have charge of their own service, and took steps in that direction. After the Japanese minister had talked with me about a treaty to that effect, I went to Grant and laid the matter before him. I found that he had but one idea — to do what was right and just toward Japan. I pointed out to him, that if he should sign such a treaty, we would be surrendering our control of the Japanese service, and would be subjected to severe criticism, especially on the Pacific coast. 'But isn't it right?' was his reply. 'Can there be any doubt about it?' I told him I only wanted to advise him of the consequences. He was satisfied that the treaty was just, and he signed it. I remember the time when he refused to sign the bill, which appeared to be a deflection from the course we have determined upon.

"For the resumption of specie payment, there was an immense pressure brought to bear on Grant to sign the bill. Republicans of prominence urged it, thinking the bill would prove a satisfactory halfway measure. I think Grant's personal inclination was to sign it. Secretary Fish and myself were the only ones in the Cabinet who opposed its approval. At the Cabinet meeting, when it was considered, Grant drew from his desk a paper and read it. It was a message to Congress, returning the bill with his signature. I said, 'I regret very much that you should have felt it your duty to pursue such a course.' 'That isn't my view of the matter,' he replied. 'I wanted to do what was best, so I wrote all I could in behalf of the bill; but it doesn't satisfy me'; and he refused to sign it. If he had signed it, it would have caused us unlimited trouble.

"Grant never lost his head when we came so near being engaged in a war with Spain on account of the *Virginius* affair. There was a good deal of excitement at the Cabinet meeting, and a war with Spain was imminent. Grant knew what war meant; and by his coolness and by his sound judgment prevented it. He was assisted in this by the Spanish representative in this country, who was a naval officer. He, too, knew what fighting meant; and these two really prevented a war."

The opposition of Charles Sumner, Horace Greeley, and others, culminated in a union of Grant's Republican opponents with the Democratic party, and the nomination of Horace Greeley for President, and B. Gratz Brown for Vice-President. Pilate and Herod became friends under this singular and unexpected arrangement—the most violent friends of slavery uniting with the most radical friends of freedom. Very bitter things were said about Grant by the Republican leaders who joined this faction. But they inflicted more injury upon themselves than they did upon him, as the election very clearly proved; for the appeal to the verdict of the people resulted in Grant's renomination *by acclamation*, and his election by an overwhelming majority. Grant and Wilson received two hundred and sixty-eight votes in the Electoral College, against eighty for other candidates. Grant's popular majority over Greeley was seven hundred and sixty-two thousand nine hundred and ninety-one. This was an unexpected endorsement of Grant's administration to those Republicans who committed themselves against it; and many of them felt the sharp rebuke.

It is not our purpose to occupy space by the details of President Grant's second term as Chief Executive. It was a successful administration, to which there was less opposition than there was to his first term of four years. His ability as a statesman was more and more apparent to the people, as his military genius became more and more manifest in each succeeding year of the war. Many who doubted the wisdom of electing a military man President, became satisfied that the measure was a fortunate one for the country. So strongly did many of the wisest leaders, both North and South, feel upon the subject, that they proposed to nominate him for a *third* term, contrary to all precedent; but Grant, supported by many of his best friends, condemned the plan as subversive of a time-honored custom, which could result in no great advantage to the country. But in 1880 a movement of great magnitude, to secure his election to a third term, was inaugurated, and would have proved successful if Grant himself had actively engaged in the canvass.

Mr. Cresswell, who was almost as familiar with the facts as Grant himself, says now, —

"He did n't desire to be President a third term for any glory or reputation, but his sole object was to reconcile the North and South, and I think he would have done it thoroughly. The 'Solid South' would have been a thing of the past."

Here, as elsewhere, Grant's unselfish spirit was manifest. He was always ready to sink himself for the good of his country. George W. Childs, Esq., of Philadelphia, one of his most intimate friends, recently said, —

"He is generous to a fault, and has given away a fortune in charities. In this, like in everything else, he was modest. The same modesty that prevented him from asking for an appointment or a promotion, caused him to maintain silence concerning his gifts to the needy. I remember that when he was on one of his visits to me during his presidency, a great many people called here to ask favors of him. Not caring to have him worried, I refused admittance to all whom I suspected of being on an errand of that kind. One day a lady who lived in the same block— in fact only a few doors from my house—called and asked to see him. 'You may see her, General,' said I, laughing, 'I guess she is not after an appointment.' He came back in a little while and said, 'You were wrong; she *was* after an appointment.' I looked at him in astonishment, and he explained that the lady wanted him to transfer the sister-in-law of Edwin M. Stanton, Lincoln's Secretary of War, from the mint, where she was then employed, and where the work was too hard for her, to the Treasury Department. He requested me to see the Assistant United States Treasurer in this city, and ask him to give her a position. I did so, and the Assistant Treasurer told me he had no vacancy. 'General Grant's request is law, however,' said he, 'and I can make room for Mrs. Stanton, by removing a lady who has no need for a position here.' This was done, and some time afterward I met a son of Mr. Stanton (the latter was dead at the time), who thanked me for getting his aunt the appointment. 'General Grant appointed her,' said I. 'Oh, no,' said he, 'General Grant himself told me that you had got the appointment for her.' This is characteristic of the General, who is continually doing good, and giving others the credit."

Thus, the Tanner Boy and humble leather merchant of Galena climbed to the top round of the ladder of fame. In eight years from the time he took his satchel and left his Galena home to enlist for the war, he became President of the United States. So unknown at the outbreak of the war that no one prophesied for him a career of even moderate distinction; yet, he outstripped the military men of whom the Nation expected great things, and carried off the garlands which had been woven for them. Though about the last man to whom his nearest friend looked for statesmanship before the war, his eight years of service at the head of the Nation abundantly vindicated his claim to be ranked with our wisest rulers of the past.

And now the problem of his life is not difficult to solve. From the standpoint of to-day it is clear as noonday how he worked his way up to the highest post of renown. He made the most of himself possible, not by the aid of friends or political patronage, but by his own personal efforts, in spite of obstacles that would have carried dismay to hearts less persistent and brave. Elements of character, to which we called attention again and again, dominating his whole life, from boyhood to manhood, wrought for him as only such qualities can. It would be quite impossible to find a public man, in all the annals of the past, with whose career what men call "acci dent," or "luck," or "fortune," had so little to do as they did with Grant. From the bottom to the top round of the ladder, it was one persistent climbing by his own unassisted efforts, patronage, fortune, and all the rest of the aids to which politicians look for help, standing aloof to let him climb. This is what distinguished his career from that of most public men, whom the accident of birth, patronage, and good fortune favored. He "earned" every promotion before it became his.

We cannot do better than to close this chapter with further testimony from Mr. Cresswell, who knew Grant so well. Being asked what he thought of President Grant as a writer, he replied, —

"He wrote with great facility. His style, like his character, was the embodiment of directness. He used few metaphors and little ornamentation, and never two words where one would do, preferring Saxon words to Latin or French. He never hesitated for a word, and always went right to the point. He wrote all his own papers, notwithstanding the reports to the contrary, and all his messages were framed and written by himself."

"What are the facts about him as a talker?"

"Those who thought Grant could n't talk made a mistake," was the reply. "When he became intimate with one, he would talk as much as any companion should. I have heard him do nearly all the talking for an hour or two. He was a good talker, but slow; sometimes hesitating for a word — something never experienced in writing. He either had implicit confidence in a man or he had none. He was quick to form an estimate of a man, and if his suspicions were once aroused, his firm jaws shut like a trap, and he would remain cold and silent, and by his appearance could chill a speaker, no matter how earnest he might be. He always was modest and unassuming — never presented himself as a hero of an occasion, and never introduced military subjects in conversation. He had a very quick eye, and it was surprising to me how he could take in the whole topography at a glance. I remember once, while he was visiting me at my farm, I took him along for a drive around the country. I took a by-road, intending to strike the main road, but missed my way. Finally, I laughingly confessed it. 'Where did you want to go?' he asked. 'I wanted to strike a road which would take me to the village which lies in that direction.' He stood up in the buggy, and, looking over the surrounding country, said: 'If you will let down the fence here, drive over this field and then through that gate up yonder, I think you'll strike the road you want on that ridge.' 'Why do you think so?' I asked. 'Well, you say the village is in that direction [pointing]; up there I see quite a settlement. The people who live there will have a way to reach the village, and they could not find a better way than along that ridge.' I did as he advised, and found the road just where he said I would. I expressed surprise at his accuracy, and he replied, 'It has been part of my business to find roads. A good soldier should be able by seeing a portion of the country to form a good judgment of what the rest is.'"

Mr. Cresswell adds, —

"I had more admiration for General Grant than

for any man I ever saw, and it grieves me to the soul that he should be ending his days in suffering. I knew Lincoln, and I knew Stanton, and those two, with Grant, made the distinguished trio. Grant, the great soldier; Stanton, the executive officer, and Lincoln, the great arbiter. Grant's qualities of true manliness were more pronounced than those of any man I ever knew. In my close relations with him, while I was a member of his cabinet, I never heard him say a harsh or petty thing; never heard him speak impulsively, or use a profane word. His relations with his family were most delightful and charming. There never was a kinder or more indulgent father, and I never saw a more devoted couple than General and Mrs. Grant. Of course everybody knows how he loved his daughter. The meeting between them the other day was very touching, and the emotion shown by the old warrior exhibited the depth of his affection."

Gen. Charles Devens, of Massachusetts, who was intimately associated with Grant, both in war and peace, paid the following tribute to him at the "soldiers' carnival" in Boston, April 12, 1885:—

"Our service to-day has an added and peculiar solemnity. With moistened eyes and quivering lips we have seemed, as we celebrated it, to stand watching and waiting by the very side of the dying couch of the illustrious chieftain who was the leader of all our armies. How great and noble he has been, how immense the debt we owe him, we have never appreciated until the time has come when we know we must part with him forever. The representative of all as he lies in the august majesty of impending death, there gather around him the tender memories of all who have gone before him. His glory and his deeds were theirs, and theirs were his, and no commander ever claimed less for himself or gave more to those who followed him than Grant. Well may a Nation swell the funereal cry of him in whom were embodied all there was of courage, of endurance, of patriotism that distinguished the national soldier; and as the sounds of our sad farewell sink away in his dying ear, we will believe there will rise the tones of glad welcome from those he goes to meet. His place is to be forever with those whom God has reared up to save great nations in their hour of peril. It is gratifying to feel that all good men have fully given him their hearts at last; that detraction has been silent; that carping criticism — its meanest form — has been dumb; that many even of those once in arms against him and the cause for which he fought have recognised his generosity and forbearance, and that we who have loved him always have been allowed to renew to him the assurances of our respect and devotion. As after a day of clouds and storm there comes a calm, the winds are still and the world is flooded with the mellow light of the descending sun, even so as this great life of toil and struggle, of labor and duty, of vast and patriotic service draws to its close, earth and sky are filled with its glorious radiance, while he that has lived it, simple, serene, and uncomplaining, waits for that final word that will indeed dismiss him from our sight, but never from our love."

XXIII.

IN THE MOTHER-COUNTRY.

GENERAL GRANT'S fame had gone out through all the world during the sixteen years of public service which he had rendered to his country. There was a very strong desire in other nations to see "the greatest general of modern times." He was repeatedly urged by public men in other lands to visit them. The request met with a glad response from his own heart; for he had become wholly absorbed in the affairs of government, and he would study other governments, and learn statesmanship as it is found in other countries. He needed, too, the relaxation from public business; for sixteen years he had been subjected to a constant strain, such as no other American ever endured for so long a period. Four years in war; four years more at the head of our armies in settling the issues of the war; and eight years President of the United States,—service that involved thought and deeds, night and day, much of the time! His fine physical organization, under the control of an immense will-power, alone could have carried him through such a strain. It is not strange that a long, unbroken rest was absolutely necessary.

It was arranged for General Grant to sail for the Old World on the *Indiana*, on the seventeenth day of May, 1877. The news of his decision to start on that day had spread over our land, and crossed the Atlantic to other lands; so that the distinguished tourist became an object of interest to the world from the time of his departure. He breakfasted with George W. Childs, Esq., of Philadelphia, to whom we referred in the last chapter; and then, in company with many friends, including the Mayor of the city, he boarded the *Magenta* to go down the Delaware to the *Indiana*, twenty-five miles distant. The banks of the river were lined with people to bid adieu to the man whose eminent service for the country had awakened their gratitude. Men cheered, ladies waved their handkerchiefs, and chil dren shouted, as the boat sped on her way.

A table was spread for lunch on the *Magenta*, and toasts were read; in reply to which eloquent speeches were made. Mayor Stokley delivered a parting address to General Grant, in which he spoke so kindly of his service to his country, and of the debt of gratitude under which the American citizen is placed, as to well-nigh overcome him. In reply the General said, with considerable emotion, —

"I do not feel myself competent to respond to so many kind words uttered, and can only express my sincere thanks."

Once on board the *Indiana*, she steamed away amid the cheers of the multitude and the thunder of cannon.

While this was transpiring on this side of the

Atlantic, on the other side distinguished leaders were discussing whether Grant should be received as a sovereign or an American citizen. Fillmore and Van Buren had visited England, and they were received as honored citizens of the United States only. But Lord Beaconsfield finally announced that he would be received as a sovereign. In his nature he was just such a sovereign as would be found beneath the jacket of almost any American citizen; and yet he was doomed to the crucial test. What a trial to his prevailing modesty none but him will ever know.

The steamer was eleven days on its voyage through rough and stormy weather. Most of the passengers were sea-sick, except General Grant, who was as quiet and self-possessed as usual in the roughest weather.

At Queenstown a steamer from Cork, Ireland, with a large delegation on board, steered alongside to tender to General Grant the hospitalities of that city. They were received on board, and conducted to the captain's cabin, where an informal reception took place, and the invitation to visit Ireland was extended. General Grant replied briefly to the ad dress, promising to visit Ireland at a future day.

In the afternoon the *Indiana* reached Liverpool, where an unexpected display greeted the honored visitor. The whole city was covered with flags, and flags of every nationality floated from the ships in the harbor. The wharves were literally crammed with people, whose loud cheers rang out upon the water long before the steamer reached her landing. With uncovered head, Grant acknowledged the ova·

tion as the steamer rode into harbor. With the wife of the Consul-General of London on his arm, he stepped upon the pier, where a cordon of police closed around him; and the Mayor advanced and read an address of welcome, to which the General briefly replied. Then, stepping into the Mayor's carriage with his wife, he was driven to the Adelphi hotel, followed by a long procession of carriages, occupied by lords and ladies, and a crowd of people completely filling the streets, and making the city ring with their plaudits. The next day he was shown the objects of interest in the city, and lunched with the Mayor at the town-hall, where speeches were made; and he replied to a toast, in which he spoke of the harmony existing between the United States and the mother-country, and then proposed the health of the Mayor, Mayoress, and ladies of Liverpool.

On the following day he visited Manchester, where the compliments, applause, toasts, and speeches were repeated; and here our modest American made the longest speech of all. He spoke as follows:—

"It is scarcely possible for me to give utterance to the feelings evoked by my reception upon your soil from the moment of my arrival in Liverpool, where I have passed two days, until the present moment. After the scene I have witnessed in your streets, the elements of greatness, as manifested in your public and industrial buildings, I may be allowed to say that no person could be the recipient of the honor and attention you have bestowed upon me without the profoundest feeling. Such have been incited in me, and I find myself inadequate to their proper expression. It was my original purpose on my arrival in Liverpool to hasten to London, and from thence proceed to visit the various points of interest in the country. Among these I have regarded Manchester as the most important. [Hear.] As I have been aware for years of the great amount of your manufactures, many of which find their ultimate destination in my own country, so I am aware that the sentiments of the great mass of the people of Manchester went out in sympathy to that country during the mighty struggle in which it fell to my lot to take some humble part. The expressions of the people of Manchester at the time of our great trial incited within the hearts of my countrymen a feeling of friendship toward them distinct from that felt toward all England, and in that spirit I accept, on the part of my country, the compliments paid me as its representative, and thank you."

A lunch followed in the programme, when the Mayor highly complimented the city's guest, and facetiously remarked, —

"We have got out of him more and longer speeches than his countrymen ever did."

General Grant replied, and as facetiously said, —

"Englishmen have drawn from me more and longer speeches than my countrymen, but they are *poorer* simply because they are *longer* than I have been accustomed to make."

Jacob Bright, a member of Parliament, was called upon for a speech, and he said, —

"No guest so distinguished has ever before visited

Manchester. General Grant is a brave soldier, and he has pursued a generous, pacific policy toward the enemy he conquered. He should be honored and beloved, and deserves the hearty reception he is sure to receive throughout the realm."

The next day, on his way to the London station, a crowd of factory-girls met him, in their working-dresses, and gave him a warm salute with handkerchief and voice.

A similar demonstration was made at Leicestershire and Bedford, on his way to London. At the latter place, the Mayor, in his address to General Grant, called him "the Hannibal of the American armies."

In reply, the General asked to be excused from making a speech, and called forth much laughter by suggesting, "I might provide a substitute, perhaps, as men do in some other positions."

But the most remarkable festivities awaited his arrival in London, — such honors as are never bestowed upon another there except crowned heads. Preparations had been making for several weeks on the most imposing scale; and for a whole week the humble leather-dealer of Galena was *fêted* by the aristocracy and royalty of the kingdom in a manner that would have touched the pride of any one but him.

Our Minister to England, Mr. Pierrepont, met him at St. Pancras Station, and took him in his private carriage to his own residence in London.

The most imposing of all the ceremonies to honor their guest, was that of conferring upon him the freedom of the city. The following is an accurate description of the affair: —

"This is the highest honor that can be paid by this ancient and renowned corporation. The freedom of the city was presented in a gold casket. The obverse central panel contains a view of the Capitol at Washington, and on the right and left are the General's monogram and the arms of the Lord Mayor. On the reverse side is a view of the entrance to the Guildhall and an inscription. At the end are two figures, also in gold, representing the city of London and the Republic of the United States;— these figures bear enameled shields. At the corners are double columns, laurel-wreathed, with corn and cotton, and on the cover a cornucopia, as a compliment to the fertility and prosperity of the United States. The cover is surmounted by the arms of the city of London, and in the decorations are interwoven the rose, the shamrock, and the thistle. The casket is supported by the American eagle in gold, standing on a velvet plinth, decorated with stars and stripes.

"The ceremonies attending the presentation of the freedom of the city of London are stately and unique. Guildhall, one of the most ancient and picturesque buildings in the city, was especially prepared for the occasion, and eight hundred guests were invited to the banquet, a considerable portion of them being ladies. There were the Members of the Corporation, the American Minister, the Chancellor of the Exchequer, Members of Parliament, and representatives of the American Colony resi

dent in London. On arriving at the Guildhall the
General was received by a deputation of four Aldermen, with the chairman and four members of the
City Lands Committee, including the mover and
seconder of the resolution presenting the freedom.
This deputation conducted the General to his place
in the Common Council on the left-hand of the Lord
Mayor. The passage leading to the library was
guarded by a detachment of the London Brigade.
The routine of business being over, the Chamberlain
arose and addressed General Grant in quite a lengthy
speech, in which he spoke of the two countries, of
Grant's military achievements, and the distinguished
position he had held as President of a great Republic, and expressed the wish that he might enjoy his
visit, and closed by adding, —

"'Nothing now remains, General, but that I should
present you an illuminated copy of the resolutions of
this honorable Court, for which an appropriate casket
is in the course of preparation, and, in conclusion,
offer you, in the name of the honorable Court, the
right-hand of fellowship as a citizen of London.'"

General Grant's reply was as follows:—

"It is a matter of some regret to me that I have
never cultivated the art of public speaking, which
might have enabled me to express in suitable terms
my gratitude for the compliment which has been
paid to my countrymen and myself on this occasion.
Were I in the habit of speaking in public, I should
claim the right to express my opinion, and what I
believe will be the opinion of my countrymen when
the proceedings of this day shall have been tele-

graphed to them. For myself I have been very much surprised at my reception at all places since the day I landed at Liverpool, up to my appearance in this, the greatest city in the world. It was entirely unexpected, and it is particularly gratifying to me. I believe that this honor is intended quite as much for the country which I have had the opportunity of serving in different capacities, as for myself; and I am glad that this is so, because I want to see the happiest relations existing, not only between the United States and Great Britain, but also between the United States and all other nations. Although a soldier by education and profession, I have never felt any sort of fondness for war, and I have never advocated it except as a means of peace. I hope we shall always settle our differences in all future negotiations as amicably as we did in a recent instance. I believe that settlement has had a happy effect on both countries, and that from month to month and year to year the tie of common civilization and common blood is getting stronger between the two countries. My Lord Mayor, Ladies, and Gentlemen, I again thank you for the honor you have done me and my country to-day."

Then General Grant signed the roll of honor, which all great men, to whom the freedom of the city was ever granted, had signed.

The inevitable lunch followed these ceremonies, when General Grant was again toasted by the Lord Mayor, another speech being expected from the General. The latter created considerable merriment by his response: —

"My Lord Mayor and Gentlemen: Habits formed in early life and early education press upon us as we grow older. I was brought up a soldier—not to talking. I am not aware that I ever fought two battles on the same day in the same place; and that I should be called upon to make two speeches on the same day under the same roof is beyond my understanding."

Yet, he made a third speech on that day—the last one being strictly voluntary. Later in the day he attended a private dinner in the Crystal Palace, where Mr. Hughes proposed his health, and said that a speech was not expected. General Grant arose and said,—

"Nevertheless I must expresss the gratification it gives me to hear my health proposed in such kind words by 'Tom Brown of Rugby.'"

There was a fine display of fireworks in the evening, in which one of the pieces was a fine likeness of Grant "drawn in blazing lines against the sky." The General gazed at the likeness until it faded from his view, and, in its place, arose the Capitol in flaming splendor,—a magnificent spectacle, worthy of so great an occasion. Turning to Lady Ripon, who was sitting beside him, he remarked, "They have burned me in effigy, and they are now burning the Capitol."

He attended a costly banquet given by the Corporation of Trinity College, and presided over by the Prince of Wales. It was here that General Grant made one of his happiest speeches. A listener said, "He said not a word too much nor too little. The United States was never represented better anywhere than General Grant represented it on this occasion."

This eventful week of festivities received its crowning glory by the reception which the Queen herself gave to the General at Windsor Castle. The inside of this grand affair was never made public, for the reason that it is the custom to treat everything of the kind as sacred; but the external ceremonies were published abroad.

Dinner was served in St. George Hall, used only for state banquets. A select royal company was present; small in numbers, because the Queen must converse with every one present. Our Minister to England, Mr. Pierrepont, introduced General Grant to Victoria, and Lord Derby introduced Mrs. Grant. The Queen shook hands with them cordially, while the ladies in waiting bowed.

Then the gentlemen led the way to the table in the Oak Room. The Queen sat at the head of the table. On her right were Prince Leopold, Princess Christian, and General Grant; on her left Prince Christian, Princess Beatrice, and Mr. Pierrepont; then, the Duchess of Wellington, Lord Elphinstone, and Mrs. Pierrepont, Lord Derby and Mrs. Grant, the Duchess of Roxburgh and Lord Biddulph, the Countess of Derby and Jesse Grant.

During the dinner conversation was free and easy, in which the Queen joined with her accustomed vivacity; and she conversed with every one present. No speech from the General on this occasion.

But on the next day General Grant was obliged to

risk another speech; for he was waited upon by a deputation of forty men, representing a million English workingmen. He was at the house of his old friend and staff-officer, Consul-general Badeau. The leader read an elaborate address to him, welcoming him to England, and assuring him of their great interest in the country which the General represented, where English workmen were always welcome. After the reading of the address, several of the deputation made speeches. General Grant's reply was apropos:—

"In the name of my country I thank you for the address you have presented to me. I feel it a great compliment paid my Government, and to me personally. Since my arrival on British soil I have received great attentions, which were intended, I feel sure, in the same way for my country. I have had ovations, free hand-shakings, presentations from different classes, — from the Government, from the controlling authorities of cities, — and have been received in the cities by the populace; but there has been no reception which I am prouder of than this to-day. I recognize the fact that whatever there is of greatness in the United States, as indeed in any other country, is due to labor. The laborer is the author of all greatness and wealth. Without labor there would be no government, or no leading class, or nothing to preserve. With us labor is regarded as highly respectable. When it is not so regarded it is because man dishonors labor. We recognize that labor dishonors no man; and no matter what a man's occupation is, he is eligible to fill an post in the gift of the people; his occupation is not considered in selecting, whether as a law-maker or as an executor of the law. Now, Gentlemen, in conclusion, all I can do is to renew my thanks for the address, and repeat what I have said before, that I have received nothing from any class since my arrival which has given me more pleasure."

We have not room to describe all the receptions and festivities of that memorable week. The Queen gave him another reception, at Buckingham Palace in the city, which was regarded a great honor. The Duke of Wellington gave him a costly banquet at the Apsley House, where lords and ladies, counts and countesses, earls and viscounts, and other royal characters, assembled to do him honor. The Prince of Wales gave him a private audience at the Marlborough House, where he was introduced to all the members of the family with little formality.

At one reception he was asked, "How does English racing compare with the races in America?"

"There is an impression abroad," answered General Grant, smiling, "that I am a great horse-racer, fond of horses, and know all about races; but, on the contrary, I really know nothing of racing, having seen only two races — one at Cincinnati in 1865, and at the opening of Jerome Park in 1867. I feel, therefore, that I am not qualified to judge of the comparison. Thus far I like London very much. I have, however, accepted so many engagements that I shall be compelled to alter my plans and remain here until the 27th, when I shall visit Ireland."

The reader will recall the sensitiveness of the boy

Grant, when neighbors called him a "jockey," and he repelled the appellation. Something akin to that appears in the incident narrated. A horse-racer was a position to which General Grant did not aspire.

He attended divine service on Sunday, at Westminster Abbey, and heard the eloquent Dean Stanley. Of course, the General scarcely expected to make a speech on this occasion, nor to have one made over him; but in the course of his sermon the preacher did say: —

"We have in this congregation to-day the chief citizen of the United States, who has just laid down the sceptre of the American Commonwealth; who, by his military prowess and generous treatment of his comrades and adversaries, has restored unity to his country. We welcome him as a sign and pledge that the two great kindred nations are one in heart and are equally at home under this paternal roof. Both regard with reverential affection this ancient cradle of their common life."

General Grant must have been satisfied by this time that *unsought* honors are of rapid and luxuriant growth. They grew on every tree. They dropped down in every place. A crop of them, ripe and luscious, waited for him in every field. Every day in the week, secular and sacred, he was forced to pluck them. Even in the house of God they fell at his feet without shaking the tree!

The reader will recollect that General Grant promised to visit Liverpool again before leaving England. That promise was redeemed. The city welcomed him to a grand dinner, at the conclusion of which the Mayor toasted him, and the General replied in quite a lengthy speech, much of which was charged with dry humor. We have space for only a paragraph:—

"I am a soldier, and the gentlemen here beside me know that a soldier must die. I have been a president, but we know that the term of the presidency expires, and when it has expired he is no more than a dead soldier. [Laughter and cheers.] But, Gentlemen, I have met with a reception that would have done honor to any living person. [Cheers.] We are of one kindred, of one blood, of one language, and of one civilization, though in some respects we believe that we, being younger, surpass the mother country. [Laughter.] You have made improvements on the soil and the surface of the earth which we have not yet done, but which we do not believe will take us as long as it did you." [Laughter and applause.]

By this time the General was thoroughly weary, and both body and mind demanded rest. Such continuous excitement tasked him fully as much as the exigencies of war; for he was more at home on the tented field than he was in the courts of royalty. He sought repose by escaping to other honors.

XXIV.

ON THE CONTINENT.

N the Fourth of July General Grant left England for a respite amid the grand scenery of the Alps. He left London for Ostend, where the royal car conveyed him to Brussels, the Belgium capital. General Badeau accompanied the party.

It is not our purpose to give a detailed account of General Grant's travels,—that would be quite impossible in a volume of the size of this. We can do little more than to record incidents of special interest; chiefly those which will show the reader more and more of Grant himself. For that is the purpose of this book, from beginning to end.

At Frankfort-on-the-Main the people turned out *en masse* to welcome him. A public dinner was served, and great enthusiasm prevailed. A committee of Americans met him at Hamburg les Bains, and conveyed him to Salburg to visit the famous Roman camp, which was discovered about one hundred and fifty years ago. The camp covers seven hundred acres, and is under the control of the Prussian Government. A singular custom prevails with the authorities. When a very distinguished visitor comes, it is the custom to open one of the graves

So, in honor of General Grant, Professor Jacobi and Captain Fischer ordered a dead Roman soldier, after his repose of two thousand years, to be dug up. The result was, ashes well-nigh undistinguishable —a delicate hint to the great American General of the inevitable to himself. We need scarcely say that the whole affair was of little interest to so practical a man as Grant, who prefers "a living dog to a dead lion."

At Geneva, beautifully situated at the foot of Lake Leman, the public honors were conducted upon a grand scale, having in the programme one incident as interesting to Grant as it was novel. An American citizen had given a site for an Episcopal Church; and it was arranged for General Grant to lay the corner-stone. A gathering of Americans at the Hotel Beau Rivage, including several Protestant clergymen, formed a procession and marched to the place. Prayer was offered, followed by an address, when a box, containing a variety of American and Swiss papers and coins, was placed under the foundation. Then General Grant took a mallet and struck the stone with it, declaring that it was well laid in the name of the Father, Son, and Holy Ghost. A lunch followed, with several appropriate addresses, alluding fully as much to the distinguished guest as they did to the Holy Trinity. In reply, General Grant said,—

"I have never felt myself more happy than among the assembly of fellow-republicans of America and Switzerland. I have long had a desire to visit the city where the Alabama claims were settled without the effusion of blood, and where the principle of international arbitration was established, and which I hope will be resorted to by other nations, and be the means of continuing peace to all mankind."

Grant had a desire to go into northern Ita.y by the Simplon Pass, — a highway over a mountain ten thousand feet high. The road is regarded as a monument of Napoleon's engineering skill. It is thirty-six miles long, and twenty-five feet wide the whole length. Thirty thousand men were employed six years in constructing it. There are six hundred and eleven bridges on it, — seventeen bridges to a mile, on the average, — some of them spanning fearful abysses. There are ten galleries cut through solid rock, and twenty houses of refuge, in which travelers can find shelter from destructive avalanches.

Though, at its highest altitude, there is perpetual snow, the average grade is but one inch per foot. The grandeur of the scenery is beyond description. When once the tourist reaches the heart of the Alps, the road winds its perilous way along the edge of deep gorges, hundreds of feet below, crawling around ragged mountain-spurs that shoot skyward, gliding under immense glaciers towering hundreds of feet above, climbing mountain-peaks that rise in solemn stateliness, and finally gaining the snow-clad summit, where perpetual winter holds carnival. Near the top is a place from which the traveler can look straight down through an awful gorge and behold Briez, the town from which he started — twenty miles away by the road traveled.

On the other side General Grant found the de

scent still more grand,—the work of God and Napoleon combining to awaken awe at one place and terror at another. The "Gorge of Gonda" is a gallery six hundred feet long, cut through solid rock; and this remarkable tunnel, together with the perpendicular cliffs and monumental rocks seeking to pierce the skies, presented a scene never to be effaced from memory.

Being perfectly familiar with the circumstances under which this road was built, and also with the career of the mighty builder, General Grant was specially interested in his trip over the Simplon Pass.

At the hotel at Lake Maggiore, a crowd assembled to greet him. He was addressed by an officer who had served under Garibaldi. In his reply, Grant said,—

"There is one Italian whose hand I wish especially to shake, and that man is Garibaldi."

A thundering applause followed this announcement; for it touched the hearts of the people.

The time was near when he had promised to be in Edinburgh, Scotland, so that he was forced to cut short his tour in Italy and Switzerland, and repair thither.

The freedom of the city of Edinburgh was presented to him by Lord Provost Sir James Falshaw, in Free Assembly Hall, in the presence of two thousand of the leading citizens of Edinburgh. Grant replied:—

"I am so filled with emotion that I scarcely know how to thank you for the honor conferred upon me by making me a burgess of this ancient city of Edinburgh. I feel that it is a great compliment to me and to my country. Had I the proper eloquence I might dwell somewhat on the history of the great men you have produced, on the numerous citizens of this city and Scotland who have gone to America, and the record they have made. We are proud of Scotchmen as citizens of the United States. They make good citizens of our country, and they find it profitable to themselves. I again thank you for the honor you have conferred upon me."

Three cheers were given "for the youngest burgess."

Grant had any amount of hand-shaking to go through in Scotland. A friend, whose sympathies for the great hand-shaker was stirred, asked, —

"General Grant, do you not tire of this endles hand-shaking?"

"Yes, I do," answered Grant. "I was under the impression that there was no such custom here; but in England the habit is as strong as in America. I think hand-shaking is a great nuisance, and the custom ought to be abolished. In 1865 it was awful with me; I thought I could hardly survive the task. It not only makes the right arm sore, but it shocks the whole system and unfits a man for writing or attending to other duties. It demoralizes the entire nervous and muscular system."

Now he may enjoy the pleasant reflection that he has shaken the hands of more people than any other man who ever lived.

On the 13th of September he arrived in Glasgow

and was presented with the freedom of the city, accompanied by a formal and complimentary address, in which he was called, "THE WELLINGTON OF AMERICA." He was praised especially for his magnanimous treatment of his enemies after he had conquered them.

"So different," the address said, "from the petty feelings of vengence which disgraced so many northern political leaders."

Grant's reply was brief; but he awakened laughter and applause by the following sentence : —

"I find that I am being made so much a citizen of Scotland it will be a serious question where I shall go to vote."

Returning to England, the workingmen of North umberland and Durham arranged to give him a splendid ovation on the town moor of Newcastle, on Saturday afternoon, September 22d. It was estimated that fifty thousand people assembled there. Twenty-two trade societies were out with badges and banners, forming a procession that was twenty minutes in passing a given point. Mr. Thomas Burt, member of Parliament for Morpeth, presented a eulogistic address to Grant, to which the latter replied.

The *Chronicle*, a racy journal of Newcastle, gave an account of the "immense crowd," the "banners, bands, rush, and roar" of the occasion, in which appears the following description of Grant : —

"Looking as much like an ordinary Tyneside-skipper as possible, open-browed, firm-faced, blunt, bluff, and honest, and unassuming, everybody at once settled in his own mind that the General would do.

"The vast concourse still rushing up from the turnpike, and which now musters at least eighty to a hundred thousand, estimate the unheard speech (speech of Grant) after their own thoughts, and applauded every now and again with might and main. When the General finishes, everybody who has not yet shouted feels it incumbent to begin at once, and those who have bellowed themselves hoarse make themselves still hoarser in their endeavors to come up to the demands of the situation. Hats are waved with a self-sacrificing obliviousness to the affection subsisting between crown and brim which is beautiful to witness. And right in the centre of the crowd, little shining rivulets glistening on his ebony cheeks, and his face glowing with intense excitement, the whole soul within him shining out through the sable skin, like a red-hot furnace seen through a dark curtain, stands a negro, devouring Grant with a gaze of such fervid admiration and respect and gratitude that it flashes out the secret of the great liberator's popularity."

At Sunderland he laid another corner-stone — that of a museum — accompanied with the usual display of bunting and buncombe, addresses, lunch, music, toasts, with more addresses, toasts, and lunches. He had knocked the corner-stone out of the Confederacy, and now he was fast becoming the great corner-stone layer of useful institutions.

Before going to Birmingham he rested several days with his daughter, Mrs. Algernon Sartoris, of

Southampton. At Birmingham the address of welcome was read by Mr. O'Neil, in behalf of the International Arbitration Union, and it referred very gracefully to General Grant's policy towards the Indians of our country. The General's reply honored both his head and heart.

"Members of the Midland International Arbitration Union: I thank you for your address. It is one that gives me very little to reply to, more than to express my thanks. Though I have followed a military life the better part of my years, there was never a day of my life when I was not in favor of peace on any terms that were honorable. It has been my misfortune to be engaged in more battles than any other general on the other side of the Atlantic; but there was never a time during my command when I would not have gladly chosen some settlement by reason rather than by the sword. I am conscientiously, and have been from the beginning an advocate of what the society represented by you, gentlemen, is seeking to carry out; and nothing would afford me greater happiness than to know, as I believe will be the case, that, at some future day, the nations of the earth will agree upon some sort of Congress, which shall take cognizance of international questions of difficulty, and whose decisions will be as binding as the decision of our Supreme Court is binding on us. It is a dream of mine that some such solution may be found for all questions of difficulty that may arise between different nations. In one of the addresses, I have forgotten which, reference was made to the dismissal of the army to the pursuits of peaceful industry. I would gladly see the millions of men who are now supported by the industry of the nations return to industrial pursuits, and thus become self-sustaining, and take off the tax upon labor which is now levied for their support."

There is much Grant in every line of this speech. His heart comes to the front, and the hand which wielded the sword with such power, bears the palm of peace. That is real "Grantism."

On the 24th of October, General Grant sailed in the yacht *Victoria* for France, and was welcomed at Boulogne by a multitude of people. He spent a month in that country, and most of the time was under the wing of our Minister Noyes and a colony of Americans who dwelt in Paris.

President McMahon showed him marked attentions, and gave an elaborate dinner in his honor. Receptions, dinners, public welcomes, and other demonstrations followed in rapid succession. If possible, there was more sight-seeing for Grant in France than there was in England, leaving him little time for repose. The French people were on tip-toe to see the great American General, and tens of thousands of them were gratified. The press was eulogistic in its comments upon the General's appearance and career. The well-known paper, *Figaro*, sent a member of the editorial staff to interview him, and published a long article relating thereto, from which we extract the following:—

"The American General, who has been the guest

of Paris for the last two days, is generally considered the most taciturn man in the world. To him Count Von Moltke, whom the Germans call the Great Silent, is quite a talker, since they often get from him speeches of fifty or sixty lines, while the longest speech which Grant is remembered ever to have made was that pronounced the day after he was first nominated President of the United States. Here it is in all its simplicity. The General appeared upon the balcony of the hotel where he was staying. Below, in the streets, more than ten thousand people were awaiting a speech. 'Gentlemen,' he said, 'I am very glad to see you.' Then he made a bow, as much as to say, I hope you will not expect anything more from me now. On another occasion he found the means of being even more concise. One of his soldier-friends, who is said to be almost as reserved as himself, was commissioned to present the General with an elegantly engraved gold cup, in the name of the soldiers who had served under him. The warrior was introduced into the Grant household, having the cup in question. He quietly placed the cup upon the side-board, remarking, 'There's the cup.' The President looked at it in a dreamy sort of a way, and after the lapse of a few seconds, replied, 'Thank you.'

"The physiognomy of the brave General, to whom I had the honor to be presented, was very curious to observe. I do not think, for example, that there is upon earth any being whatever who, under whatever circumstances, could flatter himself as having seen made upon this enigmatic figure the shortest, the slightest, the most momentary impression. I know, through a friend of the General, that this phenomenal imperturbability is never relaxed, even for a second — even in circumstances the most grave and perilous. The friend has seen him under fire, mounted on his grizzly mare, as celebrated in America as the white horse of Napoleon has been in France; and there was always the same figure — impassable, indifferent. During a series of battles, which lasted ten or twelve days, and which cost the Federals nearly sixty thousand men, Grant slept at night for eight hours at a time, as peaceably as an infant, arose in the morning and dressed, then began to give his orders about in the same way a city merchant arranges his bills. Never have circumstances more grave, never has heavier responsibility rested upon a man, than General Grant has experienced; yet a word of anxiety, trouble, or discouragement was never known to escape him. They called Wellington the Iron Duke; the Americans might well have entitled Ulysses S. Grant the Steel General.

"The conversation commenced in English about Paris, which the General now visits for the first time in his life. I inquired what his first impression was. He replied to me with much good sense and precision, to the effect that he was unable to form an opinion, as he had ridden from the railroad depot to the hotel in a covered carriage, and was unable to see anything but the cushions in the vehicle.

"'But, General, have you not paid a visit to Marshal McMahon? How did you find our President?'

"'We were unable to comprehend each other.'

"'How was that?' I said, with astonishment.

"'Simple enough. I didn't understand a word of French; the Marshal does not know a word of English. He bowed to me; I bowed to him. He extended his hand to me; I extended mine to him. Then all was over.'

"'Then the interview only lasted a minute?'

"'I remained a few minutes to speak with Madame McMahon; and I was delighted, for she speaks English admirably. I was, indeed, astonished that a French lady should speak so beautifully. The Marshal has a fine mien, and has the air of an honest man.'

"'General,' I continued, 'as you have been like our Marshal,— President of a Republic, — and you have been in an analogous situation to his, — that is to say, at variance with the legislative power, — I am sure the public would be glad to know your opinion of the present crisis.'

"'I am not a Frenchman; I am an American,' replied the General; 'and, as the Atlantic separates us, I have not studied the question in any such way that I should dare give my opinion on it.'"

The American residents of Paris gave a magnificent banquet to Grant, at which our General was requested to appear in full uniform; and he did. Several speeches were made — one by our Minister Noyes. Marquis de Lafayette and Rochambeau, both descendants of honored Frenchmen who took part in the American Revolution, were present, and spoke in terms of eulogy of General Grant.

A very expensive banquet was given, also, by Mrs.

Mackay, whose husband was known in Paris as "Bonanza," on account of his immense wealth. He is a large owner in the gold mines of California. The farewell banquet was provided by a wealthy banker, whose generosity left nothing to be supplied for the occasion.

The United States Government sent the steamer *Vandalia* to France for General Grant's use while he remained abroad. She arrived at Ville-Franchè on the thirteenth day of December, when, as soon as he could complete his arrangements, **Grant and his family embarked for Naples.**

XXV.

TO THE ORIENT.

GENERAL GRANT was in Naples on the 18th of December. He was more curious to visit Vesuvius than he was to see the ancient city. So arrangements were made early for a trip up the burning mountain. And here the General was outgeneraled for once in his life. Knowing that an army of beggars would surround him as he was never surrounded on the field of battle, he provided himself with a quantity of small coin with which to satisfy this beggarly element. At the base of Vesuvius, where they mounted donkeys for the ascent, the beggars were on hand. The General threw down several pieces of coin, when there followed such a scramble as he had never witnessed, — not even among office-seekers. He threw down more coin, and the numbers and tumult doubled. Instead of satisfying the importunate crowd, their determination to have more was only strengthened. They became terribly in earnest. He scattered more coin; and the scramblers literally swarmed, tumbling over each other, and yelling like so many cats in a fight. It looked very much as if they intended to carry the General by storm instead of by siege. He saw that he had made a grave mistake. More grape and canister would satisfy ordinary assailants, but fighting a battle with coin at the base of Vesuvius with Italian beggars was quite another affair. The more coin, the more beggars. The more effort to satisfy, the greater the scramble. General Grant was forced to retreat and change his tactics. But he won the day finally, and accomplished his purpose, as he was wont to do. He ascended Vesuvius and returned, having added another day's experience never to be forgotten.

He visited Pompeii, and wandered about among its marvellous ruins. Here he found a guide who spoke English.

"I was General Sheridan's guide when he visited Pompeii," he informed Grant. "I am a soldier, too," he added, appearing to understand all about General Grant.

A singular custom prevails here with the Italian authorities. When a great man from abroad visits Pompeii, hey order a house dug open in honor of their guest, and afterwards call it by his name. A house was dug open for Grant; but nothing except a few ornaments and a loaf of bread wrapped in a cloth was discovered. The bread was stale enough for even a chronic dyspeptic, having been baked nearly two thousand years ago.

"We'll open another house for you," suggested the guide, who seemed to be disappointed that no bones of human beings were discovered.

"I prefer to excavate a beefsteak," replied an officer of the *Vandalia*, who was exceedingly hungry

The company decided for the beefsteak instead of more ruins.

From Naples General Grant proceeded to Palermo, where he arrived in the midst of Christmas festivities. The officers of the *Vandalia* served a Christmas dinner on board the ship in true American style. Everything about it was home-like. Grant enjoyed it hugely, surrounded as he was by his own countrymen. The vessel was decorated with evergreens, and the stars and stripes made conspicuous. Mr. Young, the correspondent who accompanied the General, said of the occasion:—

"As the General sat under the green boughs of the Christmas decorations, the centre of our merry company, it seemed as if he were as young as any of the mess—a much younger man by far than our junior Dannenhower, who looks grave and serious enough to command all the fleets in the world. Mrs. Grant was in capital health and spirits, and quite enchanted the mess by telling them, in the earliest hour of the conversation, that she already felt when she came back to the *Vandalia* from some errand on shore as if she were coming home. I wish I could lift the veil far enough to show you how much the kind, considerate, ever-womanly and ever-cheerful nature of Mrs. Grant has won upon us all; but I must not invade the privacy of the domestic circle. She was the queen of the feast, and we gave her queenly honor."

From Palermo to Malta, and thence to the Orient, was Grant's programme. He reached the land of the Pharaohs and disembarked at Alexan dria, where the authorities had made preparations for his arrival.

The American consul, vice-consul, and governor, together with all the missionaries, came on board to pay their respects, before the party landed. According to an Egyptian custom, the number of guns fired is determined by the official rank of the honored guest, so that on this occasion the greatest number of guns were fired, creating such a noise that the company were forced to wait until cannon ceased to thunder, before conversation could be heard. The Governor, in the name of the Khedive, addressed General Grant, and offered him the use of a palace in Cairo and a steamer to take him up the Nile.

In the afternoon of the same day, Grant returned the official visit. On going ashore, another round of firing took place, followed by loud huzzas from the crews of all the vessels in port, including that of the *Vandalia*. A guard of honor took possession of him, and conducted him to the Pasha's palace, where a formal reception took place.

In the evening, the General and Mrs. Grant dined with the vice-consul, where they met Henry M. Stanley the African traveler. Stanley had completed his travels across the "Dark Continent," and was on his way back to England. A toast was given to him, and he replied in quite a lengthy speech, closing by saying, —

"It is the proudest moment of my life to find myself beside the distinguished guest from the United States."

The Government provided him with a special

train to Cairo, only about four hours distant by rail. This was an exceedingly interesting trip to him, not only because a view of the pyramids was novel, but the elaborate reception was unexpected, and old army acquaintances surprised him by their presence.

When he alighted at the station, he found the way carpeted for him to walk on, and a guard with a group of cavaliers were waiting to receive him. The Oriental costume and Egyptian uniform presented a novel spectacle; and yet they did not conceal from his sharp observation the features of two old acquaintances.

"Why, there is Loring, whom I have not seen for thirty years," he said with much surprise.

Loring was at West Point with him; and he was an officer in the Southern army during the Rebellion.

"And there is Stone also," continued the General. "He must have been dyeing his hair to make it so white."

Stone was the American officer who was so severely criticised in the Ball's Bluff affair. Grant knew that both of them were in the service of the Khedive, but he did not expect to meet them here. Before his surprise was abated, Stone stepped forward and welcomed him to Egypt. It was a pleasant meeting to Grant, and he shook hands warmly with both of them. There was no "bloody chasm" between him and Loring out there under the shadow of the pyramids.

At the royal dinner in honor of Grant, the latter took occasion to say to the Khedive, "I have known

General Stone from boyhood. I do not think we had an abler officer in our army; and I am happy to see him occupy so high a position in your service."

"I like General Stone very much," replied the Khedive. "He has great ability to organize troops. and I have made him a member of my privy council."

The General enjoyed sight-seeing here; and he was greatly amused by an incident which showed that human nature was about the same in Egypt as in America. Boys were plenty on the streets, with donkeys for sale. One of them accosted the General in language, which, translated into English, means, "Want to buy a donkey? His name is 'Yankee Doodle.'"

The sharp little fellow thought that such a name would take with "the great American General."

On the 16th of January, 1878, Grant started up the Nile on a steamer provided by the Khedive. At Siout, a city of twenty-five thousand inhabitants, a public reception awaited him. A sumptuous dinner was provided, with twenty courses. Several speeches were made, very eulogistic of the United States and General Grant.

He visited Giegel, Abydos, and ancient Thebes. The latter place was once called "the wonder of the world." Homer says that it once contained three hundred thousand inhabitants, and that its walls were provided with a hundred gates. "The mighty city has crumbled to ashes, and where once gorgeous equipages and a gay and busy population thronged the streets, are now only a few scattered villages, consisting of miserable huts, built in the courts of the old magnificent temples, presenting a sad commentary on the improvement of the present over past ages."

General Grant was expected here, as flying flags indicated. The vice-consul and governor welcomed him to the town; and he was conducted over the city. On one street a house was pointed out to the General, in which an American lived fifteen years, manufacturing relics of all sorts to sell to travelers. He could make "mummy-lids," "idols," and "hieroglyphic inscriptions," in imitation of the original, and found it to be a profitable business. His workmanship has gone out into all the world, adorning parlors and adding variety to museums. Relics indeed!

Grant visited the statues of Memnon, a few miles away. Quite a party accompanied him, which, with the donkey-boys and water-girls, made quite a long cavalcade. The importunities of the water-girls on the way, in their eagerness for trade, led Hassan, the conductor, to apply his whip to them vigorously.

"Hassan," exclaimed Mrs. Grant, "you shall not whip those girls; it is cruel."

"But I do not hurt them," replied Hassan. "I only wished to scare them, and make them keep be hind in their place."

"Well, then," continued Mrs. Grant, "you tell the water-girls and donkey-boys and peddlers of relics, that, unless they keep behind and out of the way, they will receive no *baksheesh* (money) at the close of the day."

Her instructions were obeyed, and they had more effect than the whip.

Grant was called by the common people here "*The King of America.*"

At Karnac he visited the "grandest ruin in the world." The chief temple "is three hundred and seventy feet broad and fifty feet deep, with a tower one hundred and forty feet high. An avenue two hundred feet long, lined with statues and sphinxes, led up to the main entrance, which conducts you to a court two hundred and seventy-five feet by three hundred and twenty-nine. Through the great western gateway across the court, with one solitary column erect over its fallen peers, which lie their length, shattered from their bases in regular rows, as if they had been piles of milestones carefully upset, we enter the great hall of Karnac, where *one hundred and thirty-four* columns, thirty feet in circumference, rise in silent majesty around you, speaking of a wondrous past, on which the light of history will never shine."

The town of Keneh was another place visited; and here Grant saw more of real life in Egypt than anywhere else — women grinding corn, and potters at work as described in the Bible. He gave a few coin to a woman for the privilege of entering her private house. He had a strong desire to see how the people lived in their homes. The following is a description of that particular home : —

"The house was a collection of rooms ; the walls made of dried mud and bricks. It was one story high, thatched with straw The floor was the ground. The walls were clay. In one room was the donkey, in another the cow, a queer kind of buffalo-cow, that looked up at us as we went in. In another room slept the members of the family. There was neither bed, nor chair, nor table. They slept on the ground, or on palm-leaves, like the donkey; they sat on the ground for meals, and ate out of the same dish . . . I suppose there were not a thousand slaves in the South, who were not better housed than these free Egyptian citizens."

Asswan was the end of their journey, a town of four thousand inhabitants. Here all sorts of articles for sale were brought in from the surrounding country on donkeys driven by naked boys. Among them were feathers of the wild ostrich much more beautiful than those of the tame ostrich in South Africa.

"Hassan," said Mrs. Grant, "inquire what is the price of this bunch which I have in my hand."

"Twenty-four dollars," he answered, after having inquired. And he took the bunch and handed it back to the owner, exclaiming, "It is robbery."

"But I don't think it is a very exorbitant price," answered Mrs. Grant, "when I recall the price for which they sell in New York. Besides the man looks poor, and probably sells but a few feathers, and has a family to support."

"That ain't it," responded Hassan. "I know them better than you do. They always have two prices, and often they don't get their lowest price."

Then Hassan harangued the crowd and denounced the feathers, whereupon the owner extolled them with equal emphasis, but closed by asking, —

"What will the gracious lady give for them?"

"Four napoleons," replied Hassan.

The merchant assumed an attitude of surprise, and then waxed eloquent over their beauty.

"See how they shine," he exclaimed; "behold their tints — white, gray, and black!"

Then waving them in the air like a plume, he continued: —

"Such feathers were never seen in Asswan. If they came from the far desert, they would be cheap at a hundred napoleons."

Another waving of the feathers, and more eloquence expended upon their value. However, after wasting fifteen minutes "on the desert air," Hassan bought the feathers for "four napoleons."

Here, too, came a letter to General Grant from the great English General Gordon, who was at Philæ, five miles distant, inviting him thither. He sent with the message a beautiful Arabian steed for the General to ride. The animal was a high-spirited, indomitable creature; and when Grant mounted him, and he began to rear and prance, Sami Bey, one of his retinue, expressed fears for the safety of the General.

"If I can mount a horse, I can ride him," replied Grant; "and all the attendants can do is to keep away."

On his return, after a month's absence, the Khedive met the General at Cairo, and showed him still further attentions. And this same Khedive was compelled to abdicate his throne a few months thereafter.

Thence General Grant proceeded to Jerusalem. Stopping at Joppa, Grant embraced the first opportunity to find the house of "Simon the tanner, by the seaside." Having followed the craft of his illustrious ancestor, and still retaining a vivid recollection of the tannery, which he honestly hated, Grant knew just how to pity Simon, and only wanted the chance to get into his house to show his sincere commiseration.

Here they obtained vehicles to convey them to Jerusalem, thirty miles distant. They crossed "the Plain of Sharon," stopped over-night at Ramleh, and the next morning pushed on, with "the Mountains of Judea" in full view. They passed the ruins of Gezer, and near to "Kirjath-Jearim," where the ark rested for twenty years, and beyond, the Valley of Ajalon, where the sun stood still to let Joshua conquer in a battle greater than Grant ever fought. Then came the deep valley through which runs a rapid brook, where David killed Goliath, and with stones enough in it to have supplied the slings of a hundred thousand Davids.

As they came in sight of Jerusalem, a courier came galloping up to announce to the General that a public reception awaited him. In a moment, cavalry appeared in the distance, leading deputations from Greeks, Jews, Armenians, and Americans. Horses were also sent to the party — the Pasha's splendid white steed, with gold trappings, for General Grant to ride.

After some delay, the procession moved forward to the city. For a whole mile before entering it, the way was lined on both sides by crowds of people, with music and banners, eager to behold the great General from America. The Pasha received him with much pomp, and dined him with great courtesy.

General Grant visited many of the places of sacred interest. He visited Calvary, passing over the road, up which the Saviour toiled bearing his own cross. He went to the Garden of Gethsemane and Mount Olivet, and passed over the hill into Bethany, where Martha and Mary lived. He visited the spot where the Saviour stood when he wept over Jerusalem, and went down the Valley of Jehoshaphat, over the brook, and around the city to Damascus gate.

He left Jerusalem for Nazareth; and the people generally turned out to pay their respects and bid him adieu. He journeyed on to Shiloh, through Nablous, where was Jacob's Well, on which Jesus sat and conversed with the woman of Samaria.

Passing through Nain, where Christ brought back the widow's dead son to life, they came to Endor, once the abode of a famous witch, whence they soon reached Nazareth — the birth-place of Christ. Tarrying here a short time, the party pushed on to Damascus by the road over which Saul of Tarsus was traveling when he was struck down by a light from heaven, and heard that mysterious voice which moved him to a new and better life.

From Damascus General Grant proceeded to Beyrout, where the *Vandalia* was awaiting his arrival. He reached there both wearied and delighted with his sojourn in the Holy Land. Here he went on board his steamer, and sailed for Constantinople.

XXVI

FLIGHT THROUGH OTHER COUNTRIES.

HE war with Russia had just closed, and the treaty been signed, when General Grant reached Constantinople. The anxieties and labors, multiplied by the termination of the war, engrossed the Sultan's time and thoughts, so that he could not bestow upon the General that attention which he desired to show. Yet, his attentions were many, and among other things he presented him with a pair of Arabian horses, full-blooded and every way superior, selected from the imperial stable, where five hundred and seventy of the finest animals that could be found in the empire were stalled. The following is a careful description of the animals : —

"One is a dappled gray of fair size, and having all the traits characteristic of the Arabian blood: small, well-set, restless ears, wide, pink nostrils, and large, soft eyes; waving mane, and long tail reaching almost to the ground, and a skin of such delicacy that the stroke of a lady's whip is sufficient to draw blood. The other stallion has all these points. He is an iron-grey, with a white star on his forehead and white hind feet. When the long forelock falls over his forehead, the large, black eyes have all the expression of a Bedouin woman's. Their gait is perfect, be it either the rapid walk, the long, swinging trot, or the tireless, stretching gallop, while a rein of one thread of silk is enough to guide their delicate mouth. Let one of these Arabs, in the mad rush of a charge or a flight, lose his rider, and that instant the docile steed will stop as though turned to stone. These horses are of the famous Lahtan race,—the purest Arabian blood, only found in and near Bagdad. The dapple-gray is appropriately named Djeyton (The Panther), and the iron-gray Missirli (The One from Cairo), which cognomen he derives from having been bought in Cairo, though foaled at Bagdad."

The Sultan had heard of Grant's love of horses, and desiring to show him the greatest favor, presented him with this pair.

Constantinople had much to interest Grant, being the city which Constantine founded in 338, and having been besieged by armies twenty-four times But his time was limited, and he hurried away to Athens, Greece, the home of Homer, Demosthenes, Socrates, and Plato, where a round of dinners and *fêtes* awaited him. The world-renowned Parthenon, Mars Hill with the Areopagus on its summit, where Paul preached to the Athenians, the Temple of Theseus, Prison of Socrates, Temple of Bacchus, Grotto of Apollo, ruins of the Temple of Jupiter Olympus; --these were among the objects of interest which the General examined. He also visited the two famous battle-grounds of Greece, Thermopylæ and Marathon.

Thence he went to Rome, where both Church and State united to do him honor. The aide-de-camp to the King was the first to call upon him with the King's congratulations. Then Cardinal McCloskey, with the respects of the Pope. The latter gave him ar audience, and treated him with marked consideration. The King invited him to a great banquet, where the dignitaries of the city assembled in Roman pomp.

The Colosseum, which seated thirty thousand peo ple before its fall, the Capitoline Hill, the Roman Forum, Basilica of Constantine, Arch of Titus, the Campagna, the hill on which stood the Palace of the Cæsars, together with galleries of art in which the works of the old masters were collected, — these were among the wonders of the Imperial City which Grant inspected. His visit to St. Peter's, which de fies description, — a church of such magnitude that a dozen of the largest churches in the United States might be set into it, — was a source of as much sur prise and pleasure as any of Rome's marvels.

He was greatly interested in one custom which prevails in Rome — that of designating where distinguished persons lived and died, by a marble slab over the door. Thus the house which Galileo occupied, the one in which Dante was born, the home of Corinne, and that of Americus Vespucius are marked by inscriptions on marble slabs. It is a custom which the people of other countries might imitate with profit.

Hasty visits to Florence and Pisa he made, and passed on to Venice, where the authorities received him in state. Here again dinners and imposing demonstrations followed in rapid succession for three days. Venice is unlike any other city in the world, being built on a collection of small islands connected by four hundred and fifty bridges, the largest of which is the Rialto, consisting of a single arch one hundred and eighty-seven feet long. The only streets it has are canals, and the only mode of conveyance is by gondolas. The city is noted for its costly churches and palaces. Many Americans reside here, and they assembled with music and banners to do Grant honor when he departed for Milan, a city that is known for having the largest and most costly cathedral in the world except St. Peter's. It is built of white marble, and there are four thousand statues on the exterior alone. Grant had time only to visit this cathedral, and the original painting of Leonardo da Vinci, representing the Lord's Supper, which is found in this city. He had promised to be in Paris near the opening of the World's Exhibition, and was obliged to hasten. On his way to Paris, the people gathered at almost every station to see and honor him. He arrived at Paris on the seventh day of May, 1878.

A day was appointed for General Grant to visit the exhibition; and it was made a gala-day. Thousands of Americans were in the city, and all that time and money could do to honor their illustrious countryman was brought into requisition. He was overwhelmed by invitations to dinners and public *fêtes*, and was obliged to decline many of them.

He paid a visit to Holland, stopping briefly at Rotterdam and Amsterdam, where public receptions were tendered him. At this time the news of the attempted assassination of the Emperor of Germany caused him to delay his early departure to Berlin for a week. But he reached Berlin on the twenty-sixth day of June. Prince Bismarck, whom most of all he desired to see, called upon him first. Grant was out, and the Prince called the second time, only to find him absent. Then, Grant sent a note to him, saying that he would call at any hour he would name. The Prince named four o'clock in the afternoon. At that hour, the two great men met.

"Glad to welcome General Grant to Germany," exclaimed Bismarck, extending both hands to meet him in the most familiar manner.

"Not more glad than I am to have the honor of meeting you," replied Grant in his cordial way.

"I am surprised to see so young a man," continued Bismarck; "much younger than I am."

"I don't know about that, not much difference in our ages, I think," responded Grant.

Comparing ages, Bismarck was surprised to find himself the senior of Grant by seven years only.

"This," remarked the Prince, "is the advantage of a military life, for here you have the frame of a young man, while I feel like an old man."

"I regard it a great compliment to be told, at my time of life, that I look like a young man," answered Grant, with a somewhat unusual smile for him.

"And what can you tell me about General Sheridan?" inquired Bismarck. "The General and I were fellow-campaigners in France, and we became great friends."

"I received a letter from Sheridan recently, and he is quite well," replied Grant.

"Sheridan seemed to be a man of great ability," added Bismarck.

"Yes; I regard Sheridan not only as one of the great soldiers of our war, but as one of the great soldiers of the world — as a man who is fit for the highest command. No better general than Sheridan ever lived." Such was Grant's noble answer.

"I observed that he had a wonderfully quick eye," continued Bismarck. "On one occasion, I remember, the Emperor and his staff took up a position to observe a battle. The Emperor himself was never near enough to the front, — was always impatient to be as near the fighting as possible. 'Well,' said Sheridan to me, as we rode along, 'we shall never stay here; the enemy will, in a short time, make this so untenable that we shall all be leaving in a hurry. Then, while the men are advancing, they will see us retreating.' Sure enough, in an hour or so the cannon-shot began to plunge that way, and we saw we must leave. It was difficult to move the Emperor, however; but we all had to go, and [laughing] we went rapidly. Sheridan had seen it from the beginning. I wish I had so quick an eye."

The European Congress on the Turkey affairs was in session in Berlin at that time; and Bismarck said, —

"I am sorry that my attendance upon the Congress will occupy much of my time, which otherwise I should give to you. And the Emperor is very sorry that he cannot see you; but the doctors have forbidden him to see any one."

"I regret very much that I could not have had the honor of meeting him," replied Grant. "I hope that he will entirely recover."

"You know that he is a very old man?" added Bismarck, inquiringly.

"That adds to the horror one feels for the crime," responded Grant.

"The Emperor has a very kind heart, a winning and generous disposition; and I wonder that any one should want to take his life," remarked the Prince.

"It was the same with President Lincoln," said Grant. "He was one of the kindest-hearted men who ever lived, and yet he was killed by an assassin. The influence which aimed at the Emperor's life is an influence that would destroy all government, all order, all society, republics, and empires."

This conversation about the Emperor and the attempt upon his life continued for some time, when Bismarck added, —

"But the old gentleman is so much of a soldier, and so fond of his army, that nothing would give him more pleasure than to display it to so great a soldier as yourself. But *I* will now invite you to a review in the morning."

"I accept your invitation," Grant replied; and then remarked, with a smile on his face, "The truth is, I am more of a farmer than a soldier. I take little or no interest in military affairs; and, although I entered the army thirty-five years ago, and have been in two wars, — in Mexico as a young lieutenant, and later in the war of the Rebellion, — I never went into the army without regret, and never retired without pleasure."

"You are so happily placed in America," said Bismarck, "that you need fear no wars. What always seemed so sad to me about your last great war was, that you were fighting your own people. That is always so terrible in wars; so very hard."

"But it had to be done," remarked Grant.

"Yes, you had to save the Union just as we had to save Germany."

"Not only to save the Union, but destroy slavery," added Grant.

"I suppose, however, the Union was the real sentiment, — the dominant sentiment, — was it not?"

"Yes, in the beginning, certainly; but as soon as slavery fired upon the flag, it was felt, — we all felt, even those who did not object to slaves, — that slavery must be destroyed. We felt that it was a stain to the Union, that men should be bought and sold like cattle."

Grant attended the review on the next morning in a pouring rain, which wet him through to his skin. Bayard Taylor was our Minister at Berlin, and he gave a great dinner in honor of Grant; and, before the latter left Germany, Bismarck invited the General and his wife to dine with him.

From Berlin he went to Hamburg, arriving there on the 2d of July. A deputation from the Senate waited upon him, showed him about the city, and *fêted* him in the evening at the Zoological Gardens where toasts were given and speeches made. The vice-consul gave an elaborate dinner on the Fourth of July, to which he invited prominent Americans in the city. There were thirty or forty guests in all. Here, too, there were toasts and speeches. The consul paid a noble tribute to Grant as a soldier and statesman, and closed by saying, "He saved the country."

This compliment brought out a characteristic speech from Grant, in which modesty, magnanimity, and nobility appear in about equal parts.

"Mr. Consul and Friends: I am much obliged to you for the kind manner in which you drink my health. I share with you in all the pleasure and gratitude which Americans so far from home should feel on this anniversary. But I must dissent from one remark of our consul, to the effect that I saved the country during the recent war. If our country could be saved or ruined by the efforts of any one man we should not have a country, and we should not now be celebrating our Fourth of July. There are many men who would have done far better than I did, under the circumstances in which I found myself during the war. If I had never held command; if I had fallen; if all our generals had fallen, there were ten thousand behind us who would have done our work just as well, who would have followed the contest to the end, and never surrendered the Union. Therefore, it is a mistake and a reflection upon the people to attribute to me, or to any number of us who held high commands, the salvation of the Union. We did our work as well as we could, and so did hundreds of others. We deserve no credit for it; for we should have been unworthy of our country and of the American name if we had not made every sacrifice to save the Union. What saved the Union was the coming forward of the young men of the Nation. They came from their homes and fields, as they did in the time of the Revolution, giving everything to the country. To their devotion we owe the salvation of the Union. The humblest soldier who carried a musket is entitled to as much credit for the results of the war as those who were in command. So long as our young men are animated by this spirit, there will be no fear for the Union."

General Grant visited Copenhagen, capital of Denmark, then proceeded to Christiana, Norway, and on to Stockholm, the capital of Sweden. In all these places public receptions were accorded to the General, and all along the way, from place to place, the people showed that they had been apprised of the coming of the American chieftain, by gathering at the stations in enthusiastic crowds, and flinging banners to the breeze. In several places triumphal arches were erected over the track, bearing the inscription, — "WELCOME TO GENERAL GRANT."

At Stockholm he took boat for St. Petersburg, across the Baltic. Prince Gortschakoff called upon him for the Emperor, and welcomed him to Russia. At an appointed hour Grant drove to the palace, where the Emperor received him warmly. When he left, the Emperor conducted him to the door and said, —

"Pleasant relations have always existed between Russia and the United States, and as long as I live nothing shall be spared to continue this friendship."

"Although the two governments are different," answered Grant, "the American people are in sympathy with Russia, and I trust they always will be."

The Grand Duke Alexis called upon him, and showed him marked attention. The Neva runs through the city, and its banks are lined with fine churches and palaces, and towers glittering with gold, and lovely gardens. The Imperial Garden is on its banks, beautiful beyond description. Grant was captivated by the Neva and the costly works of man on its banks. Here was the church known as Lady of Kazan, whose nave and cupola rest on fifty-six granite columns, with bronze capitals. The Emperor's Winter Palace attracted his special attention, — the grandest palace in the whole world. It is filled with the costliest works of art; and in the winter it is occupied by six thousand people who belong to the Emperor's household.

The Emperor placed his yacht at Grant's command, and he made a trip to Peterhoff; also to the Russian man-of-war *Peter the Great*, where he received a salute of twenty-one guns, and the band played national airs. He continued down the Neva to Cronstadt, and sailed through the Russian fleet, each vessel saluting him by running up the Stars and Stripes, while the sailors sent up cheer on cheer.

He went to Moscow, interested to behold the city which Napoleon captured and entered in 1812, with one hundred and fifty thousand men, only to see it consumed by a conflagration which the inhabitants kindled, and his mighty army fade away, and the star of his destiny set. In the centre still stands the world-renowned Kremlin, which the flames did not consume. It is two miles in circumference, — a monster citadel. Within its walls are palaces, churches, cathedrals, the treasury and arsenal, monasteries, museums, and other public buildings. Most wonderful of all is the Tower of Ivan Veliki, two hundred and fifty feet high, with forty bells, the largest of which weighs sixty tons. Originally it supported only one bell, which weighed four hundred thousand pounds. A fire burned away its supports, and it fell, and now lies at the base, cracked, and is used for a chapel, being twenty-five feet high and sixty-seven feet in circumference. When it fell it was buried in in the earth by its weight, and lay there a hundred years, when it was raised and placed on a grand pedestal, — the largest bell ever cast. If Grant could have had such a bell at Donelson, Vicksburg, Shiloh, Richmond, or Appomattox, his "boys in blue" would have made it heard over every battle-field!

From St. Petersburg Grant went to Warsaw, Poland; thence to Vienna, where there were a series of imposing receptions, dinners, and royal entertainments, consuming four days. Here he saw St. Stephen's Cathedral, whose bell was cast from one hundred and eighty cannon taken from the Turks, and weighs forty thousand pounds.

He visited the public library at Munich, the largest in the world, containing eight hundred thousand volumes, thirty-three thousand manuscripts, and three hundred thousand engravings.

Again General Grant turned his face toward France, going through Switzerland, chiefly to visit Ulm, where Napoleon captured Mack's whole army. The reader will recollect that General Halleck, in an order quoted on a former page, compared Grant's Vicksburg campaign to that of Napoleon against Ulm. Perhaps there was a connection between that order and Grant's visit.

When he reached Bordeaux, where the freedom of the city was offered him, he found a letter from King Alfonso of Spain, inviting him thither.

XXVII.

FROM SPAIN TO CHINA.

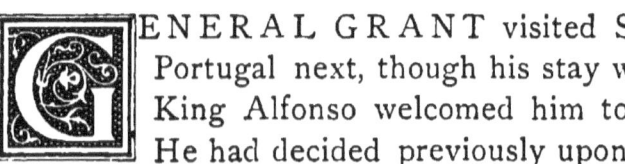ENERAL GRANT visited Spain and Portugal next, though his stay was short. King Alfonso welcomed him to Vittoria. He had decided previously upon the rank and character in which Grant should be received,— that of captain-general of the Spanish army,—next in rank to king.

King Alfonso was a young man of only twenty years, yet dignified and mature.

"General Grant," he said, "I am most happy to welcome you to Spain. I feel myself highly honored by your visit. I have read all about you, both as a great general and president, and have admired your career and have been very anxious to see you."

"I thank your majesty with all my heart for this cordial greeting," replied the General, "and I assure you that the people of my country as well as myself desire the prosperity of your government. You share our deepest sympathy in the recent death of the Queen." Alfonso had recently buried his wife.

"I have read kind words of sympathy in the American journals, and they touched my heart," responded the King. "Our marriage was one of love purely, and we were engaged from the time we were fifteen years of age. We were very happy together, and she helped me much to bear the burdens of my office, which are very irksome."

"I know how it is," remarked Grant; "the eight years of my Presidency were the most harassing and weary ones of my whole life."

"While my wife lived," continued the King, "I found in her a solace for all my cares; but now she has gone, my only comfort and relief is to be actively engaged in labor the whole of the time."

In this familiar and pleasant way the conversation continued for some time, the young King appearing to be glad to find a man to whom he could unburden nis soul.

On this visit Grant learned that Ex-President Castellar was about starting for San Sebastian, and he sent for him. Castellar came at once.

"I sent for you," said Grant on shaking his hand cordially, "to thank you personally for your noble sympathy for the United States Government in the late civil war. There is no man in Spain whom I desired so much to see as yourself. Be assured that the defenders of our Government appreciated your kindness, and were glad that, while your presidency was short and stormy, you maintained the integrity of the Spanish Government."

Castellar thanked the General for his complimentary address, and spoke words of eulogy in return.

In Madrid Grant visited the royal palace, occupying, with its gardens, eighty acres; also, the Escurial Palace, called "the eighth wonder of the world."

In Lisbon, Portugal, King Don Louis invited him to a grand banquet at the palace, the ministers and leading men of the court being present. This King's father, Don Fernando, fell in love with a Boston lady, who came to that city to sing, ana he married her. She is called the Countess d'Ella; and she took great pleasure in showing the General over the palace.

He called at Cadiz, the oldest city in Europe, founded eleven hundred years before Christ. Thence he went to Gibraltar, by invitation of Lord Napier, where he spent three days in sumptuous dinners, royal *fêtes*, and review of troops.

He now turned his steps toward England, in order to fulfil his promise to visit Ireland. At Pau, France, at the foot of the Pyrennees, he stopped a short time, and the Americans there gave him a banquet, at which Mr. Douglas introduced him as "UNCONDITIONAL SURRENDER GRANT." The General replied, —

"I never succeeded in making speeches, and think I will not make the attempt now; but will justify the epithet of Mr. Douglas by making an unconditional surrender."

This sally was received with great laughter and cheers.

On reaching England, he prepared for a hurried visit to Ireland; including Dublin, Belfast, Derry, and other cities. It was January 3, 1879, when he reached Dublin. He was welcomed, and the freedom of the city was offered to him by Lord Mayor Barrington. He was *fêted* throughout the day; and, in the evening, at a grand banquet, he made his longest speech.

General Grant returned to his daughter's home at Southampton, England, where Mrs. Grant remained while he went to Ireland. He made immediate preparations to visit India. The company was now somewhat changed, and consisted of the General and Mrs. Grant, Col. Fred D. Grant, their son (in the place of Jesse), Mr. Borie, and Doctor Keating, of Philadelphia, with Mr. Young, the *Herald* correspondent. They sailed on the twenty-fourth day of January.

At Bombay he was welcomed to India by the Governor of the Presidency of Bombay, and the use of the Government House at Malabar Point tendered to him. Here he was lionized for a week, making two or three brief speeches in reply to compliments paid him.

At Agra he visited the Tay, one of the most beautiful buildings in the world.

On leaving Jeypoor, where honors were lavished upon him, there was a great display at the public hall. "An attendant entered, bearing a tray filled with wreaths of the rose and jessamine. The Mahrajah, taking two of the wreaths, put them on the neck of the General. He did the same to Mrs Grant and all the members of the party. Then taking a string and silken cord, he placed that on Mrs. Grant as a special honor. The General, who was instructed by the English Resident, took four wreaths and put them on the neck of the Mahrajah, who pressed his hands and bowed his thanks. Another servant came, bearing a small cup of gold and gems containing attar of roses. The Mahrajah, putting some of the perfume on his fingers, transferred it to Mrs. Grant's handkerchief. With another portion he passed his hands along the General's breast and shoulders; this was done to each of the party. The General, then taking the perfume, passed his hand over the Mahrajah's shoulder, and so concluded the ceremony, which, in all royal interviews in the East, is supposed to mean a lasting friendship. Then the Prince, taking the General's hand in his own, led him from the hall, across the garden, and to the gateway of his palace, holding his hand all the time."

Next, the General visited Lucknow, memorable for the mutiny of '58 and '59, and forever associated with the name of the brave Havelock. Thence he went to Benares,—a city of alleys, not streets; so narrow that sedan-chairs, mounted on poles, and carried by four men, are the only mode of conveyance about the city. Extra chairs, ornamented with gold, were provided for Grant and his party; but the General did not fancy this mode of conveyance, and so he walked. In their perambulations they entered a temple where sacred animals were kept for worship. Mrs. Grant had a wreath of flowers on her neck, which a flower-girl had placed there as she entered. A sacred cow beheld the tempting flowers, and made a sudden dash for them, tearing them from her neck; and, but for the timely interposition of the police, the result might have been serious.

General Grant proceeded from Calcutta to Rangoon, Burmah.

At Singapore, General Grant received an invitation from the King of Siam to visit his kingdom This was an unexpected invitation to Grant, and he gladly accepted it. He sailed for Bangkok, and was met by a messenger from the King thirty miles from the city, accompanied by the American consul, and bearing the following from the King : —

"THE GRAND PALACE, BANGKOK, April 11, 1879.

"*Sir*, — I have very great pleasure in welcoming you to Siam. It is, I am informed, your pleasure that your reception should be a private one; but you must permit me to show, as far as I can, the high esteem in which I hold THE MOST EMINENT CITIZEN of that great nation which has been so friendly to Siam, and so kind and just in all its intercourse with the nations of the far East.

"That you may be near me during your stay, I have commanded my brother, His Royal Highness, the Celestial Prince Bhanusangsi Swangwongse, to prepare rooms for you and your party in the Saranrow Palace, close to my palace; and I most cordially invite you, Mrs. Grant, and your party, at once to take up residence there, and my brother will represent me as your host.

"Your friend,

"CHULAHLONG KORN, R. S.

"His Excellency, General Grant, late President of the United States."

This was giving the General full swing. And now commenced a series of honors which astonished the General beyond measure; coming, as they did, from the people of an almost unknown kingdom hitherto.

On the next day he was conveyed to another palace, to meet a king of a higher grade,—the REGENT, —who waited, in decorations of gold, the General's coming. The Regent advanced, and, taking his hand in his, conducted his guest into the gorgeous audience-room of the palace, where a file of soldiers presented arms, and the band played "The Star Spangled Banner." Then the Regent made a speech, praising Grant and his country, to which Grant replied, praising the Regent and *his* country, so that they were even now.

But it turned out that Grant had not yet seen the real, *bona-fide* King of Siam. He was conducted to him on the 14th of April, in state-carriages, with pomp and ceremony. He lived in still another pal ace; and on approaching it, troops with gay uni forms, and aids of the King in royal apparel, waited to conduct him into the presence of His Royal Highness, while the band played "Hail, Columbia."

The King gave a state-dinner in honor of Grant, at which all the dignitaries of his kingdom appeared in their royal trappings. · Everything about the banquet was regal in its splendor.

Grant returned to Singapore, where he took the steamer *Ashuelot* for Canton, China. Before he left the United States, the Viceroy had issued the fol lowing placard:—

"We have just heard that the King of America, being on friendly terms with China, will leave America early in the third month, bringing with him a *suite* of officers, etc., all complete on board the ship It is said that he is bringing a large number of rare presents with him, and that he will be here in Canton about the 6th or 9th of May."

His arrival in Canton caused such commotion as that city never witnessed before. Of course such a proclamation from the Viceroy as the above put the people on tip-toe to see the "King of America." Never was a people more disappointed in the world. They expected to see a large, portly man, covered with gold badges to denote his high position, and attended by a retinue of officers in splendid uniforms. What was their surprise when a plain man in traveling apparel, without a single badge or decoration, attended by companions equally plain in dress, disembarked and appeared in their streets!

Grant went to Hong Kong, Swatow, Shanghai, and Amoy, where public receptions were tendered. At Shanghai the display was imposing. A hundred thousand people crowded the landing; the ships in the harbor were decorated with bunting and flags from stem to stern; and salutes of cannon and strains of martial music added enchantment to the scene.

At Pekin, the great city of the eastern world, the demonstration was equally imposing. The Prince Regent sent an escort to meet him at the village of Tung Chow, ten or fifteen miles away, and from that point his march into Pekin was that of a crowned head. Grant was carried in an imperial chair by eight bearers, and he was the first guest of the country ever permitted to occupy an imperial chair. The people understood that such a thing would happen, and they turned out *en masse* to see the foreigner who was great and good enough to be carried in the chair of the Emperor.

General Grant was determined to make his visit to China of real value, politically, to both nations and to all nations. For this purpose he sought two personal interviews with Prince Kung, of two hours each; also an interview with the Viceroy at Tien-tsin. The Prince appeared to be as anxious as Grant that his visit should prove a benefit to China politically. We should be glad to insert the whole conversation, but our space is limited. One suggestion of Grant seemed to surprise the Prince:—

"I think that progress in China should come from inside, from her own people," said Grant. "If her own people cannot do it, it will never be done."

This appeared to be a revelation to the Prince, but he acceded to it.

"For that reason, I know of nothing better than to send your young men to our schools. We have as good schools as there are in the world, where young men can learn every branch of science and art. These schools will enable your young men to compare the youngest with the oldest civilization, and I can assure them of the kindest treatment, not only from our teachers, but from our people."

The conversation branched off to political questions, and, at the second interview, the government, policy, resources, and material progress of China, as compared with the United States, were discussed. At the time war with Japan was imminent, on account of her usurpation in Loochoo, and the Prince importuned Grant to intercede with the Japanese

Government, so as to bring about a settlement. Grant canvassed the whole subject with him, and promised to do all he could to prevent war; and it is believed that his interposition and counsels did prevent a war.

So anxious were the Chinese authorities to make Grant understand that they regarded him as the greatest man their country had ever seen, that the Viceroy even gave a farewell dinner to Mrs. Grant —a woman—something never tolerated in the land before; a step in modern civilization wholly unexpected in China!

XXVIII.

JAPAN AND HOME.

ENERAL GRANT had arranged for a trip to the "Great Wall of China," but, finding that he would pass the end of the wall on the sea-coast, on his way to Japan, and could anchor and go on shore to examine it, he resolved upon this course.

He found the wall a monument of human energy and enterprise. Though built two thousand years ago, to stop the invasions of the Tartars, it is in a tolerable state of preservation. It is twelve hundred and fifty miles long, with an average width of about twenty-five feet at the top, and twice that or more at the bottom. General Grant said, —

"The late Mr. Seward thought that the labor expended upon this wall would have built the Pacific railways; but I think he underrated its extent. I believe that the labor expended on this wall could have built every railway in the United States, every canal and highway, and most if not all of our cities."

On the 21st of June the *Richmond*, placed by the United States at General Grant's service, steamed into the fine harbor of Nagasaki, where an enthusiastic public welcome awaited the "American Mikado," as the people called General Grant. The wharves were crowded with people, and the vessels in the harbor were decked in gala-day attire. The *Richmond* ran up the Japanese flag and fired twenty-one guns in honor of Japan. The forts answered the salute. Then the forts and the Japanese gun-boats ran up the American flag, and fired twenty-one guns in honor of General Grant.

It was a half mile from the landing to General Grant's head-quarters, and his way was covered with red cloth, while, on both sides of the streets, thousands of American and Japanese flags were intertwined; and numerous arches of evergreen and flowers, bearing mottoes in honor of Grant, spanned the streets in fairy-like loveliness. Then followed the formal presentation of high officials, and a long, complimentary address by foreign residents of all nationalities, to which Grant replied in one of his longest and best speeches.

The merchants of the city gave General Grant an elaborate dinner of twenty courses. After the first course a very complimentary address to Grant was read by one of the leading merchants, to which he briefly replied. Then came the second course; after which the company went out of the temple in which the dinner was given, to behold the bay under the reflection of the sun setting behind the enfolding hills. In a few minutes they returned to the table for the third course, after which several girls in blue silk came in and played the harpsichord, followed by three more who sang. Then followed the fourth course, after which the company left the tables to behold the illumination of the city and the magnificent fireworks, with bonfires on the hilltops. The scene was indescribable. On returning to the table, candles had been brought into the temple and placed on costly pedestals, while the walls were draped with the costliest blue silk, richly embroidered with gold and silver, presenting a gorgeous scene under the flashing lights.

Thus the courses proceeded; some sort of entertainment being furnished between, until eight hours had been consumed by the dinner—such a dinner as had never been given before to any man; not even to a crowned head.

At Tokio a still grander reception was tendered to him. The General was conducted, in great pomp, to the Emperor's palace, where high officials introduced him and his party to their chief. The Emperor advanced and shook hands with him, which was an honor never before bestowed upon a man, however great. The Emperor only bowed slightly to others of the party, as they were presented. Then the Emperor made a signal to one of his noblemen, who advanced, and, with bowed head, was instructed to read to General Grant the following address:—

"Your name has been known to us for a long time, and we are gratified to see you. While holding the high office of President of the United States, you extended toward our countrymen especial kindness and courtesy. When our ambassador, Iwakura, visited the United States, he received the greatest kindness from you. The kindness thus shown by you has always been remembered by us. In your travels around the world you have reached this country, and our people of all classes feel gratified and happy to receive you. We trust that during your sojourn in our country, you may find much to enjoy. It gives me sincere pleasure to receive you; and we are especially gratified that we have been able to do so on the anniversary of American independence."

General Grant replied:—

"Your Majesty: I am very grateful for the welcome you accord me here to-day, and for the great kindness with which I have been received ever since I came to Japan, by your Government and your people. I recognize in this a feeling of friendship toward my country. I can assure you that this feeling is reciprocated by the United States; that our people, without regard to party, take the deepest interest in all that concerns Japan, and have the warmest wishes for her welfare. I am happy to be able to express that sentiment. America is your next neighbor, and will always give Japan sympathy and support in her efforts to advance. I again thank your Majesty for your hospitality, and wish you a long and happy reign, and for your people prosperity and independence."

The Emperor proposed to give a breakfast to General Grant at Shila Palace on the 7th of July, and devote the day to his honor. A grand military review was arranged for that day, both the Emperor and American General to be present. A review of the troops by the Emperor was always an occasion of great interest; and now to have a review by the Emperor and General Grant together, created an unprecedented interest. We have no space for a description of the military scene; but it excelled anything of the kind Japan had ever witnessed. And the breakfast was sumptuous and royal through out, such as only kings can serve.

General Grant desired to have a familiar conversation with the Emperor on public affairs, including national troubles with China; and such a conference was secured. It lasted two or three hours; and the dispute about the sovereignty of Loochoo was particularly canvassed, with the most favorable results.

"I know of nothing," said Grant, "that would give me greater pleasure than to be able to leave Japan, as I shall in a short time, feeling that between China and Japan there is entire friendship."

A resident American facetiously remarked that "everything had been brought in to honor Grant except an earthquake." Earthquakes are common in that country, but not the slightest shock of one had been experienced for more than two months, when the above remark was made. But, finally, an earthquake honored Grant. At one of the last dinners, a shock swayed the chandelier, shook the table, and made the building tremble. That was a characteristic feature of the country, which could not have been omitted without leaving the knowledge of it incomplete.

Grant resolved to leave the East and turn his steps homeward. But he must pay his respects to the Emperor, and bid him farewell, according to the custom. Preparations were made, therefore, for him to take leave of the Head of the Nation ; and it was on a grand scale too. A cavalcade of titled dignitaries escorted him to the palace. The Prime Minister, the Cabinet, Princes of the Imperial Family, foreign ministers, and other royal personages, waited to receive him at the door. He was ushered into the presence of the Emperor, his party following; and now the Emperor stepped forward and shook hands with both the General and Mrs. Grant; and the Empress did the same.

General Grant's addresses had been wholly extemporaneous hitherto; but, on this occasion, he desired to be more particular, and do greater honor to the Emperor, so he carefully wrote his address, and read it. It was as follows : —

"Your Majesty — I come to take my leave and to thank you, the officers of your Government, and the people of Japan, for the great hospitality and kindness I have received at the hands of all during my most pleasant visit to this country. I have now been two months in Tokio and the surrounding neighborhood, and two previous weeks in the more southerly part of the country. It affords me great satisfaction to say that during all this stay and all my visiting, I have not witnessed one discourtesy toward myself, nor a single unpleasant sight. Everywhere there seems to be the greatest contentment among the people ; and while no signs of great individual wealth exist, no absolute poverty is visible. This is in striking and pleasing contrast with almost every other country I have visited. I leav-

Japan greatly impressed with the possibilities and probabilities of her future. She has a fertile soil, one-half of it not yet cultivated to man's use, great undeveloped mineral resources, numerous and fine harbors, an extensive seacoast abounding in fish of an almost endless variety, and, above all, an industrious, ingenious, contented, and frugal population. With all these nothing is wanted to insure great progress except wise direction by the Government, peace at home and abroad, and non-interference in the internal and domestic affairs of the country by the outside nations. It is the sincere desire of your guest to see Japan realize all possible strength and greatness, to see her as independent of foreign rule or dictation as any Western Nation now is, and to see affairs so directed by her as to command the respect of the civilized world. In saying this, I believe that I reflect the sentiments of the great majority of my countrymen. I now take my leave without expectation of ever again having the opportunity of visiting Japan, but with the assurance that pleasant recollections of my present visit will not vanish while life lasts. That your Majesty may long reign over a prosperous and contented people, and enjoy every blessing, is my sincere prayer."

The Emperor replied by reading his own address, which was as great a departure from the imperial custom as shaking hands with his guest. His address was as follows:—

"Your visit has given us so much satisfaction and pleasure, that we can only lament that the time of your departure has come. We regret, also, that the heat of the season and the presence of the epidemic [cholera] have prevented several of your proposed visits to different places. In the meantime, however, we have greatly enjoyed the pleasure of frequent interviews with you, and the cordial expressions which you have just addressed to us in taking your leave have given us great additional satisfaction. America and Japan, being near neighbors, separated by an ocean only, will become more and more closely connected with each other as time goes on. It is gratifying to feel assured that your visit to our empire, which enabled us to form very pleasant personal acquaintance with each other, will facilitate and strengthen the friendly relations that have heretofore happily existed between the two countries. And now we cordially wish you a safe and pleasant voyage home, and that you will on your return home find your Nation in peace and prosperity, and that you and your family may enjoy long life and happiness."

Great preparations were made to receive General Grant at San Francisco, Cal. The people of that State were determined to make it the grandest reception ever given to an American in this country. Time and money were lavished upon the arrangements, as if the managers had resolved to eclipse all demonstrations of honor in the East.

About three o'clock, P. M., on the twentieth day of September, the bell on the Merchants' Exchange rang out the glad tidings. As if by magic the whole city was astir at once, and from every direction the multitude surged toward the harbor.

It was nearly dark when the General landed at the foot of Market Street, where the Mayor of the city welcomed him in a brief address, to which Grant replied. Then the procession started, which was signalled by another boom of cannon, ringing of bells, and screaming of steam-whistles. Market and Montgomery Streets, through which it passed, weie converted into one long, magnificent archway of flowers, banners, festoons, flags, and draperies, more beautiful than any oriental display which the illustrious guest had seen. The city was illuminated, and bonfires blazed on surrounding hills and even at the corners of streets, while Roman candles, electric lights, rockets, and other fireworks poured the light of day upon the host of people in the streets.

A week was given to receptions, dinners, and other public demonstrations in honor of Grant.

On the 25th, Oakland received him. Sixty thousand people were added to her population of forty thousand on that day.

After dinner at Tubb's Hotel, the General addressed the multitude in a brief but fitting speech. On his return to the wharf the crowd followed him. A bright little girl, who pleaded to be lifted up that she might see the General, was passed along from one to another, over the heads of the throng, to Grant, who took her in his arms, kissed her, and passed her back, creating the wildest applause possible.

On the 29th TWENTY THOUSAND children of the public schools welcomed him at Woodward Gardens. It was a memorable day.

On his way from the West to the East, the whole population seemed to be waiting to do him honor At Chicago the reception was on a grand scale The Mayor's address of welcome and Grant's reply elicited hearty applause.

At Philadelphia, whose citizens hoped that he might make the "Quaker City" his home, and to that end, had presented him with a fine house, his welcome was not inferior to that of San Francisco. The procession which escorted him was four hours passing a given point.

Among the demonstrations were, a grand dinner given by George W. Childs, Esq.; a reception at Independence Hall; a camp-fire reception by the Grand Army of the Republic; another reception by the Chamber of Commerce; and a farewell reception ball and banquet, the latter of which, it is claimed, surpassed in brilliancy anything of the kind ever given in this country. All of them were worthy of the occasion — that of honoring the most renowned general and statesman in the world!

At nearly every dinner and public demonstration, from the time Grant reached San Francisco until he left Philadelphia, he addressed the assemblies. Some of these speeches were his longest and best; all of them were worthy of the man and the occasions. Our limited space has compelled us to omit most of them.

Very appropriately, the General left Philadelphia to pay a visit to his aged mother in New Jersey.

XXIX.

MISFORTUNE AND SICKNESS AT LAST.

GENERAL GRANT did not sit down in idleness after his tour round the world. He was too active a man by nature to waste time with "nothing to do," and too much of a patriot to be indifferent to the welfare of his country. All public matters connected with reconstruction, the relations of the United States Government to foreign powers, the commercial intercourse of our country with the West Indies, Mexico, and other nations, — these and kindred questions enlisted his undivided attention.

The construction of railroads in the interest of American traffic was a subject upon which he bestowed much attention; and he was offered the presidency of one of the largest railroad enterprises of the day, to establish better commercial relations between our country and the republic of Mexico. He visited Mexico twice, for the sole purpose of enlarging the fraternal and commercial relations of the two countries. It was universally conceded that his great influence did turn the attention of the two countries to each other, and that here is found the secret of the promise which now invests that republic, especially in respect to its future intercourse with the United States.

General Grant took up his residence in New York after his return from abroad. He was a poor man then. The few thousands he had saved from his salary as General and President, were spent in his trip around the world. The great attentions shown him largely increased his expenses. The railroad trains and hotels, provided for him often by the governments he visited, only served to increase his obligations to be more generous in other directions. Had he paid his railroad fares and hotel bills, as other travelers do, he would have been in a better pecuniary condition at the close of his tour.

But General Grant was too much honored and beloved to remain a poor man. It was said that the railroad presidency which was offered to him, would have brought him a salary of *fifty thousaud dollars annually*. But wealthy friends thought a wider field of usefulness awaited him. Some of them were then hoping to see him elected President of the United States for the third time in 1880. The work of reconstructing the South had not progressed as rapidly and successfully as they desired; and they saw an early solution of difficult problems in a third term of the presidency by General Grant. Hence, they were opposed to his undertaking railroad enterprises, or any other, however important they might be for the public welfare. Besides, they were willing, in common with many others, to give the General all the money he wanted. Wealthy men were glad to guarantee a fund which would enable him to live as a great general and statesman should, the remainder of his days. The result was that a fund of two hundred and fifty thousand dollars was raised and invested in trust, the income of fifteen thousand dollars annually to be paid to him.

The National Republican Convention of June, 1880, to nominate a candidate for President, was commanding public attention. General Grant was put forward for a third term by his friends. There was wide-spread opposition to the measure, on the ground that a third term was a radical departure from the custom—that even Washington declined the nomination for a third term, and considered it as impolitic. Chiefly this reason, and not lack of confidence in General Grant, induced many leading Republicans, and many of the most prominent journals, to oppose his nomination. And yet, in the convention, he developed unexpected strength. On the first ballot he received more votes than any other candidate— THREE HUNDRED AND SIX. His opponents saw that only a union of hostile elements could defeat him in the convention. The friends of other candidates must sacrifice their choices, and unite on the best man available, in order to prevent the nomination of Grant. James A. Garfield had made a very favorable impression upon the delegates by his eloquent appeal for John Sherman, as candidate for President. Moreover, he was known to the convention as one of the ablest generals in the late war, in whom Grant himself reposed great confidence; and, in addition, had been one of the foremost men in Congress for nearly twenty years, and was already looked upon by many as a future President. To him the friends of other candidates turned as their only hope of success against Grant; and in this they were not disappointed.

Grant did not want the office. The country could not add to his honors by another term of the presidency. He consented to leave himself in the hands of his friends, for nomination or otherwise, only upon the ground which they claimed,—that he could be of greater service than any other man in completing the work of reconstruction, and cementing peaceful relations with foreign powers.

A year or more later, one of his sons entered into business with Ferdinand Ward, whose reputation in financial circles was high. The General put in a large amount of money, and thereby became a special partner. James D. Fish, the president of the Marine bank, and a man of excellent reputation, became a special partner also. The business was managed by Ward, on account of his superior business qualities and unusual experience for one of his age. General Grant knew little or nothing about the business; indeed, it was not legitimate that he should know about its details. Neither did his son feel competent to manage it, while one of so much larger ability and experience was not only willing to manage it, but claimed the right to do it for the reasons suggested. The result was, that Grant and Ward went down in one of the most disastrous crashes ever known in the financial circles of this country. General Grant, and other persons who put money into the firm, lost every dollar.

On the day before the crash, Ward told his partner that they must raise one hundred and fifty thousand dollars more to tide them over the next day; and he went to the General to ask if he could not raise it for them. "It will be returned in two days," said Ward. General Grant obtained the money of Vanderbilt, and gave his note for it; not even cherishing the shadow of a suspicion that anything was wrong. The next day the firm failed, and Grant was a poor man.

"Ward was arrested. The true character of the 'government contracts' was exposed. They were entirely and absolutely without foundation — were mythical in character, and the 'profits' a lie. New loans had constantly to be made to pay dividends on sums previously borrowed, or placed in Ward's hands for investment; and it is clear that each new sum must be greater in amount than that preceding."

The crash of the firm was stunning to Grant. It came near crushing him, as he was suffering at the time from a serious cancerous trouble at the root of the tongue. The fear that his world-wide reputation for uprightness might suffer, more than the loss of all his property, overwhelmed him. But his mighty will-power, commanding every faculty of his soul, which made him invincible in war, now came to his relief; and he sat down, with his noble wife at his side, to convey, legally, their home and all their personal property, to the last dollar, to Mr. Vanderbilt, to secure him against loss. Poverty was a welcome boon to him, and to his devoted companion, could they but repay a friend who kindly loaned the General one hundred and fifty thousand dollars.

The sympathies of friends in every part of the country, and in other lands, too, were enlisted for General Grant and his family. It was proposed to raise a second fund for his benefit; and the project would have been readily consummated, but the General signified that it would not be agreeable to him; so it was abandoned.

As soon as General Grant found himself embarrassed, he turned his attention to literary work. Conductors of magazines were ready to pay him an extravagant price for articles on the late war; and book-publishers were eager to secure his memoirs for publication. He applied himself to the production of both,—magazine articles and his memoirs.

He felt that his disease would prove fatal, sooner or later; and he desired to leave his family in comfortable circumstances. A publishing house offered him a large sum for his autobiography. Although he knew that the grateful people of his country would see that his wife and family were provided with both the necessaries and luxuries of life, he preferred that his own personal efforts should make them independent.

Here is another illustration of his tremendous will-power. That he was able to rise above the depression occasioned by the loss of his property and the inroads of a fatal disease, and devote himself to literary work, is a marvel. Few men ever lived who could master circumstances like that. Probably he could never have done it, but for his terrible discipline in the late war.

History affords few parallels to the case of General Grant. He stood upon the top of worldly success. There was nothing more of honor, wealth, confidence, fame, that a nation could add, to exalt his earthly lot. Suddenly he was plunged down, down, by misfortune and disease, to an experience more appalling because of the height to which he had attained. History furnishes no parallel to it.

He was now seriously ill. The people of the United States and the world had just learned of the dreadful malady that was so sure to result in death — cancer in the throat. For months it had been progressing, though he kept it a secret from his family. But the Grant and Ward troubles aggravated the disease, and soon it assumed the most alarming aspect. The tidings spread over the land, that General Grant was seriously ill. This was followed immediately by more definite news — that cancer in the throat was his trouble, and that his death must be near.

From the Atlantic to the Pacific, the honest grief and lamentation were unprecedented. South, as well as North, there was a profound feeling of sadness, that he, to whom the Nation owed its life, in an important sense, was thus stricken. State legislatures in session, secular and Christian conventions, Grand Army Posts, Ministerial Associations, Boards of Trade, and all sorts of assemblages bore testimony of their sorrow, in resolutions of grief and sympathy adopted. The press of the country, secular and religious, joined in the universal expression of sadness, and filled their columns with a rehearsal of his deeds, both in war and peace. Opponents forgot their hostility in recalling the indebtedness of the country to the heroic sufferer. The living comrades of the Union army felt a personal affliction in the sudden and unexpected prostration of their old commander. It was taking away one for whom many of them would willingly die. The Nation was ready to wear the deepest mourning when its great leader should pass away.

Seldom have a people waited upon the mails and telegraphs more eagerly and tearfully, from day to day, than they did to catch the last report from General Grant's sick-room. The slightest news of more favorable symptoms was hailed with unmingled joy. News of declining strength awakened corresponding sorrow. Night and day the street in front of his residence was besieged with interested parties waiting for the last tidings from the sick man. Neither physician nor friend could come out of the house without being beset by eager inquirers about the General's condition. Such a demand was made upon the press, for the latest news from Grant, that a room was rented close to his residence, where the reporters gathered and waited for reports from his physicians and nurses.

Soon after the public were made acquainted with the General's malady, his old friend, George W. Childs, Esq., of Philadelphia, called upon him. Mr Childs, speaking of the interview, said, —

" He realized that his life was drawing to a close

but seemed to regard the approach of death calmly and without the slightest fear."

The reader will recall the General's reply to the inquiry how he could keep so cool, and be so self-possessed in war, when its fortunes seemed to turn against him, — "When I have done the very best I can, I leave it." Here, as elsewhere, we discover the man of few words committing his cause to Providence. Under the strongest conviction that his cause was right, he believed that Providence would finally vindicate it. All through his war life this element of strength appears. And here it predominates in the presence of his last enemy — Death.

Mr. Childs inquired about the progress he had made on his book.

"I hope that I shall be able to complete it before I die."

"Your friends, in Congress and out, are deeply concerned to have you placed upon the retired-list," suggested Mr. Childs.

"Yes; and I feel very grateful to them for their efforts," replied the General. "The newspapers, too, speak very kindly of the measure."

"Why; it is half-past eleven o'clock," said Mr. Childs with surprise, as he looked up to the clock.

"Yes; and I suppose the Senate is about adjourning now," added the General.

Just then a telegram was brought in to Mr. Childs, from Mr. Drexel, stating that Congress had placed General Grant on the retired list.

"There, General, read that," said Mr. Childs, passing the telegram to him

The General read it, and a smile of satisfaction lit up his countenance, while his emotions were too deep to admit of speech.

Mrs. Grant came into the room, when Mr. Childs told her of the action of Congress. With a countenance beaming with delight, she exclaimed, "They have brought us back our old commander."

Mr. Childs says of the interview, —

"The scene was very affecting. The General could hardly express the delight he felt at the compliment which had been paid to him. He bore not the slightest ill-will toward those who had opposed the bill, for he is the most magnanimous man I ever knew. The greatest soldier that ever lived, he is as kind and gentle as a woman. He frequently told me how much it pained him to be accused of butchery. He said he was always overcome by a feeling of sadness before a battle, at the thought that many a poor fellow would never return from the field. He is the most wonderful man in combating disease I ever heard of. He walks about the room unaided, notwithstanding his extremely weak condition. A short time ago he walked into an adjoining room and affixed his autograph to four pictures. The strokes of his pen were as bold and firm as they were when the General was in health."

During these days of intense anxiety, the crowd began to gather at daylight in the street front of the Grant residence. All day long, day after day, continuing until midnight, the people waited in the streets to hear from the sufferer. The stoops of the houses were filled; and not a few people went into the houses opposite and watched from the windows. Every person who came out of the General's house, night or day, was beset with earnest, honest inquirers. They must know what hope was left.

When the second severe attack threatened the General's life at once, Mrs. Grant said,—

"Send for Doctors Sands and Shrady immediately."

The General was cool and collected as ever, and he said to Doctor Douglas, who was rendering every possible attention, —

"It can do no good to send for them; you are enough."

But his son, Col. Fred Grant, hastily wrote two notes, and sent them by messengers to Doctor Sands and Doctor Shrady.

Mrs. Sartoris, his daughter, came into the room after the severest struggle was through, and the General looked up and smiled, at the same time extending his hand. She took his hand between both of hers and sat down by him, holding it until he fell asleep. When he awoke, in a few minutes, liquid food was brought to him, of which he partook sparingly, and pushed it aside.

"You have not taken enough to do you any good," said Doctor Shrady. "Take more."

"Very well, Doctor, just as you say," the General replied; and then drank freely of the nourishment. He had not forgotten how to obey a superior officer.

The little daughter of Colonel Grant came into the room, ready for a walk. With a face fu'l of sunshine and joy, she ran up to the chair of the General and said, "Good bye, grandpa, I'm going out to the park." The General patted the golden-haired girl upon the head, his eyes glistening with tears, and said, in a voice full of emotion, "Good bye, my child; good bye." As Mrs. Sartoris raised the child to kiss his forehead, the General smoothed away the ringlets from her brow, took a long look at her face, and then turned his head away and closed his eyes, while his lips faintly uttered the words, "Bless you, my child; bless you."

Colonel Grant repaired to the library, and reported the views of the doctors to his mother. Although expecting to hear the worst at any moment, she was quite overcome by these unfavorable tidings; but, speedily rallying from her paroxism of grief, she said,—

"Well, let us take courage, and look to God for strength."

"Now, I would like to see Dr. Newman," said the General, after he had become quiet, and the doctors had retired to the library. A messenger was sent to his house, and Dr. Newman came immediately.

"I am very glad to see you, Dr. Newman," said the General, in a strong voice, at the same time extending his hand.

"How are you feeling now?" inquired Dr. Newman.

"Very tired and weak. This long struggle has worn me out."

Conversation followed upon his physical and spiritual condition, when Dr. Newman remarked:—

"You have friends everywhere who are remembering you in their prayers in your sufferings, General; and in fact, it seems as if every one was your friend at present."

"Yes," replied the General, "I have many friends here; and I have also many friends on the other side who have crossed the river before me."

"Yes, General, that is so," said Dr. Newman; "they have taken the journey before you, and now they stand waiting to receive you."

"It is my wish that they may not have long to wait for me, and that the end will soon come."

His chair was drawn up to the window so that he could look into the street. In that position he fell asleep; and people on the opposite side could distinctly see his pale, death-stricken face; and many of them were seen to wipe unbidden tears from their eyes, as if experiencing a personal sorrow.

The following day, although the General was more comfortable in some respects, Doctor Shrady said, —

"The General's condition indicates that he is sinking rapidly; and, so far as I am able to judge from appearances, he is liable to go at any moment."

Doctor Douglas said, —

"There is little doubt that the end is near. I don't think that stimulants will be used to a great extent; for, though we may tide over the night possibly, the end is close at hand, and is looked for at any moment.

These opinions show that General Grant lay at death's door for several days; and yet his wonderful recuperative power asserted itself, and he rallied;

but only temporarily, as it was supposed. On tne 12th or 13th of April, Dr. Newman called, and, after an interview, said to a reporter, —

"His mind is perfectly calm. He knows that the end is coming, and calmly sits, awaiting death. He has no fear, and looks upon death as a mere change that happens as ordained by the Creator, as a part of the grand scheme of creation. I have attended many cases of sickness, and generally the patients have some hope and expect to recover as long as they are possessed of their reason, but in General Grant's case, there is no hope."

Telegrams and letters of sympathy had been pouring into the Grant home, by the hundred, for many days. They came from every part of the country, and even from foreign lands. Among them was a kind, loving message to Mrs. Grant, from Queen Victoria.

One day eight hundred unopened letters of this kind were in the General's home. And one who has been much in the family says, that "these many tokens of confidence and true sympathy touched the General's heart, and often moved him to tears. They aided much to remove the depression with which he brooded over the Grant & Ward failure, as they showed him that he still commands the hearts of the people."

One day a poor old man in seedy garments, who said he traveled on foot from Galena, Ill., and had known and fought under the General, paused in front of the house at 6.30 A. M., and doffing his weather-beaten hat, prayed loud and fervently for his recov ery. When he turned to go the tears were coursing each other down the old man's cheeks. He refused assistance offered him by those present and would not give his name.

General Grant was very much affected when this incident was related to him.

Strange as it may appear, General Grant rallied, so that when his sixty-third birthday occurred, on the 27th of April, he was in a very comfortable condition ; and the occasion was celebrated in many parts of our land. In some places it was made a holiday. In some schools special exercises were arranged in honor of Grant. Messages from individuals and societies were forwarded to him, and resolutions adopted by public bodies on that day. Many tokens of friendship, prompted by sincere affection, were also sent. And he was very much affected by these expressions of tender regard for him.

The General was soon able to attend to his literary work; and, though his medical attendants could not express the slightest hope of his recovery, yet he devoted himself to the preparation of his autobiography with as much singleness of purpose and enthusiasm as he could display if sure of living twenty years longer. This is one of the remarkable things about the General — an element of character which made him equal to any emergency during the war, so that he never provided for defeat.

Said one of his able generals recently, —

" General Grant never knew defeat ; and it begins to look as if neither doctors nor death would defeat him."

If there is any reliance to be placed upon the highest medical and surgical authority, his recovery is impossible. Soon, at longest, he must die; and no one is more thoroughly convinced of the fact than Grant himself. But his work is not quite done; he is bending his energies to the last task of his life.

Working — suffering — waiting! That is the heroic record.

And what a life! A hundred years and more compressed into sixty-three! Deeds, victories, achievements, honors in rich profusion crowding one mortal span!

Tennyson's ode, to England's great Wellington, may well be sung in honor of General Grant.

> "Our greatest, yet with least pretense,
> Great in council, and great in war,
> Foremost Captain of his time,
> Rich in saving common sense,
> And, as the greatest only are,
> In his simplicity sublime.
>
> "Who never sold the truth to serve the hour,
> Nor paltered with eternal God for power;
> Who like the turbid stream of rumor flow
> Through either babbling world of high or low;
> Whose life was work, whose language rife
> With rugged maxims hewn from life.
>
> "He on whom, from both her open hands,
> Lavish Honor showered all her stars,
> And affluent Fortune emptied all her horn."

XXX.

HIS LAST JOURNEY.

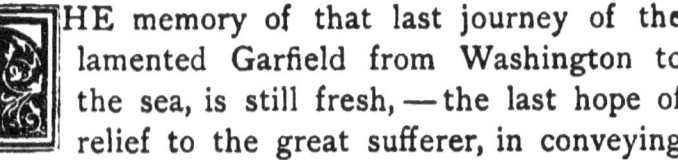HE memory of that last journey of the lamented Garfield from Washington to the sea, is still fresh, — the last hope of relief to the great sufferer, in conveying him to Francklyn Cottage, Long Branch, where the bracing sea-air afforded another possible chance of life. But the ocean only joined the Nation in bemoaning his expiring life, and soon sung a doleful requiem over his death.

In like manner, General Grant took his last journey, not to the sea, but from New York city to the mountains. His departure was hastened on account of a sudden and unexpected change for the worse. The symptoms were so alarming that his medical attendants feared speedy death, unless immediate removal to Mount McGregor should extend his furlough.

Mount McGregor is situated thirty miles from Saratoga Springs, and is reached from the latter place by a narrow-guage railway, which winds around it until the ascent is accomplished. The owner of the now famous Drexel Cottage, Mr. Drexel, tendered the use of it to the General as soon as it became apparent that he might survive to breathe the country air of summer. The location is beautiful, and the air pure, crisp, and invigorating.

At half-past nine o'clock, on the morning of June 16, 1885, the General left New York city, in a private car, accompanied by his family and Doctor Douglas. When passing Stony Point, Colonel Grant, the General's son, spoke so as to be heard above the clatter of the train, —

"When Anthony Wayne stormed Stony Point, my great-grandfather, Captain Dent, was commander of the forlorn hope, and when they reached the walls he had his men stand on each other's shoulders and then the Captain scaled the rampart over their backs, and stood on the wall and pulled his men up one by one over the human ladder. They then descended and opened the gates of the fortress and let in Wayne's men."

General Grant smiled assent to the statement, and the son added, —

"And up here at Ticonderoga, father's great-grandfather and his brother were killed in the French and English war, about the year 1754."

The General nodded assent.

Passing West Point, the scene of his cadetship, the General smiled and nodded to his wife to look across the river to that military home of his youth ; and he continued to take in the view until it was swept out of his sight.

Reaching his destination before night, the General was found to have borne the journey full as well as his friends expected.

The next morning Colonel Grant said: "Father had considerable rest last night. When I went to his room a little while ago he whispered, very faintly, that he found his voice a little stronger to-day, but that he should not try to use it; hoping that with caution it would grow strong enough so he could talk again. But the failure of his voice is owing to debility, and he is growing weaker all the while."

Yet, on that day, June 17th, with the assistance of Harrison, his faithful attendant, he walked to the brow of the mountain, a hundred yards away, and returned, with so little exhaustion as to surprise Doctor Douglas.

Near the cottage a little white tent was pitched, with small flags fluttering over it; and the tent was occupied by an old soldier in uniform,—S. W. Willet. He was employed to protect the General from intrusion by strangers.

On the evening of the eighteenth, after the arrival of his son Jesse, with Doctor Newman, he wrote: "It is just a week to-day since I have spoken. My suffering is continuous. The doctors, Sands and Douglas, say my ailment is improving."

Within three or four days he was able to perform some labor on his book, though with the utmost care. On the twenty-fourth he received two telegrams, which afforded him much pleasure. The first was from the State Teachers' Association of Missouri, representing thirty thousand teachers, tendering their heartfelt sympathies to him in his affliction. The other was from the Grand Army of the Republic, assembled at Portland, Me., for their nineteenth national encampment, conveying renewed expressions of love and sympathy for their old commander. The General read these telegrams with evident satisfaction, and returned his thanks over his own signature.

He wrote, on June 29th, to comfort his wife,— ".Do as I do—take it quietly. I give myself not the least concern. If I knew that the end was to be to-morrow, I would try and get rest in the meantime. As long as there's no progress, there's hope."

On the thirtieth, Doctor Douglas said, "General Grant's life has been prolonged by the invigorating air here. The disease has progressed in the natural way. As I have said before, his condition is one of increasing debility. His present weakness is the natural result of the disease. He is each day less strong; and though the step from day to day is scarcely perceptible, the aggregate of fourteen days becomes noticeable."

On the following day Doctor Newman, who spent much time with him, inquired, "General, are you sensible of increasing weakness?"

He wrote in reply: "I do not know as there is any special weakness. I worked a good four hours to-day, and wrote a short chapter for my book. I scarcely use my cane in going about my room. Often when I go out I have to look about for it to find it."

Before leaving, Doctor Newman, at the General's request, read the eighth and ninth chapters of Matthew, and offered prayer.

For sometime thereafter he seemed to renew his

strength; yet, he was not able to converse even in a whisper. On July 8th a visitor called upon him, when the General motioned him to a seat.

"I am a Catholic clergyman from Baltimore," he said. "We are all praying for you."

The General wrote: "I regret very much that I am not able to converse, not even in a whisper."

The caller repeated his kind message.

"Yes, I know," continued the General in writing, "and I feel very grateful to the Christian people of the land for their prayers in my behalf. There is no sect or religion, as shown in the Old or the New Testaments, to which this does not apply. Catholics, Protestants, and Jews, and all the good people of the Nation, of all politics as well as of religions, and of all nationalities, seem to have united in wishing or praying for improvement. I am a great sufferer all the time, but facts I have related are compensation for much of it. All that I can do is to pray that the prayers of all these good people may be answered so far as to have us all meet in another and a better world. I cannot speak even in a whisper.

"July 8, 1885. (Signed.) U. S. GRANT."

In the afternoon of the same day, twenty editors of the Mexican Associated Press called upon him, and, one by one, were introduced to him. Then, Señor Augustin Arroyo de Anda addressed him as follows : —

"In the name of the Visiting Committee of Mexican journalists who are visiting this country, I desire to say that they could not pass so near to a great friend of Mexico without coming to pay their re spects to the hero of Richmond, — he who broke the chains of slavery in order that the iron of the chains around the slaves might be made into rails for the progress of the country, and thus unite the two republics by bonds of steel, — he who did so much to make the two republics one."

In response General Grant wrote: —

" My great interest in Mexico dates back to the war between the United States and that country. My interest was increased when four European monarchies attempted to set up their institutions on this continent, selecting Mexico, a territory adjoining. It was an outrage on human rights for a foreign nation to attempt to transfer her institutions and her rulers to the territory of a civilized people without their consent. They were fearfully punished for their crime. I hope Mexico may soon begin an upward and a prosperous departure. She has all the conditions, — she has the people, she has the soil, she has the climate, and she has the minerals. The conquest of Mexico will not be an easy task in the future."

Notwithstanding the unusual strain of this day upon his strength, he was full as comfortable on the next day, and conversed, by writing, with a caller, for some minutes. Among other things he wrote this: —

" I am glad to say that while there is much unblushing wickedness in this world, yet there is a compensating generosity and grandeur of soul. In my case I have not found that republics are ungrateful, nor are the people."

After this his strength seemed to increase, and on

Sunday, the 12th, he startled his daughter, as she returned from religious service, by asking audibly,— " Nellie, did you have a good sermon, to-day ? "

Three days later, the following resolution, adopted by a Democratic convention in Vicksburg, Miss., was telegraphed to the General : —

"*Resolved*, That all join in the Nation's grief for the sad affliction which has befallen Gen. U. S. Grant, America's most illustrious citizen, who was as magnanimous in peace as he was great in war."

This message was very grateful to him, coming as it did, from those whom he fought and conquered.

On Sunday, the 19th, Doctor Douglas consented that the General should be drawn in his bath-chair to a locality on the mountain, where he might once more take in the magnificent view.

" Not on Sunday," said the General.

So the trip was deferred until Monday, when it was accomplished with unexpected exhaustion. It was only a short distance, but it proved too much for him. He did not rally from it. At five o'clock, on the morning of the twenty-second, Doctor Douglas said, —

"He cannot possibly survive over twenty-four hours."

He was fully conscious of the approach of death, and remarked in the afternoon, —

" I cannot hold out much longer."

At nine o'clock in the evening, his pulse only fluttered, and the family gathered about him. Doctor Newman, who arrived in the afternoon, knelt beside him and offered prayer amid the solemn stillness. But his pulse rallied again, and an hour afterward, he signified to his daughter that he wanted to write a message. She brought his pad, and he wrote a private message to the family. Colonel Grant read it, and replied, —

"Father, I have attended to that already."

An hour later, he looked up to Doctor Douglas and whispered, —

"Tell them all to go to bed; there is no reason why they should sit up longer."

He knew full well that they were sitting up in momentary expectation of his death; and, evidently, he thought he might live through the night. And he did.

At eight o'clock, on the morning of the 23d of July, however, the family were hurriedly summoned to his bedside to see him die. He had relapsed into a state of unconsciousness as they gathered; and he quietly and peacefully passed away. The scene was impressive and overwhelming at the moment the devoted wife and children realized that the husband and father was no more. It was equally impressive to the millions of people whose hearts were in sympathy with the afflicted family around the great man's bed. The tidings flashed over the wires, "General Grant is dead!" and the land was filled with mourning. Symbols of the honest grief that pervaded the land, from Plymouth Rock to the Golden Gate, began to appear, within a single hour, in town and city. Flags drooped at half-mast, bells tolled, public buildings were draped, badges of crape

appeared on banners and the arms of veteran sol
diers. Everywhere the habiliments of grief told the
touching story of the Nation's loss. The mourners
went about the streets, saying to each other, as of
old, "Know ye not that there is a prince and great
man fallen this day in Israel?"

The President issued the following proclama
tion : —

"The President of the United States has just received
the sad tidings of the death of that illustrious citizen and
ex-President of the United States, Gen. Ulysses S. Grant,
at Mount McGregor, in the State of New York, to which
place he had lately been removed in the endeavor to prolong his life. In making this announcement to the people
of the United States the President is impressed with the
magnitude of the public loss of a great military leader
who was in the hour of victory magnanimous; amid dis·
aster serene and self-sustained; who in every station,
whether as a soldier or as a chief magistrate, twice
called to power by his fellow-countrymen, trod unswervingly the pathway of duty, undeterred by doubts, single-
minded, and straightforward. The entire country has
witnessed with deep emotion his prolonged and patient
struggle with painful disease, and has watched by his
couch of suffering with tearful sympathy. The distined
end has come at last, and his spirit has returned to the
Creator who sent it forth. The great heart of the Nation that followed him when living with love and pride,
bows now in sorrow above him dead, tenderly mindful of
his virtues, his great patriotic services, and of the loss
occasioned by his death. In testimony of respect to the
memory of General Grant, it is ordered that the Executive
Mansion and the several Departments at Washington be

draped in mourning for a period of thirty days, and that all public business shall on the day of the funeral be suspended, and the Secretaries of War and of the Navy will cause orders to be issued for appropriate military and naval honors to be rendered on that day.

"In witness whereof, I have hereunto set my hand and caused the seal of the United States to be affixed.

"Done at the city of Washington this twenty-third day of July, A. D. one thousand eight hundred and eighty-five, and the Independence of the United States the one hundred and tenth. GROVER CLEVELAND.

"By the President.

"T. F. BAYARD, Secretary of State."

State governments and city governments throughout the country joined in the universal expression of sorrow. Public bodies, secular and religious, courts of justice, political organizations, commercial, philanthropic, and religious societies, adopted glowing tributes of respect to his memory.

Victoria, the Queen of England, sent a message by the British Minister:—

"WASHINGTON, D. C., July 24, 1885.

"*Mrs. U. S. Grant*,—Her Majesty the Queen requests me to convey to yourself and family her sincere condolence on the death of General Grant.

"(Signed.) BRITISH MINISTER."

The Prince and Princess of Wales sent a message of condolence:—

"LONDON, July 24, 1885.

"*To Mrs. U. S. Grant*,—Accept our deepest sympathy in the loss of your distinguished husband. We shall al ways look back with gratification at having had the advantage of knowing him personally.

"THE PRINCE AND PRINCESS OF WALES."

Among others was the following:—

"TOKIO, JAPAN, July 24, 1885.

"*Mme. General Grant,*—I learned with much sorrow of the death of your husband. I tender you my sincere condolence and deep sympathy. PRINCE TOWPITO."

The death of no other living man could perhaps have touched so many hearts as that of Grant. Surviving war-veterans mourn for him as children mourn for a dead father, and in their families his name is a household word. And loyal citizens everywhere feel that the country was saved by his great generalship, and their gratitude is surpassed only by their grief over his death. Even the South, over which the great General bore his victorious banner, join in the universal lamentation. They recall his unparalleled magnanimity in the hour of triumph towards them, and they weep that one so generous and noble has fallen. He is the Nation's dead — the world's lamented benefactor!

Doctor Douglas has made public the following communication, written by General Grant on the second day of July, with the understanding that it should be withheld from his family until after his death:—

"I know that I gain strength some days, but when I do go back it is beyond where I started to improve. I think the chances are very decidedly in favor of your being able to keep me alive until the change of weather toward winter. Of course there are contingencies that might arise at any time, that would carry me off very suddenly. The most probable of these is choking. Under the circumstances, life is not worth the living. I am very thankful [for thankful glad was written, but scratched out and thankful substituted] to have been spared thus long, because it has enabled me to practically complete the work in which I take so much interest. I cannot stir up strength enough to review it and make additions and subtractions that would suggest themselves to me and are not likely to suggest themselves to any one else. Under the above circumstances, I will be the happiest the most pain I can avoid. If there is to be any extraordinary cure, such as some people believe there is to be, it will develop itself. I would say, therefore, to you and your colleagues, to make me as comfortable as you can. If it is within God's providence that I should go now, I am ready to obey his call without a murmur. I should prefer going now to enduring my present suffering for a single day without hope of recovery. As I have stated, I am thankful for the providential extension of my time to enable me to continue my work. I am further thankful, and in a much greater degree thankful, because it has enabled me to see for myself the happy harmony which so suddenly sprung up between those engaged but a few short years ago in deadly conflict. It has been an inevitable blessing to me to hear the kind expressions toward me in person from all parts of our country, from people of all nationalities, of all religions and of no religion, of Confederate and of national troops alike, of soldiers' organizations, of mechanical, scientific, religious, and other societies, embracing almost every citizen in the land. They have brought joy to my heart, if they have not effected a cure. So to you and your colleagues

I acknowledge my indebtedness for having brought me through the valley of the shadow of death, to enable me to witness these things.
"(Signed.) U. S. GRANT."

Doctor Tiffany was General Grant's pastor in Washington, at one time ; and, in some reminiscences, since the General's decease, he said, —

"On one occasion a friend whom I wished to hear was to preach for me on a Sunday night. I called upon the President to inform him of this fact, and said that I had done so because I had observed that he attended service only once on a Sunday, and thought that if he knew of this arrangement for the pulpit he might prefer to attend the evening service. He said to me : ' I am glad of an opportunity to explain this matter to you. Secretary Fish and some others have an absurd notion that I ought not to walk about the streets of Washington at night, and consequently I never get to the evening service, though I should be glad to do so. And perhaps you think that I might have the carriage and ride to service ; but, Doctor, when I was a poor man, long before I ever thought that I should have a servant, I made up my mind that if I ever did have one, he should have his hours of Sunday for worship ; and no servants or horses are ever called into use by me upon that day for my own personal convenience.'

. . . .

"He was a man of religious habit and thoroughly honest and earnest in his belief in a Superintending Providence, regarding certain facts in history as inexplicable without this, and admiring the firm faith of a devoted sister, and reverencing with a sacredness that was beautiful in its exhibition the piety of his parents. He made a visit of a week to Martha's Vineyard, which was then as now my summer home. I preached a sermon on the victory of faith, from the text: 'They overcame him by the blood of the Lamb.' He was more moved than I had ever seen him under a discourse, and, at the close of the sermon, at his suggestion, we wandered away from the crowd and engaged in earnest and serious conversation. He said: 'Why is there so much stress laid upon the blood in your preaching and in the New Testament?' I explained to him in the simplest terms the doctrine of atonement, and he seemed fully to comprehend it. The giving up of life as a test of love was an incontrovertible argument to a man who had led thousands through death to victory, and I have always had a strong confidence that on that day the General had a personal realization of the truth as it is in Jesus."

The President requested, in behalf of the Nation, that, after the bereaved family had paid their last tribute of affection to the dead, they should commit the remains to the Government representatives for national obsequies. This request being granted, plans were at once adopted for the most imposing military funeral on record, and General Hancock was appointed by the President to conduct it. The funeral was arranged to begin with the family's private obsequies, in the Drexel cottage on Mt. McGregor, on the fourth of August, and to close with the national rites in New York city on the eighth day of August, and preparations were thus made on the most elaborate scale.

In the afternoon of the last Sabbath the remains were at Mount McGregor, Mrs. Grant summoned Doctor Newman to the cottage, that he might lead the family in their devotions, as they gathered about the remains in the parlor. The General had been embalmed, and was lying in a rich casket made of polished oak, lined with copper, covered with dark purple velvet; strengthened by solid silver bars the whole length, on either side, and ornamented with solid silver handles, and a solid gold plate. When the family were seated around the catafalque, Mrs. Grant passed her husband's Bible to Doctor Newman; and it opened, as she passed it, at the eleventh chapter of Job, which the Doctor read; and, after a pause, re-read the sixteenth and seventeenth verses — "Because thou shalt forget thy misery, and remember it as waters that pass away; And thine age shall be clearer than the noonday; thou shalt shine forth, thou shalt be as the morning." A brief pause followed, when the man of God knelt down with the family, amidst a silence that was as impressive as that of the dear husband and father in the casket. He then thanked God for the beautiful life that was ended, and the divine comforts vouchsafed to the sorrowing household; pleading that the father's mantle might fall upon the sons, and the blessing of the widow's God attend the solitary one whose walk must henceforth be alone; and closing with a pledge of renewed consecration to Him who "doth not afflict willingly, nor grieve, the children of men."

The morning of August 4th dawned auspiciously, and sunrise was heralded by thirteen guns, the original number of States, followed by one gun each half hour, and thirty-eight at sundown, the present number of States in the Union. Before the time of the family's funeral in the cottage arrived, more than a thousand people assembled, including the military escort, to listen to Doctor Newman's discourse. At ten o'clock Bishop Harris read the nineteenth Psalm, and offered an impressive prayer. "My Faith Looks up to Thee" was then sung by the audience, with many eyes bedimmed with tears.

Doctor Newman's sermon followed, from Matthew 25:21: "Well done, thou good and faithful servant; enter thou into the joy of thy Lord."

"And what were the elements of that character, so unique, symmetrical and now immortal? God had endowed him with an extraordinary intellect. For forty years he was hidden in comparative obscurity, giving no indication of his wondrous capacity; but in those four decades he was maturing, and at the appointed time God lifted the veil of obscurity, called upon him to save a nation and give a new direction to the civilization of the world."

. . . .

"He had this double advantage over all this world heroes — he possessed the solid virtues of true greatness in a larger degree than other men of renown, and possessed them in greater harmony of proportions. Temperate without austerity, cautious without fear, brave without rashness, serious without melancholy, he was cheerful without frivolity. His constancy was not obstinacy; his adaptation was not fickleness; his hopefulness was not Utopian. His love of justice was equaled only by his delight in compassion.

. . . .

"In private life, he bore many of the fruits of the Spirit. Of all men known in a pastoral experience of thirty years, he displayed the spirit of forgiveness more than any other man. He caught the spirit of the Saviour's prayer: 'Father, forgive them; they know not what they do.' There is one high in official position in our nation who had traduced him at the point of honor whereat a great soldier is most sensitive, and the wrong done was made public, to the mortification of all. Grieved at what he had done, and confined to his sick room, he who had offended was nigh unto death. But himself a man of proud and sensitive spirit, he sighed for reconciliation. 'Would the President forgive the offense and call on the sick?' anxiously asked interested friends. A suggestion from me that it would be a Christian act to call was sufficient. The call was made; the sick man revived, and old friendship was restored. And rising to a magnanimity worthy a saint, he would not withhold an honor due, even from those who had done him a wrong. Who does not regret the death of such a man? Heaven may be richer; but earth is poorer."

. . . .

"How tender was that scene, in the early dawn of that April day, when all thought the long-expected end had come. He gave his watch to his wife, and tenderly caressed her hand. And the dying hero whispered, 'I did not have you wait upon me, because I knew it would distress you; but now the end draws nigh.' And out from the 'swellings of Jordan' he rushed back to the shore of life, to write this tender message to his son : 'Wherever I am buried, promise me that your mother shall be buried by my side.' It is all a wife could ask; it is all a husband could wish.

"And how tender was his care! He thought not of himself, but of her. To his son he said, 'I hope mother will bear up bravely.' To quiet her anxiety he wrote, 'Do as I do; take it quietly. I give myself not the least concern. If I knew the end was to be to-morrow, I would try just as hard to get rest in the meantime.' Would she keep holy vigils through the livelong night? He wrote her: 'Go to sleep and feel happy; that is what I want to do, and am going to try for. I am happy when out of pain. Consider how happy you ought to be. Good-night.'

"And such was the tenderness of his love and solicitude for her and hers, he surprised her by a letter found after his death. It came as a message to her from him after he had gone. When his spirit had returned to the God who gave it, there was found secreted in his robe his last letter to her, enveloped, sealed, and addressed. He had written it betimes; written it secretly, and carried the sacred missive day after day during fourteen days, knowing that she would find it at last. In it he poured forth his soul in love for her and solicitude for their children : —

"'Look after our dear children and direct them in

the paths of rectitude. It would distress me far more to think that one of them could depart from an honorable, upright and virtuous life than it would to know that they were prostrated on a bed of sickness from which they were never to arise alive. They have never given us any cause for alarm on their account, and I earnestly pray they never will. With these few injunctions and the knowledge I have of your love and affection, and of the dutiful affection of all our children, I bid you a final farewell until we meet in another and, I trust, a better world You will find this on my person after my demise. Mt. McGregor, July 9, 1885.'

. . . .

"'Honor thy father and thy mother,' was in perpetual obedience in that home. What reverence for that honored father shown by those devoted sons and that precious daughter! What blissful love they manifest for that dear mother, to-day a widow! What pure delight in each other's company; what mutual pride in each other's future welfare! Such a home is worthy to be called an American home. Give us such homes of purity, love, and joy, and our republic shall live forever."

At the close of Doctor Newman's sermon, "Nearer, my God, to Thee," was sung with tearful interest.

The funeral cortege started immediately for New York,—the train consisting of several cars, being deeply draped from locomotive throughout. Every city, village, and hamlet on the way wore mourning emblems in profusion; and the people turned out *en masse*, and stood, with uncovered heads, in solemn silence as the train swept by. At Albany the dead lay in state at the capitol, where a stream of people continued to view the remains through the night until ten o'clock on the following day. Seventy thousand persons filed past the catafalque.

The funeral-train from Albany to New York co sisted of eleven heavily draped coaches; and body was borne to it on a mounted catafalque dra by six black horses, wearing funeral trappings. T whole distance was marked by symbols of sorrow.

At five o'clock P. M., the sombre train reached New York, which was arrayed in mournful emblems so elaborate that the market of black fabrics was exhausted. Nothing like it was ever witnessed in that city. The expense of the funeral to the city was not less than a million dollars.

From the time the remains were deposited in the City Hall of New York, on Wednesday night, until the lid of the casket was closed at one o'clock on Saturday morning, there was one unbroken column of people mournfully passing through the gates to view the face of the illustrious dead. Thirty-four thousand, by actual count, availed themselves of this privilege during the first four hours the body lay in state. At this rate, several hundred thousand people must have viewed the remains.

The floral tributes were elaborate and numerous. The simplest and least expensive, however, was the most conspicuous on account of its history. It was a wreath of oak leaves furnished by little Julia Grant, daughter of the Colonel. After the death of her grandfather, Julia, accompanied by Josie Douglas, daughter of the physician, wandered out into the woods on Mt. McGregor, where they gathered the oak leaves and wrought them into a wreath. Julia carried them to her father, and said, —

"Josie and I have made this for grandpa, and won't you please give it to him?"

Its value was in its history; and that value was so great, that, of all the floral tributes in City Hall, this alone was carried with the casket to the tomb.

City Hall was fragrant with the perfume of flowers, so profuse and remarkable was the floral exhibition. The large piece — "The Gates Ajar" — was placed at the head of the casket, and it completely filled the space between two pillars. Its beauty will linger long in the memory of all who viewed the dead. There were many crosses and crowns, wreaths and pillows and columns, made of the rarest flowers and laid about in tasteful display. There were horseshoes of red and yellow rosebuds scattered around here and there, adding novelty as well as beauty to the scene. A tall clock of flowers, presented by the "Women's Relief Corps of the Grand Army," was as appropriate in its design as it was beautiful in workmanship. An elaborate piece from Galena, General Grant's old home, attracted much attention. It was a large, oblong panel of white flowers, edged with green leaves, and bearing across the middle the word "GALENA" wrought in purple flowers. Rising above it was the costly floral device presented by the City Council of New York, consisting of the city coat-of-arms, a liberty-cap, crossed flags, and other designs. All these floral offerings together consti tuted a scene so marvelously attractive that a journey across the continent to see them could well be made.

Saturday, the day of the National obsequies, was a memorable day in the annals of our country. New York never placed on record such a day before. For two weeks the most labored preparation had been made for the mournful occasion. The best part of the city was densely draped; and every variety of honest tribute, which a sorrowing people could pay to the dead, appeared. Indeed, this was true of the whole country, even throughout the South. Funeral services were observed in towns and cities of every State and Territory of the Union, amidst a display of mourning emblems unparalleled; and none more sincere and tender than those of the conquered South.

The route of the procession to the tomb was nine miles long, and the whole distance was so profusely hung with funeral symbols as to present a scene of solemn grandeur. The whole way, too, was densely packed with people, eager to see the sable cortege on its way to the silent house. Not only the sidewalks, but the doorways, balconies and windows of houses and stores, the vestibules and porches of churches, the trees, lamp-posts, fences, and roofs of low buildings, all were occupied by people who were willing to forego one day of food and rest for the sake of paying their respect to the departed hero. It was estimated that three million persons saw the funeral procession on its nine miles of march to the grave.

When the time for the cortege to move arrived,

the funeral car, drawn by twenty-four black horses, each one led by a colored servant, and each covered with sable trappings that swept the street, drew up to the City Hall. The arrival of General Hancock in full uniform, with his staff, and the movements of the battalions of the army and navy, announced that the time was at hand for the procession to form and move.

Thirty thousand military men, with their officers, fell into line. Minute-guns from the war-vessels in the harbor sounded; fire and church bells throughout the city, and in the suburbs, tolled; the numerous bands played solemn dirges; the great bugler, Krouse, blew the marching signal, and the imposing cortege moved.

The military pageant, led by General Hancock and his staff, preceded the funeral car; and the head of it reached the tomb three hours and a half before the funeral car arrived,—a fact that conveys to the reader some idea of the magnitude of the procession. The war veterans occupied a conspicuous position in the military display, bearing aloft their tattered ensigns on which victory perched under their victorious leader. Their whole appearance indicated that an honest sentiment of grief controlled their hearts, and that they paid their last tribute of respect to the memory of their old commander with unfeigned sorrow.

The pall-bearers, preceding the funeral car, were Gen. William T. Sherman and ex-Confederate Gen. Joseph E. Johnston; Gen. Philip H. Sheridan and Gen. Simon B. Buckner, who surrendered to Genera

Grant at Fort Donelson; Admiral Porter and Vice-Admiral S. C. Rowan; George S. Boutwell, ex-Secretary of the Treasury, and Gen. John A. Logan; George W. Childs and George Jones; Oliver Hoyt and A. J. Drexel. The three attending physicians, with Doctor Newman and a representative clergyman from each denomination, including the Catholic and Jewish, followed.

The family, relatives, and friends joined the procession immediately behind the sable hearse, followed by General Grant's Staff and Cabinets. Next, the President of the United States, accompanied by Secretary Bayard, in a barouche drawn by six bay horses, took his place, with his Cabinet behind him. Then followed two ex-Presidents of the United States, with their Cabinets; the Supreme Judges of the United States, various commissioners, and ex-ministers, together with the representatives of foreign Governments at Washington. Committees of the national Senate and House of Representatives, diplomatic and consular officers, the Governors of some fifteen States, with their staffs, the Mayors and Aldermen of many cities, with other officials of rank from nearly every State in the Union, were next in order.

Without delaying to describe the organization of the cortege, it is sufficient to say, that over ten thousand public men, from the President down to the humblest officer, rode in carriages in the remarkable procession.

Fifty thousand persons joined in the solemn and imposing march to the grave. It was such a demonstration as never was accorded to departed greatness in any nation before. In some respects it was like the tribute which England paid to Lord Wellington, though more elaborate and grand. The London papers agreed that the demonstration was "something wonderful." The *Times* highly commended the American people for honoring the memory of Grant so sincerely and grandly; and it pronounced the funeral "a spontaneous outburst of national admiration and gratitude, which, although it can do nothing for its actual object, is not, therefore, the less to be commended."

An observer wrote : " Many a touching scene was observed, for veterans of the war and others, whose memories carried them back to those days when their own households were bereft by the fate of bat tle, could not restrain their emotion. As the lofty, crape-covered vehicle bearing the coffin turned into Broadway, and proceeded slowly along its way, the demeanor of the crowd was that of silent reverence. The car stood for a time near Chambers Street, and a white-haired colored man who had come to the city from the South too late to see the General's face, obtained permission to approach the vehicle, and gazed long at the coffin. As he turned away, his head was bowed, and the tears could be seen rolling down his cheeks. Many of the women, as they heard the solemn music of the band, and witnessed the slow approach of the funeral-car, felt their eyes moisten and hid their faces in their handkerchiefs, and not a few stalwart men wept. The poorer people who were unable to obtain vantage ground from which to view the whole procession, and who were compelled to catch glimpses of the car from the crowded streets, were observed to be more moved to expressions of grief than the richer or more influential occupants of the windows along the route. It was interesting to observe faces which had been hardened by lines of anxiety, become softened for the moment as they paid the last tribute of respect to the man whose name for twenty-two years had been so frequently heard and spoken by them."

The site chosen for General Grant's tomb is at Riverside Park, on a promontory overlooking the Hudson River,—the highest point in Manhattanville. The summit is a level plateau of about twenty acres, which can be converted into one of the most charming spots in the country.

It was past four o'clock in the afternoon when the "Chariot of Death," as one called it, reached the tomb. The casket was placed in its cedar case at the door of the tomb, when the family, clergy, and war veterans closed around it, and the ritual of the Grand Army and the burial service of the Methodist Episcopal Church were read.

Chaplain Wright prayed: "God of battles, Father of all! amidst this mournful assemblage we seek thee, with whom there is no death. Open every eye to behold him who changed the night of death into morning. In the depths of our hearts we would hear the celestial word, 'I am the resurrection and the life; he that believeth in me, though he were dead, yet shall he live.' As comrade after comrade departs, and we march on, with ranks broken, help us to be faithful unto thee and to each other. We beseech thee, look in mercy on the widows and children of deceased comrades, and with thine own tenderness console and comfort those bereaved by this event which calls us here. Give them 'the oil of joy for mourning, the garment of praise for the spirit of heaviness.' Heavenly Father! bless and save our country with the freedom and peace of righteousness, and through thy great mercy, a Saviour's grace, and thy Holy Spirit's favor, may we all meet at last in joy before thy throne in heaven, and to thy great name shall be praise for ever and ever."

The comrades said, "Amen!" and the band played a dirge.

Post Commander Alexander Reed: " One by one, as the years roll on, we are called together to fulfill the last sad rites of respect to our comrades of the war. The present, full of the cares and pleasures of civil life, fades away, and we look back to the time when, shoulder to shoulder, on many battlefields, or around the guns of our men-of-war, we fought for our dear old flag. We may indulge the hope that the spirit with which, on land and sea, hardship, privation, and danger were encountered by our dead heroes, may never be blotted out from the history or memories of the generations to come,—a spirit uncomplaining, obedient to the behest of duty, whereby to-day our national honor is secure, and our loved ones rest in peace under the protection of the dear old flag. May the illustrious life of him whom we lay in the tomb to-day prove a glorious incentive to the youth, who, in the ages to come, may be called upon to uphold the destinies of our country. As the years roll on, we, too, shall have fought our battles through, and be laid to rest; our souls following the long column to the realms above, as grim death, hour by hour, shall mark its victims. Let us so live that when that time shall come, those we leave behind may say above our graves, 'Here lies the body of a true-hearted, brave, and earnest defender of the republic.'"

Senior Vice Commander Lewis W. Moore (laying a wreath of evergreen upon the coffin): "In behalf of the post I give this tribute, a symbol of undying love for comrades of the war."

Junior Vice Commander John A. Wiedersheim (laying a rose or flower upon the coffin): "Symbol of purity, we offer at this sepulchre a rose. May future generations emulate the unselfish devotion of even the lowliest of our heroes."

Past Post Commander A. J. Sellers (laying a laurel wreath upon the coffin): "Last token of affection from comrades-in-arms, we crown these remains with a symbol of victory."

Rev. J. W. Sayers (Chaplain-in-Chief, Department of Pennsylvania, G. A. R.): "The march of another comrade is over, and he lies down after it in the house appointed for all the living. Thus summoned, this open tomb reminds us of the frailty of human life and the tenure by which we hold our own. 'In such an hour as ye think not, the Son of Man cometh.'

"It seems well we should leave our comrade to rest where over him will bend the arching sky, as it did in great love when he pitched his tent, or lay down weary by the way, or on the battlefield, for an hour's sleep. As he was then, so he is still, in the hands of the Heavenly Father. 'God giveth his beloved sleep.'

"As we lay our comrade down here to rest, let us cherish his virtues and strive to emulate his example. Reminded forcibly by the vacant place so lately filled by our deceased brother, that our ranks are thinning, let each one be so loyal to every virtue, so true to every friendship, so faithful in our remaining march, that we shall be ready to fall out here to take our places at the great review, not with doubt, but in faith; the merciful Captain of our salvation will then call us to that fraternity which, on earth and in heaven, may remain unbroken. (A pause for a moment.) Jesus saith: 'Thy brother shall rise again. I am the resurrection and the life.' (The body is deposite in the tomb.) Behold, the silver cord having been loos. the golden bowl broken, we commit the body to the ҫ·· where dust shall return to the earth as it was, an. spirit to God who gave it. Earth to earth, ashes to a.. dust to dust, looking for the resurrection and the li.. come through our Lord Jesus Christ."

Prayer by Rev. H. Clay Turnbull, Post Chaplain, followed, when the bugler sounded taps,—lights out, — and the beautiful and impressive service of the military orders was brought to a close.

Bishop Harris, surrounded by the clergy of different denominations, then read the burial service of the Methodist Church, and Doctor Newman added the commitment, "Dust to dust," and pronounced the benediction. Three volleys of musketry and a national salute by Fessenden's United States Battery added weird solemnity to the closing scenes. Again Bugler Krouse sounded "Rest"; and the bugle-notes echoed over land and water, announcing to the tearful multitude that the solemn rites were ended.

> "The stars on our banner grow suddenly dim,
> Let us weep, in our darkness, but weep not for him!
> Not for him,—who, departing, leaves millions in tears!
> Not for him,—who has died full of honor and years!
> Not for him, —who ascended Fame's Ladder so high,
> From the round at the top he has stepped to the sky!
> It is blessed to go, when so ready to die."

www.ingramcontent.com/pod-product-compliance
Lightning Source LLC
Chambersburg PA
CBHW030321020526
44117CB00030B/318